MW00979773

Pulling Apart :

The Deterioration of Employment and Income in North America Under Free Trade

BRUCE CAMPBELL
EXECUTIVE DIRECTOR, CANADIAN CENTRE FOR POLICY ALTERNATIVES

MARIA TERESA GUTIÉRREZ HACES
SENIOR RESEARCHER, INSTITUTE FOR ECONOMIC RESEARCH,
NATIONAL AUTONOMOUS UNIVERSITY OF MEXICO (UNAM)

ANDREW JACKSON
SENIOR ECONOMIST, CANADIAN LABOUR CONGRESS

MEHRENE LARUDEE
PROFESSOR, ECONOMICS DEPARTMENT, WILLIAMS COLLEGE, MASSACHUSETTS

Published by

The Canadian Centre for Policy Alternatives
804-251 Laurier Avenue West, Ottawa, Ontario K1P 5J6
Tel (613) 563-1341   Fax (613) 233-1458
e-mail: ccpa@policyalternatives.ca

$19.95

Canadian Cataloguing in Publication Data

Main entry under title:

Pulling apart: the deterioration of employment and income
in north america under free trade

Includes bibliographical references.
ISBN 0-88627-935-6

1. Labor market--North America. 2. Wages--North America.
3. Free Trade--North America. I. Campbell, Bruce, 1948-
II. Canadian Centre for Policy Alternatives.

HD5722.P84 1999   331.12'097   C98-901299-9

Printed and bound in Canada

Contents

Pulling Apart :

*The Deterioration of Employment and Income
in North America Under Free Trade*

Preface

It has been 10 years since the Canada-US Free Trade Agreement was implemented and five years since it was renegotiated, extended to Mexico and renamed NAFTA. NAFTA is the template for the Free Trade for the Americas initiative (FTAA) scheduled for completion in 2005, as it is for the Multilateral Agreement on Investment (MAI) and other agreements.

The prevailing orthodoxy is that free trade has been good for Canada, Mexico and the United States. Trade has increased. Cross-border investment has increased. Capital is freer to move to where returns are highest. Inflation is low or nonexistent. Business is more competitive. Productivity is growing. Governments are less intrusive. Without free trade, the conventional narrative goes, unemployment would be even higher, recessions even deeper, public spending cuts even greater.

Both Canada and Mexico have experienced a major increase in trade and in their dependence on trade in the 1990s. Canada's trade (exports plus imports) rose from 51% to 71% of GDP. Canadian exports grew five times as fast as GDP. Mexican trade doubled, from 24% to 48% of GDP. US trade dependence, low to begin with, grew modestly from 21% to

24% of GDP. Both Mexico's and Canada's dependence on the US, already high, grew to over 80% of total exports. Canada's merchandise trade surplus with the US rose throughout the decade, including in a majority of manufacturing sectors (more than half of all manufacturing output was now exported). But this did not stop manufacturing employment from falling further than in the US.

All three countries have seen a substantial increase in the inflow of foreign direct investment during the 1990s compared to the previous decade, although proportionately, the increase has been most dramatic in Mexico. Both Canada and the US have experienced large increases in the flow of outward-bound direct investment. And all three countries have seen even faster growth in inflows and outflows of portfolio capital. For Mexicans the consequences of mobile capital exiting *en masse* are still being felt.

The 1990s have been mostly years of recession or low growth for Canada and Mexico, much more so in the case of Mexico. The US fared modestly better. It also had lower unemployment, although inequality and poverty continued to rise during the 1990s. NAFTA has not ushered in a new dawn of prosperity hailed by political leaders in all countries. Far from it.

Employment and income have deteriorated in the free-trade 1990s. GDP per capita fell in the first half of the decade in both Canada and Mexico and rose modestly in the US. This was the first time Canada had experienced such a prolonged decline since the 1930s. For Mexico it was the continuation of the previous decade's disastrous decline. Average real wages have been more or less stagnant in the 1990s in both the US and Canada and have dropped sharply in Mexico. The already huge gap between CEO earnings and average workers' wages continued to widen in all three countries. The minimum wage has dropped in all three countries, most dramatically in Mexico.

In all three countries the growth of low wage precarious employment—part-time, temporary, contract and self- employment has accelerated.

Labour productivity has increased in all three countries, far outpacing any wage gains. The delinking of productivity and wages has been greatest in Mexico, the continuation of the previous decade's trend.

Official unemployment in Canada has averaged around 10% in the 1990s, almost double the US rate. This reflects a major widening of the gap from the previous decade. Mexico has a much lower rate of open unemployment but the effective rate is estimated at around 25%. There has been a net destruction in manufacturing jobs in the US and Canada, though most deeply in Canada. Although manufacturing employment in Mexico was stable overall, it masked a deep restructuring, namely, the explosive growth of lower paid export manufacturing jobs in the maquiladora sector offset a by huge loss of jobs in the domestic manufacturing sector.

There has been a drop in public sector program spending in all three countries especially with respect to the social wage. This decline has been dramatic in Canada if only because its social safety net was far more generous than its NAFTA partners. Both Canada and Mexico experienced large declines in the size of their public sectors in the 1990s.

In all three countries *market* income inequality (from earnings and investment) has deepened, accelerating the trend of the previous decade. It has been most pronounced in Mexico. Earnings of the poorer half of the populations have fallen, while those of the richest 10% have risen steadily. Overall income inequality in the US and Mexico (after taxes and transfers) continued to grow in the 1990s. In Canada, overall income inequality remained stable through the 1980s and midway through the 1990s. It has since begun to widen, reflecting the decline in public transfers.

These so-called trade deals are a central component of a neo-liberal policy agenda which has, since the late 1970s been transforming national economies, restructuring the roles and relationships among governments, markets and citizens in the march to an integrated market-centred global economy. The neo-liberal family of policies is well known: privatization, deregulation, investment and trade liberalization, public sector cutbacks, tax reductions, monetary austerity, and so forth. With a view to bringing about the "structural adjustment" of societies everywhere, they have rolled back the post-war gains of working people in Canada, the US, Mexico and many other countries. They have lowered people's expectations of governments, disciplined unions, and freed markets.

Causality is complex. Outcomes are the result of neo-liberal policies interacting with each other in mutually reinforcing ways. They are shaped by technological forces, corporate strategies, and a varied landscape of social and labour market institutions. The deterioration of employment and income for most in the region is not in dispute. Nor is this outcome surprising given an agreement like NAFTA and its sibling policies which transfer power from workers to corporations, boost profits at the expense of wages, and weaken the public sector while giving free reign to the market.

Beyond specific provisions, the drumbeat of competitiveness is at the heart of the NAFTA dynamic affecting employment and income. Several mechanisms are summarized below.

1. Competitive corporate pressure: As national markets with different cost and regulatory structures are brought into closer contact with each other, the pressure on companies to cut costs and restructure through takeovers, downsizing, closures, and relocations increases. More acute competition also intensifies the pressure on employers to demand worker concessions. Workers are legally confined by national borders and culturally bound to their communities. Capital has the upper hand. It can move effortlessly under the new regime, or threaten to move if labour does not make wage and other concessions. It also increases the pressure to lower costs through production and work reorganization—increasing the use of part-time, temporary and contract workers, and outsourcing to non-union firms in low wage jurisdictions.

2. Competitive pressure on governments and regulatory structures: By opening national economies NAFTA intensifies pressure on hundreds of national and sub-national governments to compete with each other by raising subsidies (most of which remain legal under NAFTA), and lowering regulations and standards to maintain and attract investment. There are no *common* rules governing acceptable and unacceptable subsidies or limiting subsidy wars among governments. At best there are ineffective protections limiting competitive bidding down of labour and environmental regulations. Policy levers, such as performance requirements and tariffs, once served as sticks to nudge investors to behave in accordance with public policy priorities and discourage capital outflows. However, these instruments have been removed; governments are increasingly confined to offering rewards as a way of influencing the behaviour of capital. Thus, the need to attract investment creates dual stresses: downward pressure on regulations and standards and increased fiscal pressure.

3. Fiscal pressure: The competitive drive to attract and maintain investment increases the pressure to reduce taxes and increase subsidies to capital. The increased fiscal pressure tends to crowd out social spending: The pressure on workers' wages also negatively affects the tax base. The enhanced ability of "elite labour" to move or threaten to move, either to work in other jurisdictions or transfer savings, puts additional pressure on fiscal capacity. Also, by enhancing the ability of transnational corporations to internalize their operations, NAFTA increases the volume and relative importance of intra-firm trade and accompanying transfer pricing (where prices of imports and exports are set to show minimum profits in high tax jurisdictions and maximum profits in low tax areas). As such, it adds to the pressure to lower corporate tax levels.

4. Competitive pressure and monetary policy: Competitiveness imperatives under NAFTA affect monetary policy priorities, especially the need for wage control. Competitiveness priorities in a NAFTA environment require disciplining labour through unemployment-inducing monetary policy austerity, reducing the "natural rate of unemployment" by cutting back social benefits, weakening labour standards, unions and what neo-liberals refer to as eliminating "labour market rigidities."

NAFTA has made it easier for Canadian and Mexican policy makers to bring about the "structural adjustment" of their social and labour market institutions in line with the dominant US model. Thanks to NAFTA, what has been a concerted domestic US policy agenda since Reagan has been extended to the whole of North America. Entrenching these policies in a treaty has provided insurance against future backsliding, secured investor rights, reined in interventionist government impulses and the demands of organized labour.

On this tenth anniversary of its implementation the question needs to be posed: issues of equity and social justice aside, is the NAFTA model of development sustainable? Can it deliver on its promise of improving general prosperity and stability? On the evidence to date, the answer is, unquestionably, no. The NAFTA model is pulling apart the social and economic fabric of North American societies.

An earlier version of this document was commissioned by the International Labour Organization, Employment and Labour Market Policies Branch, in Geneva. However, the views expressed herein represent those of the authors. We appreciate the financial assistance provided by the ILO.

Bruce Campbell, Ottawa, November, 1998

CUFTA/NAFTA and North American Labour Markets: A Comparative Inquiry

by Bruce Campbell

INTRODUCTION

In its broadest sense, the North American Free Trade Agreement (NAFTA), which absorbed and replaced the Canada United States Free Trade Agreement (CUFTA), is an international treaty which advances and consolidates the restructuring and integration of national economies in North America along neoliberal lines. It provides a legal framework which embeds the principles of market supremacy and international competitiveness.

As Donald Johnston, the Canadian head of the OECD, said: "These free trade agreements are designed *to 'force adjustments on our societies.'* Countries, he said, should push the pace of adjustment...by reducing social benefits that encourage the unemployed to turn down low-paying jobs."[1]

North American integration is a corporate-driven process. Trade and foreign investment growth among the three countries has far outstripped the growth of the three economies. Fifty large corporations (mainly US-owned) account for 70% of US-Canada trade. FDI is even more concentrated. It should come as no surprise, therefore, that NAFTA and the accompanying restructuring of the state reflects the strategic interests of transnational capital.

NAFTA's role and its effects can only be fully understood within a broader policy and historical context. Moreover, any assessment of its labour market impacts must take into account the different economic, social, and political structures and institutions in each country, and the strategies and actions of the main actors. These differences help to explain differences in labour market responses.

We will attempt in our analysis to capture these complexities and contribute to an understanding of CUFTA/NAFTA's role in the larger constellation of policies that have induced the "structural adjustment" of North American labour markets.

Policy matters decisively in determining labour market outcomes. Neoliberal policies (of which CUFTA/NAFTA is central) operate in a mutually reinforcing and cumulative way. These policies also interact and reinforce with corporate strategies and technological changes. Our thesis is these policies have had a generally adverse effect on employment and income conditions of a majority of working people and their families in all three NAFTA countries. This is not an unintended consequence of these policies. Underlying these policies are relations of power and its transfer, from workers to corporations, from low and median income to high income earners, from wages to profits, from governments to the market.

What benchmark date should we use in assessing the Agreements' impact? CUFTA negotiations began officially in 1986, although the Canadian government had publicly declared its intention to negotiate more than a year earlier. The deal was signed January 1, 1988 and came into effect on January 1, 1989. The neoliberal era in Canada is generally thought to start with the Mulroney government in 1984, although it had been gaining ascendance in policy circles for the previous ten years.

The Mulroney government brought in significant privatization and deregulation measures during its first term of office—the deregulation of the energy, financial, transportation and foreign investment sectors, the privatization of public airline, oil, aircraft, telecommunications and satellite companies, etc. These measures were then entrenched in CUFTA, which in turn provided the impetus for further restructuring—for example, in banking, telecommunications, rail transport—which continued under NAFTA and the subsequent Liberal government.

Full employment policies were supplanted by "natural rate of unemployment" policies. Monetary austerity cut inflation in half (to under 5%) by the mid-1980s. In the 1988-91 period, the monetary screws were tightened even further, squeezing inflation down to under 2% and jacking up unemployment into the 10-12% range, four points above the US rate. The federal corporate tax rate was cut in the late 1980s from 36% to 28% and the top federal income tax bracket was reduced from 35% to 29%.

The formal benchmark for neoliberal ascendancy in the US dates from the Reagan presidency in 1980, although the consensus among policy makers had been building throughout the 1970s. Paul Volker preceded Reagan by a year as chair of the Federal Reserve and had already initiated the era of extreme monetary austerity. It was Reagan, in his presidential campaign, who first floated the idea of a continental "common market" stretching from "the Yukon to the Yucatan."

The Reagan Administration launched an aggressive drive to deregulate, privatize and downsize the US civilian public sector, particularly social programs like unemployment insurance and welfare, while massively increasing military spending. Monetary austerity created a major recession and huge foreign capital inflow, both with worldwide reverberations. Together with tax cuts, these policies created a huge fiscal deficit and foreign debt build-up. Reagan also took a hard line against unions, inspiring a wave of corporate and legislative attacks on organized labour.

The Reagan government also attacked the Canadian government's interventionist orientation, especially its national energy and foreign investment review policies. US monetary policy in large part triggered the 1982 Mexican financial crisis, and then, along with the IMF, put together a financial bailout package which pushed Mexico to alter its economic development path.

The structural adjustment program contained the basic neoliberal prescription[2]: investment and trade liberalization, domestic deregulation and privatization, public sector cutbacks, and inflation-controlling monetary policy and other forms of wage restraint.

Mexico's structural reforms began in 1983-84. The first stage cul-
minated with GATT membership in 1986, followed by a dramatic opening of the Mexican economy—lowering of tariffs and non-tariff restrictions on trade, and loosening of foreign investment rules. The Salinas
regime (1988-94) accelerated these policy changes and in 1990 entered
into NAFTA negotiations with the US (which Canada subsequently joined)
to consolidate and lock-in the transformation of the Mexican economy.

NAFTA was signed on December 17, 1992 and, after the negotiation of the labour and environment side-accords demanded by incoming
US President Bill Clinton, was ratified and came into effect January 1,
1994. Almost a year later, triggered by massive capital flight, Mexico was
engulfed in a severe financial and economic crisis.

In summary, the key benchmarks in the history of neoliberal restructuring and integration (depending on the country) are: 1980, 1982,
1984, 1986, 1989 and 1994. The periods of economic recession for the
US were 1981-82 and 1991-92. Canada's slumps were roughly coinci-
dent with those in the US, though deeper and longer during the 1990s. For
Mexico the deepest periods of economic crisis were 1982-88 and 1995-
96. The transformation in Mexico has been more extensive and the crises
much more severe and prolonged than were those in the US or Canada.

Reforms (including NAFTA) have been supported by a consensus
of élites in all three countries, though they have met with widespread
resistance among the general population. For example, it is unlikely that
CUFTA in Canada or NAFTA in the US would have survived a referen-
dum. The Salinas government sold NAFTA to the Mexican people as their
ticket to first world-style prosperity, stifling critical political debate on its
merits.

Once in place, NAFTA serves as what Grinspun and Krecklewich
(1994) call an external *conditioning framework*, limiting the range of political choices and enabling the implementation of unpopular measures.
For example, major social program cuts undertaken as part of the "war on
the deficit" in Canada were rationalized with the claim that: "there is no
alternative in this era of free trade and globalization." The choice of policy
measures to deal with the peso crisis were similarly justified.

It should also be kept in mind that CUFTA/NAFTA is an agreement in progress. Many of its provisions are being phased in over time (10 years in the case of CUFTA and 15 years in the case of NAFTA.) It mandates a large number of negotiations on a variety of areas, from government procurement to standards harmonization and common subsidies rules. It provides the legal architecture which locks in subsequent neoliberal restructuring by the NAFTA countries, and of course prevents backsliding.

KEY PROVISIONS OF NAFTA AFFECTING LABOUR MARKETS

NAFTA, like its predecessor CUFTA, is a complex set of documents comprising a text of more than 1,000 pages and even larger volumes of national implementing legislation, hundreds of pages of tariff schedules, statements of administrative intent, regulations, a long record of dispute panel rulings, and side-agreements on labour and the environment.

NAFTA removes tariffs and other non-tariff barriers on all goods and services, impeding governments' ability to protect strategic or vulnerable sectors from import competition. It also prevents governments from granting conditional exemptions from tariffs or duty remissions to foreign transnationals as a way of strengthening domestic productive capacity and employment.

Although the two are interrelated, NAFTA's most important provisions apply to investment, not trade liberalization. It entrenches a set of rules protecting private property rights of investors (corporations, banks, mutual funds etc.) and their investments. Virtually all types of ownership interests, financial or non-financial, direct or indirect, actual or potential, are covered.

It liberalizes investment, enhancing its ability to operate free of non-commercial considerations. Codification of these provisions in treaty reduces the risk of a future government unilaterally imposing new conditions or regulations on their investments.

The reduction of investment risks is central, enabling, for example, transnational corporations to locate production more and more on the basis of cost consideration—labour, taxes, transport, infrastructure, etc., free from "non-market" or political impediments. It enables portfolio or money market managers to freely transfer assets and income into and out of member countries.

The very broad national treatment provisions of NAFTA oblige each member country to treat foreign investors exactly the same as it treats its own national investors, regardless of their contribution to the national economy. They create the impetus for powerful alliances between foreign and domestically-owned businesses, since any policy to regulate foreign capital will have to be applied equally to national capital.

Their combined power to promote further deregulation and resist new regulation is greatly enhanced. Moreover, they remove important industrial policy tools, such as subsidies to domestic high-tech firms with stronger linkage effects to the economy than foreign firms have.

NAFTA prevents governments from imposing a wide array of performance requirements (from local sourcing and product mandating to trade balancing and technology transfer), tools which have attempted to channel foreign investment to strengthen national industrial capacity and create jobs. It formally maintains, though in vestigial form, Canada's and Mexico's foreign investment screening mechanisms, designed to ensure, with the help of performance requirements, that potential benefits from foreign investment, including job creation, were in fact realized. (It also entrenches US "national security" foreign investment prohibitions.)

NAFTA prevents governments from regulating the outflow as well as the inflow of capital. It prevents governments from placing any restrictions on the transfer within the region or outside by any investor at market currency exchange rates, any kind of financial transfer including profits, dividends, royalties, fees, proceeds of sale of an investment, payments on loans to subsidiaries. It also prevents governments from restricting the transfer of physical assets including technological assets.

There is a partial exception which allows governments experiencing balance of payment difficulties to impose limited trade and financial controls (excluding investment transfers such as profits and dividends), but only after consulting with the IMF and adopting only those measures which the IMF prescribes.

Finally, NAFTA provides comprehensive intellectual property protection (patent, copyright, trademark, etc.) for corporations' technology.

NAFTA guarantees investors the right to prompt compensation at "fair market value" for expropriations or measures which are seen to be "tantamount to expropriation"—a vague term for measures which are seen in some way to impair commercial benefits, including any future benefits which might be expected. Claims under these provisions may be adjudicated through various dispute panels, including an international tribunal at which corporations can directly challenge government measures.

It limits the ability of public or state-owned enterprises to operate in ways that are inconsistent with commercial practice and in any way impair benefits expected by private investors of the other countries. This clearly affects the ability of public enterprises to pursue public policy goals that may override commercial goals. It also limits the ability of future governments to re-regulate or re-nationalize industries once they have been deregulated or privatized (as has occurred, for example, in the airlines, telecommunications, electrical utilities, transportation and energy sectors.)

Thus, NAFTA has a built-in bias in favour of the private over the public sector, one which compresses the public space, ratchet-like, locking in every subsequent privatization or deregulation. It provides the legal framework for greater private (foreign and hence domestic) penetration into traditionally public areas, notably health care and education.

NAFTA facilitates and accelerates the realization of a privatized, continentalized transportation/communication infrastructure. It facilites the development of high-speed transportation systems that greatly reduce time and costs to the major consumer markets, important factors in industrial location decisions. It contains provisions which facilitate border-crossing for trucks, the conduit for almost three-quarters of NAFTA trade. (Although the US has thus far delayed the implementation of key trucking provisions.)

Various north-south highway and rail corridors from Mexico through to Canada are in the process of being constucted or expanded. NAFTA also provides the legal *framework* for a continentalized telecommunications infrastructure which Mexico and Canada have moved closer to reality in subsequent deregulation/privatization measures.

Finally, NAFTA enables investors to challenge directly through an international investor-state disputes tribunal (if they do not wish to go through a national government) government measures at all levels which they claim violate their rights. This further reinforces the bias of private sector interests over public policy considerations, putting a chill on any policy or regulation that might be perceived as infringements on investor rights.

The North American Agreement on Labour Cooperation (NAALC)

The NAFTA labour side-agreement was finalized in September 1993, nine months after NAFTA was negotiated. It came into being in response to warnings by US critics that NAFTA would facilitate the Mexican government's low-wage foreign investment-led development strategy—in part by repressing fundamental labour rights—and thereby accelerate the loss of US jobs and incomes.

This position was supported by incoming US President Bill Clinton who, as a candidate, expressed concern that transnational corporations could take advantage of "their ability to move money, management and production away from a high-wage country to a low-wage country. We could also lose income because those companies which stay at home can use the threat of moving to depress wages, as many do today...if you look at the experience of the maquiladora plants...there is certainly cause for concern." (Clinton 1992, cited Levinson 1996.).

The inclusion of an agreement on labour rights as part of NAFTA was indeed an historic precedent, with signatories for the first time in an international trade agreement acknowledging the link between the exchange of goods and services and the people who produce them; and promising to enforce their own labour laws and promote the 12 labour rights identified.

However the NAALC itself fell short of critics' expectations. Its prime weakness—inadequate enforcement— stands in stark contrast to the strong enforcement of protections accorded to investors. [see Stanford et al 1993, Robinson 1993; Levinson, 1996, Bolle 1997] It dealt only with non-enforcement of *existing* national laws, failing to address problems caused by the absence of laws or regulations.

Most important, it did not provide effective means for changing the Mexican record of not enforcing its own labour law, or of changing the propensity of US and Canadian governments to weaken their labour laws to attract investment. Neither the National Administrative Organizations (NAOs) housed in each country's labour department, nor the NAALC Council of (Labour) Ministers, nor the NAALC Secretariat, were given sufficient independence or investigatory power to function effectively.

Canadian provinces, which have primary jurisdiction over labour law (90% the work force), were not covered under the NAALC. Thus, only if a sufficient number of provinces agree (as determined by a complex threshold formula) will the NAALC review and enforcement apply to Canada. To date, just three provinces have signed on, making it only partially in force.

NAALC created three groups of labour rights. Group III rights— workplace health and safety, and illness protection, protections for children and youth, minimum wages—have penalties for violation determined by an arbitration panel only after a lengthy (more than two years) dispute process. The monetary penalties themselves, the equivalent of 0.007% of the value of one year's goods trade between the Parties, were seen by many as insufficient.

Group II rights—the prohibition of forced labour, minimum employment standards pertaining to overtime, employment discrimination, gender pay equity, workers' compensation, protection of migrant workers—contain no penalties for violation, only review and consultation among the NAOs, the Secretariat and the Ministerial Council, and evaluation by an outside committee of experts (ECE).

Group I rights—the right to associate, to organize, to bargain collectively and the right to strike—are subject only to NAO review and ministerial consultation. No penalties are provided for violation of these fundamental rights. Allegations of violations cannot even be evaluated by a committee of outside experts. *Thus NAALC provides a limited set of penalties for a limited group of rights.*

As of mid-1997, nine complaints had been filed with the NAOs. Two were combined in a single submission and one was withdrawn before hearings were held. All but one were filed with the US NAO. All but one alleged non-enforcement violations in Mexico. All but one pertained to one labour right, the right to organize (i.e., intimidation and firing of workers attempting to join independent unions.) As such, no complaint has gone beyond the NAO review and ministerial consultation stage. Only the most recent complaint, involving pregnancy testing, has the possibility of going to the next stage, independent expert committee evaluation (ECE).

The single complaint filed with the Mexican NAO was against *Sprint* (February 1995) for closing down a San Francisco telemarketing facility that workers were attempting to organize. The Mexican NAO requested ministerial consultations. One outcome of the consultation was a report by the NAALC Secretariat on *Plant Closings and Labor Rights* (June 1997) which found that anti-union tactics were widespread in the US. Another was a US National Labour Relations Board ruling that the closing was motivated by anti-union bias and an order to the company to rehire the affected workers and compensate them for lost wages. The case is now being appealed by Sprint in the US courts.

The first two petitions (February 1994) were filed as one by the Teamsters, against *Honeywell,* and by the United Electrical Workers (UE) against *General Electric,* alleging that the US companies had dismissed workers for trying to organize an independent union, and that the Mexican government had failed to enforce its laws protecting the right to organize.

The US NAO report did not recommend ministerial consultations, concluding that it was not able to make a decision as to whether or not the Mexican government was enforcing its own laws, in part because the Mexican government itself had not made a judgment on the allegation of the employees. Instead, it recommended a series of tri-national workshops to promote discussion regarding freedom of association and the right to organize.

In the *Sony* case (August 1994), the International Labour Rights Fund, along with three other US and Mexican groups, alleged that the company fired workers who tried to organize an independent union at five Sony-owned maquiladora plants. An allegedly rigged election conducted by the official union, the CTM, in collusion with the company, subsequently reconfirmed the government union despite worker protests.

A second attempt to form an independent union also failed when the government's *Conciliation and Arbitration Board,* on which members of the government, the corporations and the CTM sit—all with a vested interest in keeping out independent unions—refused to register the union.

The US National Administrative Office found in its report that Sony had in fact intimidated the workers for trying to organize an independent union, and agreed that the workers were gravely hampered by the registration procedure in setting up an independent union. The NAO recommended consultations among the US and Mexican Labour Ministers. Ensuing consultations resulted in workshops, conferences, and reports on union registration.

Mexico's long-standing practice of blocking the formation of independent unions through its conciliation and arbitration boards was not altered by the NAALC review. No workers have been rehired as a direct result of this complaint.

The *Pesca Union* complaint (June 1996) alleged that the union which represented the Mexican Fisheries Ministry workers was improperly deregistered in the wake of a government reorganization, and recognition was granted to a rival union. Complainants alleged that members of the arbitration board were in a conflict of interest, violating ILO Convention 87. Studies, reports and ministerial consultations ensued.

In October 1996, a complaint was launched after a Mexican arbitration board allegedly denied union registration to workers at *Maxi-Switch* (a computer keyboard maker) after the company fired 400 workers for trying to organize an affiliate to an independent union and break the "contract of protection" with the official government- sponsored union. However, the complaint was withdrawn after the board reversed its decision and registered the independent union, one of the complainants.

Some have seen this outcome as the result of the publicity brought to bear on Mexican labour practices through the NAALC process. However, the company subsequently closed and then reopened under a different name, with the government union (CTM) once again the registered union in the plant.

In May 1997, a complaint was brought by three US and Mexican human rights groups, alleging "a pattern of widespread state-tolerated sex discrimination against prospective and actual female workers in the maquiladora sector..." Specifically, it involved *mandatory pregnancy testing* and denial or withdrawal of employment to those who test positive, thereby avoiding payment of the legal three-month maternity benefit. The US NAO, as of June 1997, was still reviewing the case.

Many critics dismiss NAALC as ineffectual. Others argue that their criticism stems from unrealistic expectations about what was achievable and how it could be used. Compa (1997) and Herzenberg (1997) conclude that, while *common enforceable norms* would have been desirable, the reality of wide income disparities and the overwhelming domination of one NAFTA partner made *effective enforcement of domestic law* the more practical goal.

They emphasize the importance of NAALC as a forum for subjecting countries' labour law to the glare of public scrutiny, as well as its value in stimulating communication, information exchange and building solidarity among labour rights advocates, particularly between Mexico and the United States. (Canadian labour activists have only recently become engaged in NAALC. In September 1998, the United Steelworkers filed a complaint with the Canadian NAO charging violation of fundamental labour rights in Mexico. The case involves Echlin Industries, a Canadian-owned auto parts maker and the Mexican government's violation of the right to organize.) They emphasize that its potential capabilities have not been sufficiently tested thus far and point out that the Secretariat and other institutional structures are still in their formative stage.

Herzenberg argues that "labour advocates' inability to use the NAFTA side-agreement to reverse specific worker rights violations should be neither surprising nor a primary basis for judging [its] usefulness. Effective use of the side agreement must be understood as part of broader organizing and political mobilization to challenge the ideological dominance of neoliberalism and gain the power to replace it with an alternative development model." [p.6]

NAFTA MECHANISMS WHICH AFFECT EMPLOYMENT, INCOMES AND STANDARDS

NAFTA, in essence, codifies a shift in the balance of power in favour of capital and away from governments the kind that intervene in markets and labour. (It strengthens the power of governments to enforce market disciplines.) By weakening public policy instruments and labour's power at the bargaining table, it increases the pressure to level down employment conditions, wages and standards. These changes are being observed globally and as such are key elements of the process of globalization.

NAFTA is not a separate phenomenon, but rather *the concrete expression of globalization on the North American continent.* Thus, when the ILO Director General said several years ago that globalization is eroding government policy instruments "which have such a decisive impact on the level and quality of employment and on domestic policies for social progress," (ILO, 1994:90-94), he could just as easily have substituted NAFTA which is, in effect, *continental globalization.*

It should be reiterated, however, that national social, political and economic institutions and structures differ from nation to nation, as do the strategies of key actors. Therefore, national responses to NAFTA pressures, like the response to broader globalization pressures, can also be expected to differ.

We identify the following mechanisms associated with NAFTA-style integration:

Competitive pressure among corporations: The concurrent deregulation and integration of the continental economy, driven by expanding trade and foreign investment, intensifies competition not only among transnational corporations themselves, but also among national companies in trade-sensitive industries. As national markets with different costs and regulatory structures come into closer contact with one another, the pressure to cut costs and restructure through mergers and takeovers, downsizing, closures, relocations, etc., increases.

In Canada, the largest wave of corporate restructuring occurred during 1989-1993. Although comprehensive statistics on plant layoffs and closures are not available for the country as a whole, Ontario, which contains 40% of Canada's manufacturing capacity, reported between January 1989 and August 1993 452 permanent closures of major manufacturing facilities. Almost half of these plant closures were by foreign-owned (mainly US) companies.

Significantly, 65% of all layoffs during this period were the result of *permanent* rather than temporary closures, compared to the 1981-82 recession where only 25% of the layoffs were the result of permanent closures.

Increased competition also intensifies the pressure among employers to demand worker concessions—wages, benefits, conditions of work—as well as tax, spending and regulatory concessions from governments, especially programs such as unemployment insurance which strengthen the bargaining power of workers.

Finally, it increases the pressure (to the extent that technology permits) to lower costs through production and work reorganization—increasing the use of part-time, temporary and contract workers, and outsourcing to non-union firms in low-wage jurisdictions.

Immobile labour-mobile capital: Labour's bargaining power is disadvantaged under NAFTA-style integration because, with the exception of a few élite categories (business executives, entrepreneurs and certain professional and technical categories), workers are legally confined by national borders. Culturally, workers are bound to their communities and internal migration, let alone immigration, occurs only in exceptional circumstances.

Capital, on the other hand, being inherently footloose, can move much more effortlessly under its new regime, or threaten to move if labour does not make concessions. There is much anecdotal reporting from both unions and employers and survey research providing evidence of this kind of pressure.

For example, a *Wall Street Journal* survey of 455 senior corporate executives (September 24 1992), taken just after NAFTA was initialled, found that 25% would use NAFTA to bargain down wages and 40% would move at least part of their companies' production to Mexico as a result of NAFTA.

A 1997 study for the North American Commission on Labour Co-operation (NAALC) by Cornell University researcher Kate Bronfenbrenner found that "NAFTA has created a climate that has emboldened employers to more aggressively threaten to close or actually close their plants to avoid unionization."

Her study of 500 organizing drives and 100 first contract campaigns in the US found that, in the manufacturing and transportation sectors, 62% of employers threatened to close and move all or part of their operations instead of negotiating with the union; 10% explicitly threatened to relocate to Mexico, and many more implied as much.

Where such threats were made, companies were substantially more successful in keeping out unions than where they were not made. (See also Larudee in this volume.) Since unionized workplaces in the US and Canada pay their employees 20% to 30% more on average than non-unionized workplaces, it is clear that this is having a depressing effect on wages.

Increased competitive pressure on governments and regulatory structures: NAFTA, by opening up national economies, intensifies pressure on hundreds of national and sub-national governments to compete with one another to maintain and attract investment by increasing subsidies (most of which remain legal under NAFTA) and lowering regulations and standards.

There are no *common* rules governing acceptable and unacceptable subsidies or limiting subsidy wars among governments, and only ineffective protections limiting competitive bidding-down of labour and environmental regulations to the lowest common denominator.

Policy levers, such as performance requirements and tariffs, which served as sticks to nudge capital to behave in accordance with public policy priorities and discourage capital outflows, have been removed and only carrots remain. Thus, the need to attract investment creates dual stresses: downward pressure on regulations and standards and increased pressure on existing fiscal resources.

This reality is not disputed in official circles. In fact, at times it is used to justify specific measures to downgrade regulatory structures (whether or not objectively valid) contrary to commitments made by governments prior to NAFTA. NAFTA provides the external conditioning framework which allows policy-makers to claim there is no alternative in the new economic reality.

For example, a 1996 report by the Canadian government on key issues facing Canada to the year 2005 noted, "As we become more integrated with the US, the efficiency of our regulatory framework...will take on greater importance in corporate decision-making, increasing pressure to harmonize with the US...[For example] labour laws and policies in Canada tend to impose a higher regulatory cost on employers and reduce the flexibility and dynamism of labour markets in Canada relative to those in the US.

According to the report, what specifically puts Canada at a disadvantage? "Minimum wages tend to be higher and hours of work and overtime regulations tend to be more restrictive, advance notice and severance rules tend to be more stringent, and domestic labour laws are more conducive to the formation and retention of unions."

The social safety net is under the same pressure, according to the government's report. "The basic affordability of the system and the benefits payment regime..has a direct consequence on competitiveness...By raising the cost of labour as a productive input, such programs can either drive jobs south or encourage further substitution of capital for labour."[3]

The government has already taken this advice to heart. Public spending cuts, which accelerated after 1989, moved into high gear under the Liberal government, whose "war on the deficit" reduced federal program spending by one-third in relation to GDP during 1995-97. Program spending by all governments was cut from 40% of GDP in 1992 to 33% of GDP by 1997.

Among the most prominent cuts have been those to unemployment insurance, most of which occurred under the current government—after 1993. As a result, the proportion of the unemployed eligible to collect unemployment insurance dropped from 87% in July 1990 to 36% as of July 1998, and is expected to fall to one-third once the reforms have been fully implemented (CCPA Monitor, October 1998). In an environment of high unemployment, the impact of such measures on wage demands is obvious.

Pressure on fiscal capacity: The competitive drive to attract and maintain investment increases the pressure to reduce taxes and increase subsidies to capital. The resulting fiscal pressure tends to crowd out social spending: from unemployment and disability insurance, welfare and pensions to education, training and health care. The pressure to compress workers' wages and reduce their purchasing power also weakens the income and consumption tax bases. The enhanced ability of élite workers to move or threaten to move, either to work in other jurisdictions or to transfer their savings, puts additional pressure on fiscal capacity.

Moreover, NAFTA, by enhancing the ability of transnational corporations to internalize their operations, increases the volume and relative importance of already high levels of intra-firm trade and accompanying practices of transfer pricing (where prices of imports and exports are set by managers to show minimum profits in high-tax jurisdictions and maximum profits in low-tax areas), and so too the pressure to lower corporate tax levels. (Vernon, 1994.)

NAFTA and Macro-Economic Policy: NAFTA-style integration and macro-economic policies are bound together as mutually reinforcing pillars of neoliberal strategy. Locking in a regime that allows largely unregulated capital flows (the hallmark of NAFTA) limits macroeconomic policy control, especially for the smaller partners. The fiscal pressures engendered by NAFTA have been outlined above, as have the constraints on public spending.

In Canada, competitiveness imperatives under NAFTA also shape monetary policy priorities, especially the "need" for wage control. (The rationale for tighter monetary policy in Canada, for example, is that the "natural rate" of unemployment—the rate at which inflation is triggered—is higher than in the US due to larger labour market impediments: more generous social benefits, stronger unions, etc.)

Competiveness priorities in a NAFTA environment require disciplining labour through unemployment-inducing monetary policy in the short term, and in the longer term, harmonizing the "natural" rate of unemployment with that in the US through cutbacks to social benefits, weakening labour standards and the removal of other "impediments" to a competitive labour market.

Moreover, severe monetary tightening during 1988-91, by depressing domestic demand, forced business to export to the more buoyant US
economy, thereby hastening the integration of the Canadian economy with
its larger partner. The interest rate-driven rise in the Canadian dollar added
to the pressure on import-competing industries to adjust to the new reality
or close down.

Similarly, the interplay of macro-policy and NAFTA was evident
during the 1994-95 Mexican financial crisis. The Mexican growth and
structural adjustment strategy depended on attracting sustained inflows
of foreign investment. These flows had stalled in the late 1980s, despite
massive structural adjustment. NAFTA's role was to deepen and make
permanent the liberalized trade and investment climate and thereby attract larger and sustained inflows of foreign capital. A central requirement of the strategy was to preserve and enhance its major competitive
advantage: low-cost labour. This was done with the help of several domestic policy tools for constraining wages, outlined later.

The anticipation of NAFTA raised expectations among foreign investors eager to participate in a new era of Mexican growth. FDI inflows,
the productive capital that the government was seeking, did increase in
the pre- and immediate post-NAFTA period (1989-94). However, three-
quarters of the inflows were portfolio and other short-term capital eager
to benefit from the expected post-NAFTA boom, and lured by high interest rates on Mexican government bonds.

Only 15% of the inflow was invested in production, and much of
that was invested in export production with weak linkages to the domestic economy. (cited Dillon, 1997, 63). Moreover, NAFTA had removed
most industrial policy tools to strengthen backward linkages from the
export sector to the domestic economy.

Foreign mutual funds flooded into the previously closed Mexican
stock market, which was now flush with issues of newly privatized state
enterprises, sending their values soaring. It also poured into Mexican government bonds, which had been bolstered by a peso-dollar exchange rate
guarantee. The surge of capital into Mexico prompted a huge increase in
imports unmatched by exports, and with it a succession of current account deficits rising to $29 billion in 1994.

It also kept the peso high and stable, a key element of the government's inflation control strategy. The high peso and growing external gap reflected the effect of growing import competition on an already precarious domestic sector.

NAFTA, while putting in place a legal framework conducive to the inflow of foreign capital, also removed any capacity to control capital outflow. And flow out it did, with growing magnitude in 1994, nervous in the wake of peasant uprisings and political assassinations, wary of the ballooning trade gap, and lured out by rising US interest rates.

The fragile underpinnings of the Mexican growth strategy quickly unravelled at the end of 1994. Within weeks the peso lost nearly half its value and $28 billion fled the country. The contraction of the Mexican economy was deeper than anything the country had experienced since the 1930s.

The peso crisis prompted a quick response by the US Administration, which put together, with the help of the IMF, the World Bank and various central banks, an unprecedented $50 billion bailout package.

The crisis shattered what has been called the "NAFTA effect," the widely-held perception both inside and outside Mexico that the creation of a NAFTA-type environment was the way for countries to embark on a sustained growth path, enabling the prolonged restructuring to finally bear fruit. (See Morales 1997.) Despite the collapse of the euphoria around NAFTA, the official line in Washington and Mexico City denied any connection between the financial crisis and NAFTA, except to contend that without the Agreement the crisis would have been worse.

Both the US and Mexican governments had much at stake in protecting the credibility of the NAFTA option. The extension of NAFTA-type arrangements throughout the hemisphere is the centerpiece of US foreign policy in the area, and a key strategic goal for corporate America. To acknowledge a connection would be to undermine the credibility of the NAFTA model as a viable solution to their economic problems.[4]

For its part, politically destabilized and ever more deeply indebted ($173 billion in 1995), the Mexican government, dependent on US political and financial support, also denied the link between the crisis and an Agreement for which it had gambled so much of its political credibility.

The huge financial support package assembled by the US government stemmed the hemorrhage and prevented a default on its external debt payments. Observers, citing the benefits of NAFTA, noted that the collapse of Mexican imports from the US (and Canada) during the crisis was proportionately much less than from non-NAFTA countries. This is not surprising, given an export sector that had come to rely so heavily on imported US inputs and as such, was greatly insulated from internal instability. Mexican exports to the US and Canada grew far more than to NAFTA countries.

The subsequent inflow of direct investment was also to be expected in light of plummeting labour costs and the new commitment to deregulate the banking, communications and petro-chemical sectors imposed as a condition of the bailout.

DOMESTIC MECHANISMS AFFECTING EMPLOYMENT, INCOMES AND STANDARDS

These mechanisms interact with and reinforce the NAFTA mechanisms affecting employment, incomes and standards.

The mechanism of choice in Canada for disciplining wages has been high unemployment, maintained primarily through tight monetary policy.[5] Formal wage and price controls were used in the 1970s to deal with the stagflation problems of that era. Since then, explicit wage controls, along with the suspension of collective bargaining rights, have been confined to the public sector.

Monetary austerity from the beginning of the 1980s steadily forced up unemployment into the 9-10% range where it has remained throughout most of the 1990s. As Jackson argues in this volume, extreme monetary contraction was deemed necessary by policy-makers in Ottawa to force a compression of wage growth which had gotten out line with wage growth in the US, and was deemed detrimental to Canada's long-term competitiveness in a free trade environment.

Public sector cuts, through the mechanism of the "war on the deficit," have also played a key role in disciplining wages, particularly during 1994-97. This has occurred primarily through the erosion of the non-wage income system (social wage), especially unemployment insurance, welfare and pensions. This increased dependence on wage income at a time of profound restructuring and a harsh labour market, serves as an effective restraint on wage pressure in an environment where international competitiveness preoccupations reign supreme.

Canadian unions maintained their numbers throughout the 1980s and so far in the 1990s, in contrast to their US counterparts whose numbers have fallen sharply. During 1988-1993, overall union density has been stable at 32.6% of the labour force, although in the manufacturing sector unionization fell from 35% to 33.4% during a period of rapid restructuring.

The presence of union-friendly social democratic governments in several provinces has helped. More recently, hostile governments have attacked labour legislation in several provinces, making it more difficult to organize and to bargain effectively.

In the United States, internal mechanisms for constraining wages and other labour costs go back to changes to the National Labour Relations Act in the early post-war period, which weakened the ability of unions to organize and bargain collectively. Particularly damaging were "right-to-work" laws which permitted workers in many of the southern states to opt out of union membership. These right-to-work states were characterized by low wages compared with northern states, and very low levels of unionization. The existence of this "union free zone" has had a chilling effect on wages and labour rights nationally, and has served as a testing ground for both governments' and companies' labour relations nationally.

The US tariff exemptions which enabled the creation of the Mexican maquiladora program in 1965 provided another mechanism for companies wanting to escape the higher wages and hassle of a unionized work force. As we shall see in the next section, the maquiladora has evolved into an effective vehicle for disciplining labour in the high-wage areas of North America, as well as within Mexico itself.

Fractious relations between US employers and unions in an atmosphere of growing international competition in the 1970s and 1980s spawned aggressive union-busting and union avoidance campaigns. They were assisted by the anti-union rhetoric and measures of the Reagan and Bush administrations, and by a weakly enforced National Labour Relations Act. The consequence was a further decline in union density (from 25% in 1979 to 15.5% in 1995), a key factor driving the decline of American wages and growing inequality since the late-1970s. (Mishel et. al. 1997:199.)

The deterioration of labour market conditions, notably the growth of non-standard work, has also played a role in constraining wages and increasing inequality. For example, the growth of non-standard work has greatly reduced the proportion of workers with adequate medical coverage. Medical care, unlike Canada where coverage is universal, is a workplace benefit in the US. In 1993, 58% of the US population had employer-sponsored health insurance, down from 66% in 1980.

Health coverage for workers with a college degree dropped from 79% to 73% during 1979-93. Coverage for workers with less than high school dropped from 52% to 36% during the same period. One half of private sector wage and salary workers working less than 20 hours per week did not have a health plan; one-quarter working between 20 and 43 hours did not have a health plan. (NAALC, 1997) One-third of full-time workers in small companies (less than 100) did not have a health plan. Fear of losing health insurance has clearly contributed to the general employment insecurity and to a chilling effect on wage demands.

The US minimum wage, like Mexico's, has consistently lagged behind inflation. The 1995 US minimum wage was 13% below its 1984 level. (NAALC, 1997.) Proportionately more women in all three countries earned the minimum wage or less.

The US unemployment insurance system and adjustment and training programs were greatly cut back during the 1980s, as were welfare and anti-poverty programs. (Recent modest improvements in the minimum wage and unemployment insurance, and the NAFTA adjustment program have been overshadowed by further cuts to welfare programs.) Changes in the tax system under Reagan greatly reduced the burden on the top 10% and especially the top 1% of income earners, weakening fiscal capacity and accentuating income inequality.

Monetary policy has also been an important device for disciplining wages. However, the more advanced decline of labour market institutions and social supports has made the need for monetary policy less compelling than in Canada.

Domestic mechanisms of wage control in Mexico start from the fact that the unions are part of the governing party, the PRI. The leadership of the CTM, the official union confederation, are also PRI politicians and members of the government.

Thus, the annual tripartite solidarity agreements (Pactos Sociales) between government, business and labour which have been in place since 1987 have been a very effective vehicle for holding down wage increases below inflation and productivity growth. So has the national tripartite Minimum Wage Commission which, between 1982 and 1988, reduced the real minimum wage by over 70% (US—Office of Technology Assessment 1992:81). The 1995 Mexican minimum wage was 51% below its 1984 level. (NAALC, 1997). Real average hourly wages in 1994 had fallen 30% below their 1980 levels; by mid-1996 they had dropped another 25% (Shaiken, 1997, 3).

Unions have been an important government policy tool for controlling worker demands. Furthermore, tripartite labour regulatory bodies have effectively blocked the formation of independent unions and thus more effective worker representation. Practices where companies sign contracts with union agents, without the knowledge of workers to keep any union presence out of their workplaces, are commonplace.

Periodic currency devaluations have also been an effective tool for maintaining and enhancing Mexico's competitive advantage in low wages.

The maquiladora has several additional devices for controlling wages besides those already mentioned, including: collusion between employers and CTM officials to keep workplaces union-free; employer collusion to set wages; segmentation of skills such that the vast majority of workers are placed in the unskilled category; and a preference for young women who have tended to be more compliant and less militant in terms of workplace demands. (J. Carillo 1990, cited in Kopinak, 1996: 13-14).

Lower maquila wages exercise a drag on wages in the rest of the manufacturing sector, and, as maquila-like production expands, it increasingly sets the tone for employment relations throughout the economy.

Macro-policy instruments, especially monetary austerity, have helped to keep the domestic economy in chronic stagnation and has squeezed profit margins, pushing employers to take a hard line against wage increases. The lack of unemployment insurance in an atmosphere of a rapidly growing labour force and few formal sector jobs is a powerful deterrent to worker militancy. Moreover, policies of fiscal austerity and privatization have greatly cut back the Mexican system of social protection (medical care, housing, food subsidies education, pensions) since 1982, reducing both the proportion of workers covered and the extent of coverage.

As with the other NAFTA countries, non-standard work has grown apace with competitiveness pressures and capital mobility, leaving fewer workers with access to benefits. The huge labour surplus has increasingly been pushed into the informal sector, particularly into self-employment. Although open unemployment has doubled since 1993, complementary measures show the real level of unemployment to be much higher nudging 25% in 1996. (See Gutierrez in this volume.)

In Mexico, 34% of the labour force received workplace benefits in 1995, down from 39% in 1991, due mainly to the rise in non-standard and unpaid work and the decline of the public sector. In 1993, 63% of salaried workers received social security benefits, down from 66% in 1991. Among the self-employed, small employers, etc., only 2% received employment benefits.

THE MAQUILADORA

The maquiladora industrial program was established in 1965 to spur industrialization in the Mexican border region with the US, though it was soon expanded to include non-border areas as well. The program took advantage of the US tariff exemptions which allowed US components to be assembled abroad and re-exported back to the US duty-free. Its importance as a deregulated export zone stems not only from the profound effect it came to have on wages and jobs, both within Mexico and north of the border, but also as a precursor of the approach taken in NAFTA.

Ironically, a much different approach was taken in an agreement signed the same year, the Canada-US Auto Pact, a managed trade agreement which contained production and employment guarantees.

In the early years, maquila plants did exclusively routine assembly using unsophisticated and obsolete equipment, with a preference for hiring young women. During the 1970s, maquila plants were granted exemptions from the rules limiting foreign ownership and exemptions from Mexican labour laws; for example, lengthening the probation period during which an employer did not have to pay minimum wage, allowing dismissals without having to pay severance, etc.

The maquiladora grew, if unevenly, throughout the 1970s, experiencing declines in periods of recession in the US. It was certainly not perceived as a potential replacement to Mexico's dominant form of import-substituting industrial development. By 1981 it employed 131,000 and generated a considerable amount of foreign exchange.

Under pressure from the IMF, the World Bank and the US government to move to a deregulated, export-oriented model of economic development (post-1982), the maquiladora became a more important focus for Mexican policy-makers. Electrical and electronic equipment, machinery and automotive sectors became priority areas for maquiladora production. The massive devaluation of the peso sharply reduced the cost of Mexican labour, making it highly attractive to transnational capital.

While the domestic economy stagnated and businesses failed in large numbers throughout most of the 1980s, the maquiladora sector grew quickly. Also, a growing number of foreign-owned transnational plants, not originally set up under maquila rules, reoriented their production from the depressed domestic market toward exports, becoming, in effect, de facto maquiladoras.

US auto companies, the main example, exported back to the US under the reduced tariff provisions, its general system of preferences (GSP).

We discussed earlier how the characteristics of employment relations in the maquiladora kept wages down and have increasingly come to shape employment relations throughout the economy. Since 1975, wages in the "maquilized" industry have been about one-half of wages in the non-maquila manufacturing sector. (Gambril 1994, cited in Kopinak, 1996:14.)

The expansion of more capital-intensive production and more flexible work methods in the 1980s has been accompanied by a reduction in wages. Carrillo's study of auto plants (cited Kopinak, 150) showed that, when a company converted to export production and transferred operations north to the border area, workers' wages decreased even as advanced technology was introduced.

Workers in border plants received on average 60% less than their colleagues making finished products near Mexico City. An unskilled worker in the "old" automotive sector made the same wage as a skilled maintenance mechanic at the border. Carrilllo observed a homogenization of wages in all maquila sectors, regardless of the technology used.

The position of women in the maquiladora labour market was not improved by the changes in the 1980s. Women were much more likely to have unskilled jobs. Few were able to gain entry into the new supervisory or technician jobs that became available. (Kopinak 1996: 183.)

By the end of the 1980s, exemptions which had been granted to the maquila sector in the previous decade were extended to the entire economy. For example, foreign ownership limits were removed for all sectors except mining, petrochemicals, auto parts and communications. The maquiladora sector, which had once been the exception, had become the rule in terms of Mexican industrial strategy. It was the vehicle through which Mexico would become integrated into the global economy. The domestic component of value added in the non-maquiladora export sector dropped steadily from 90% in 1980 to 39% in 1994. (Dillon 1994:74.)

The 1989 government Decree on the Maquiladoras prepared the groundwork for the NAFTA that was to follow, creating in microcosm the rules that would later be generalized to the whole economy. Firms that were not legally maquiladoras could shift to export production if they had idle capacity, creating part-time maquilas.

The legislation was broadened to include agro-industry, mining, fishing and forestry. This blurring of the lines between the export and domestic production would further facilitate the maquilization of the economy.

NAFTA extended the maquila rules of duty-free import and re-export (with duty only on the value-added—almost entirely labour) to the whole economy. By 2001, all duties will be removed. Companies that were able, under maquila rules, to import components and materials from third countries for maquila assembly and export, duty-free, into the US, will no longer be able to do so unless they meet the NAFTA rules of origin, or content requirements.

As a result, many of these companies are shifting production from other locations, mainly in Asia, to North America, mainly Mexico. NAFTA increases in stages the ability of maquila companies to sell in the domestic market, removing all restrictions by 2001, when the name "maquila" will officially be dropped and become part of Mexico's domestic manufacturing industry.

Non-maquila companies will have virtually no protection and will either have to adapt their operations or fail in the new maquilized environment. Survival will likely entail entering into some kind of an alliance with foreign capital for access to technology and intermediate inputs.

Historically, the maquiladora has been delinked from the domestic Mexican economy, sourcing less than 2% of its non-labour value-added from within the domestic economy. This applies as well to nationally-owned maquilas which are generally sub-contractors to transnationals, providing the labour, the premises and the administration, while the transnational provides the capital, machinery, parts, components and supervision. There is evidence that under NAFTA the tie to the domestic economy has become weaker still, falling from its historic average of 1.73% to 1.45% (Dillon, 1997:74.)

Despite the widely held perception of chronic labour shortage throughout the maquila zone, wages have in fact fallen steadily throughout the 1980s and 1990s. The reason, according to Kopinak (1997: 146) and others, is employers who collude to set the terms of employment, unions which don't adequately represent workers, and the government which determines what constitutes a fair day's pay through the minimum wage. This labour market control to keep wages low was pioneered in the maquiladora and is key to the maquilization of the Mexican economy.

Perceived labour shortages have been the result of employers' unwillingness to pay higher wages. The absence of effective unions to bargain collectively on their behalf has, according to Kopinak (1996, 194-95), led workers to pursue individual and household strategies to maximize their income, notably by having more members working. The maquila labour market is heavily tilted against workers. The high turnover rates are indicative of worker's frustration and the price employers are willing to pay to keep wages from rising.

The 1994-95 crisis brought another collapse in wages, prompting a new wave of expansion and a new migration north to the border region and across to the US. The jump in illegal arrests prompted and renewed a toughening of enforcement measures by US officials and measures such as proposition 187 in California to discourage immigration by denying newcomers any form of state assistance.

The peso devaluation aided the maquila producers (who conduct their operations in US dollars) by lowering their labour costs. The enclave nature of their production insulated them from the internal turmoil of the high inflation, high interest rates and collapse of internal demand. It accelerated the foreign takeover of Mexican business, and the conversion of Mexican-owned business itself to maquiladora status.

Fuelled by NAFTA and the peso collapse, the maquiladora entered another boom period. Employment jumped by 407,000 or more than 75% since NAFTA's implementation, from 542,074 in 1993 to 980,430 by December 1997 (INEGI). In 1981, the year before the Mexican debt crisis, there were 131,000 employed in the maquila sector. By 1988, employment had grown to 369,489. Since then, another 579,000 workers have been added to the ranks of the maquiladora work force. In 1982, maquila employment made up 5% of manufacturing employment. By 1995 it had surpassed non-maquiladora manufacturing employment. (See Gutierrez in this volume.)

ECONOMIC OPENING UNDER CUFTA/ NAFTA

Both Mexico and Canada have undergone a major opening of their economies since 1990. Mexico's trade (exports plus imports) doubled as a proportion of GDP, from 24% to 48%, during 1990-95. Canada's trade rose from 58% to 71% of GDP during this period. The US, whose trade openness was by far the lowest, saw a moderate increase in trade openness, from 21% to 24% of GDP during this period. (NAALC, 1997.)

TABLE 1

MACRO-ECONOMIC AND TRADE INDICATORS

	Canada	Mexico	United States
GDP (US$ billion) 1995	500	252	6,743
Population (million) 1995	30	95	263
GDP per capita (US $)	20,401	7,239	25,512
GDP growth (average annual) 1980-90	3.4%	1.0%	3.0%
GDP growth (average annual)1990-95	1.8%	1.1%	2.6%
Annual population growth 1980-90	1.2%	2.3%	0.9%
Annual population growth 1990-95	1.3%	1.9%	1.0%
GDP per capita growth 1980-90	+24.2%	-14.3%	+19.8%
GDP per capita growth 1990-95	-2.8%	-6.0%	+7.4%
Inflation rate (average annual) CPI 1984-89	4.3%	79.2%	3.5%
Inflation rate (average annual) CPI 1990-95	2.6%	19.5%	3.9%
Real Interest rates (average annual) 1989-96	5.6%	6.1%	1.2%
Exports of goods & services (% of GDP) 1989	27.9%	18.5%	9.8%
Exports of goods & services (% of GDP) 1995	41.8%	26.9%	11.5%
Trade Balance (goods & services) US$B			
1984-89 (average annual)	9.2	6.4	-130.3
Trade Balance (goods & services)			
USB 1990-95 (average annual)	9.1	-8.2	-125.3
Inward Foreign Direct Investment (FDI)			
$US B (average annual) 1989-96	6.2	6.2	49.0
Inward Foreign Direct Investment (FDI)			
$US B (average annual) 1983-88	4.2	1.8	34.4
Outward Foreign Direct Investment (FDI)			
$US B (average annual) 1989-96	5.6	-	-57.2
Outward Foreign Direct Investment (FDI)			
$US B (average annual) 1983-88	-4.3	-	-13.6
Inward Portfolio Investment (average annual) $USB 1989-96	+21.2	+7.7	+139.1
Inward Portfolio Investment (average annual) $USB 1983-88	+11.5	-0.3	+56.8
Outward Portfolio Investment (average annual) $USB 1989-96	-6.7	-1.0	-69.5
Outward Portfolio Investment (average annual) $USB 1983-88	-1.5	-0.5	-6.1

Sources:
International Monetary Fund, International Financial Statistics.
International Monetary Fund, Direction of Trade Statistics.
World Bank, World Development Report, 1997.
North American Commission for Labour Cooperation, Secretariat, North American labour Markets: A Comparative Profile, 1997.

Both Canada and Mexico were already very trade- dependent on the US prior to CUFTA/NAFTA. Nevertheless, the share of Canadian exports going to the US rose sharply, from 71% in 1989 to over 80% in 1996. Imports from the US, although less concentrated, also rose significantly, from 64% to 67% in 1995 (IMF).

With the most open economy to begin with, Canada's exports of goods and services, as a share of GDP, rose steadily from 28% in 1989 to 42% in 1995 (NAALC,1997). Imports rose at a similar pace in relation to GDP, from 31% to 42%, indicating a major reorientation of economic activity. Exports of goods and services grew twice as fast as overall GDP growth during the 1980s and five times as fast as GDP during the first half of the 1990s.

Foreign investment flows also increased sharply in the free trade era. Canada, the industrialized country with by far the highest level of foreign ownership, saw inflows of FDI rise from $US 4.2 billion per year during 1983-88 to $6.2 billion annually during 1989-96.

Outward flows of Canadian-owned FDI also grew rapidly, from $4.3 billion per year during 1983-88 to $5.6 billion per year during 1989-96. Inflows and outflows of portfolio capital grew far more.rapidly. Inflows rose from $11.5 billion per year during 1983-88 to $21.2 billion per year during 1989-96; and outflows rose from $1.5 billion per year to $6.7 billion per year between these two time periods.

Mexico's exports to the US, like Canada's, became more concentrated, growing from 70.4% of total exports in 1990, as NAFTA negotiations began, to 82.9% in 1993 and continuing to rise to 83.7% by 1995. Import concentration from the US also rose, though from a smaller base and at a less rapid rate.

Mexico's exports as a share of GDP did not change much during the pre-NAFTA period (1989-93), fluctuating between 18% and 19% of GDP, although they had risen during the early years of the trade liberalization—from 15% in 1985. (NAALC, 1997.) However, exports rose sharply to 27% of GDP in 1995, reflecting the structural jolt in the economy. Imports, on the other hand, rose in the pre-NAFTA period—from 12% to 18% of GDP—reflecting the deepening of trade and investment liberalization and high peso monetary policy during these years. (Imports rose during the first stage of trade liberalization, from 10% of GDP in 1985 to 12% in 1989.) Imports fell in the wake of the 1995 crisis to 15%, but remained substantially above their pre-1989 level, reflecting the increased dependence of Mexican manufactured exports on imported inputs.

Comparing the growth of the Mexican economy overall to growth of the export sector, GDP in both the 1980s and 1990s grew at an average annual rate of just 1%. (Growth picked up moderately in the 1990s until 1995, when it contracted by 6.2%.) However, throughout the 1980s and 1990s annual exports of goods and services grew rapidly—6.6% and 6.8%, respectively. (World Bank, 1997.)

The inflow of foreign direct investment into Mexico also increased dramatically during the 1990s, the annual inflow rising from $US1.8 billion during 1983-88 to $6.2 billion per year during 1989-96. Portfolio inflows also increased massively, from a negative $-0.3 per year during 1983-88 to an average $7.7 billion per year during 1989-96. (Of course, these more volatile and speculative flows resulted in a sudden $10 billion outflow in 1995.)

Mexico used its oil wealth to borrow heavily in international markets in the late 1970s. In 1980, shortly before the debt crisis, it had $58 billion worth of external debt. Fifteen years later, its external debt had soared to $166 billion and more than doubled from 31% to 70% of GDP. However, Mexico was a much more export-oriented economy and the ratio of external debt to exports had declined from 232% to 171%. The ratio of debt servicing costs to exports fell in half, from 44% to 24%. (World Bank, 1997.)

The transformation of the Mexican economy, driven by trade and investment liberalization, stems from the policies implemented in the wake of the 1982 crisis, a decade before NAFTA came into effect. A key structural change associated with this economic opening was the growth in manufactured exports to the US, using imported inputs or intermediate goods from the US.[6] While manufactured exports rose from 13% of total exports in 1982 to 84% in 1995, intermediate goods imports rose from 53% to over 80% of total imports in 1995. (Hinojosa et al., 1996: 39.)

The changes were driven by the crisis and the IMF-mandated structural adjustment program agreed to and implemented by Mexican policy-makers. But they were also driven by the fact that US transnationals had decided to make Mexico an integral part of their global competitiveness strategies, as a low-labour-cost export platform close to the US market.

The change in the structural relationship between imports and exports was evident during the 1995 crisis, when intermediate goods imports from the US fell only momentarily before resuming their growth in line with manufactured exports. Consumer and capital goods imports from the US, on the other hand, experienced a deeper and prolonged compression after the peso collapse. Intermediate goods imports used for domestic production fell to a much greater extent during the 1982 crisis. (Hinojosa, 1996,38.)

Thus, the demand for Mexican exports (i.e., US demand) is now the key determinant of Mexican imports, rather than changes in domestic demand. This, according to Hinojosa, is the main structural difference between the two Mexican financial crises. Moreover, this new import-export relationship is growing even faster than the growth of maquila exports "as this strategy of manufacturing for export is adopted by many other regions, sectors and types of firms in the Mexican economy" (ibid, 9) seeking insulation from the demand weakness of the domestic Mexican economy.

In 1986, Mexico joined the GATT and by 1988 the average tariff had dropped to 10% from 25%.[7] At about the same time, Mexican policy-makers began to deregulate financial and investment flows. During 1989-94, foreign capital inflows supported a high peso and expansion of imports, resulting in a widening of trade and current account deficits. NAFTA was seen by policy-makers as a tool for enlarging and stabilizing these foreign capital inflows [Hinojosa, 1996:36]. However, this time the financial inflows were largely portfolio capital—equity and bonds rather than bank loans or direct investment. Greater openness has meant greater dependence on international financial markets.

The United States economy, the world's largest, was only moderately dependent on Canada, its largest trade partner—21.5% at the beginning of CUFTA. By 1995 it had barely moved, to 21.6%. Slightly lower dependence on Canadian imports, 18.2% of total imports in 1989, rose slightly to 19.2% in 1995 (IMF).

US export dependence on Mexico, its third largest trade partner, also low, increased significantly from 6.9% to 9.0% of total exports during 1989-93, falling back to 7.8% in 1995. US imports from Mexico as a share of its total imports rose steadily throughout the pre- and post-NAFTA periods—from 5.6% to 6.8% in 1993 and to 8.1% in 1995.

The US economy is far less open than those of Mexico and Canada. There was, nevertheless, a steady overall trade opening, exports rising from 7.2% to 12.4% of GDP during 1984-94, falling back moderately to 11.5% in 1995. Imports also rose steadily during this period, from a larger base of 10.3% of GDP in 1984 to 14.4% of GDP in 1994, falling back to 13.1% in 1995. (NAALC, 1997.)

Comparing US export growth to overall economic growth, exports grew during the 1980s at an annual rate of 5.2%, substantially above the annual 3% rate of GDP growth. During the first half of the 1990s, the divergence widened—with annual growth slowing to 2.6% and exports rising at an annual rate of 7.3%. (World Bank, 1997.)

There was also a large increase in inward FDI into the US during 1989-96 ($49 billion per year), compared to the 1983-88 period ($34.4 billion per year). More striking, however, was the rise in outward flows of US-owned FDI, from $16.6 billion per year during 1983-88 to $57.2 billion per year during 1989-96.

Both inflows and outflows of portfolio investment increased even more rapidly. The former jumped from $ 56.8 billion to 139.1 billion per year, and outward flows soared, from $6.1 billion per year to $69.5 billion per year between these two time periods.

Trade and Manufacturing Employment

As economic liberalization and integration have proceeded under NAFTA, manufacturing sector employment has fallen in all three countries—not only in relation to the rest of the economy, but also in absolute numbers. Canada has been hardest hit, with a contraction of 255,000 or 12.8% during 1988-96, more than three times the US decline of 802,000 or 3.8% during this period (see tables 2 and 3).[8]

The first phase, 1988-93, saw the biggest shrinkage, 375,000 or 18.8% in Canada and 1,763,000 or 8.3% in the US. During this stage there was a recession in both countries, although more severe and prolonged in Canada due to deeper restructuring and to a tighter monetary policy. In phase II (1993-96) there was a partial recovery of employment in most sectors in both countries.

In Mexico, the manufacturing sector as a whole declined only slightly, from 1.32 million to 1.31 million during 1988-1996. However, after growing to 1.44 million in 1993, it fell back 8.8% in the following three years. (INEGI, Encuesta Mensual.) Moreover, these numbers mask a major structural shift in the Mexican economy. Maquila sector employment more than doubled during this period, adding 384,000 workers during 1988-96, while the non-maquila sector employment lost 388,000, 41% of its work force.

Mexican manufactures exports, mainly to the US, grew rapidly, from 18.6% of total exports in 1985, the beginning of the economic opening, to 37.5% in 1988. By 1995, manufactured exports had grown to $80 billion from $38 billion in 1988, increasing its share to 83.7% of the total. Intermediate imports grew at a similar pace, reflecting the high import content of exports.

In the transportation equipment sector (mainly automotive), which accounts for about 30% of NAFTA trade, Canadian employment was steady (-0.4%), with some fluctuation during 1988-96, while US employment fell by 300,000 or 12.7%. The maquila auto sector grew by 86,000 or 116% during this period. Electrical/electronics sector employment in Canada fell by 40,000 or 25% during 1988-96, and in the US it contracted by 133,000 or 6.5%. Maquiladora employment in the electronics sector (the largest) grew by 94,632 or 98% during this period. Textile and clothing employment in Canada contracted by 47,000 or 26% during 1988-96, and by 323,000 or 17% in the United States. Maquiladora employment in this sector as well grew rapidly during this period.

Both Canada and Mexico (post-1994) have seen their merchandise trade surplus with the US increase under free trade, though their current account surplus is much smaller because of the large net outflow of interest and dividend payments to the US. However, the relationship between

TABLE 2
CANADA: MANUFACTURING EMPLOYMENT

	1988 Thousands	1993 Thousands	1996 Thousands	1988-1993 % Change	1993-1996 % Change	1998-1996 % Change
Manufacturing	1,992.3	1,617.2	1,737.7	-18.8%	7.5%	-12.8%
Food	207.7	179.6	188.5	-13.5%	5.0%	-9.2%
Beverages	32.5	24.6	22.5	-24.3%	-8.5%	-30.8%
Rubber products	23.0	20.8	23.8	-9.6%	14.4%	3.5%
Plastic products	55.2	47.6	57.6	-13.8%	21.0%	4.3%
Leather & allied products	22.3	12.8	11.8	-42.6%	-7.8%	-47.1%
Primary textiles	24.9	17.2	19.7	-30.9%	14.5%	-20.9%
Textile products	33.7	27.6	28.0	-18.1%	1.4%	-16.9%
Clothing	120.8	85.1	85.0	-29.6%	-0.1%	-29.6%
Wood	119.8	99.7	123.2	-16.8%	23.6%	2.8%
Furniture & fixtures	64.1	43.7	50.4	-31.8%	15.3%	-21.4%
Paper & allied products	127.0	101.5	99.0	-20.1%	-2.5%	-22.0%
Printing, publishing & allied ind.	152.3	147.1	140.1	-3.4%	-4.8%	-8.0%
Primary metals	103.3	80.0	83.7	-22.6%	4.6%	-19.0%
Fabricated metal Products	174.3	135.4	154.0	-22.3%	13.7%	-11.6%
Machinery (ex. leect. mach.)	84.9	64.9	89.4	-23.6%	37.8%	5.3%
Transportation equipment	224.1	196.9	223.3	-12.1%	13.4%	-0.4%
Electrical & electronic products	157.0	115.6	117.3	-26.4%	1.5%	-25.3%
Non-metallic mineral products	55.2	41.2	44.1	-25.4%	7.0%	-20.1%
Refined petroleum & coal products	21.5	13.9	12.6	-35.3%	-9.4%	-41.4%
Chemical & chemical products	90.6	84.1	82.0	-7.2%	-2.5%	-9.5%

Source: Statistics Canada; Employment Earnings and Hours

TABLE 3

UNITED STATES: MANUFACTURING EMPLOYMENT

	1988 Thousands	1993 Thousands	1996 Thousands	1988-1993 % Change	1993-1996 % Change	1988-1996 % Change
Manufacturing	21,320	19,557	20,518	-8.3%	4.9%	-3.8%
Food and kindered products	1,701	1,763	1,708	3.6%	-3.1%	0.4%
Textile mill porducts	714	620	619	-13.2%	-0.2%	-13.3%
Apparel and other finished textile products	1,182	1,004	954	-15.1%	-5.0%	-19.3%
Lumber and Wood Products, except furniture	758	705	759	-7.0%	7.7%	0.1%
Funiture and fixtures	685	624	661	-8.9%	5.9%	-3.5%
Paper and allied products	735	721	668	-1.9%	-7.4%	-9.1%
Printing, publishing and allied products	1,899	1,784	1,846	-6.1%	3.5%	-2.8%
Chemicals and allied products	1,257	1,205	1,309	-4.1%	8.6%	4.1%
Petroleum and coal products	179	176	160	-1.7%	-9.1%	-10.6%
Rubber and miscellaneous plastics products	813	783	862	-3.7%	10.1%	6.0%
Leather and leather products	140	122	140	-12.9%	14.8%	0.0%
Stone, clay, glass, and concrete products	610	530	607	-13.1%	14.5%	-0.5%
Primary metal industries	802	727	785	-9.4%	8.0%	-2.1%
Fabricated metal industries	1,332	1,212	1,305	-9.0%	7.7%	-2.0%
Machinery and computing equiptment	2,532	2,224	2,410	-12.2%	8.4%	-4.8%
Electrical machinery, equipment and supplies	2,039	1,760	1,906	-13.7%	8.3%	-6.5%
Transportation equipment	2,645	2,289	2,308	-13.5%	0.8%	-12.7%
Professional and photographic equiptment, and watches	695	686	758	-1.3%	10.5%	9.1%
Toys, amusements,sporting goods	129	142	158	10.1%	11.3%	22.5%

Source: U.S. Department of Labor. Bureau of Labor Statistics

changes in trade balances and employment changes is complex. An improvment in trade balances does not necessarily mean an increase in employment.

Employment also depends on a variety of interrelated factors, most of which are affected by integration under NAFTA. These include: changes in trade and investment with non-NAFTA countries; macroeconomic policy and performance (including output, income and productivity); the nature and changes in the structure of wages (e.g., the displacement of high-income jobs and replacement with lower income jobs, or the decline in union bargaining power); cross-border movement of capital (e.g., production facilities); the level and changes in import content of exports (affected by, for example, the ownership structure); changes in the labour intensity of exports and imports, changes in its sectoral composition; level and changes in intra-firm trade (and accompanying transfer pricing).[9]

By way of example, we looked at the changes in trade balances between Canada and the United States in the 21 major manufacturing categories (two-digit SIC codes) during 1998-96 and compared these to Canadian employment changes in these sectors [See Appendix: Table 5]. Bear in mind that the export share of manufacturing output in Canada rose from 40% to 60% during this period.

The total loss of Canadian manufacturing employment during 1988-96 was 254,500. The Canadian surplus in manufactures trade with the US improved by $29.4 billion—from $5.5 billion to $34.9 billion—during 1988-96. A rough estimate based on the Canadian Foreign Affairs Department calculation that $1 billion of exports to the US supports 11,039 jobs suggests that the improvment in manufactures trade balance translated into an employment increase of 325,000. This implies that other factors (also NAFTA-related in large part) were responsible for destroying 579,000 manufacturing jobs, given the net overall decline of 254,500 jobs.

Of the 14 manufacturing categories showing an improvement in Canada's trade balance with the US, three showed an increase in employment, a combined increase of 6,600 or 3.3%. The other 11 manufacturing sectors had a combined decline in employment of 162,700. Thus, sectors showing an improvement in their trade balance with the US, accounting for 60.3% of manufacturing employment in 1988, showed a net employment loss of 156,100, or 61% of total manufacturing losses.

The other seven sectors experienced a deterioration in their trade balance with the United States. One of these (non-electrical machinery) actually showed an improvement in employment of 4,500. The other six showed a combined decline in employment of 102,900. Thus, sectors which experienced a deterioration in their bilateral trade balances, accounting for 39.7% of manufacturing employment in 1988, had a combined net employment loss of 98,400, 39% of total losses. Thus, in aggregate, job loss was proportionately the same regardless of whether the sectors' bilateral trade balance improved or deteriorated.

COMPARATIVE PORTRAIT OF NAFTA ECONOMIES AND LABOUR MARKETS[10]

The United States was the world's largest economy in 1995, 12 times larger than the Canadian economy, and 27 times larger than the Mexican economy. Canada's GDP per capita was four-fifths of the US level. Mexico trailed far behind at just over one-quarter of the US level and just over one-third of Canada's per capita GDP (NAALC 1997).[11]

The Mexican economy grew hardly at all during the 1980s and mid-1990s, and with population growing rapidly, GDP per capita fell 14% during the 1980s and another 6% during the first half of the 1990s. This is a staggering collapse of living standards, especially when compared with the three previous decades when growth averaged close to 7% per year and per capita GDP grew almost 4% per year.

The Canadian economy slowed considerably in the 1980s compared with the post-war "golden age." Nevertheless, with a slower growing population, GDP per person still grew 24% during the decade. The situation changed markedly in the free trade era as the economy stagnated and GDP per capita actually declined 2.8% during 1990-95. [Personal income per capita declined even more rapidly—by 5.1% during 1989-96.]

The United States economy maintained a steady if slower growth path in the 1980s, declining somewhat during the 1990s. Consequently,

TABLE 4

LABOUR MARKET INDICATORS

	Canada	Mexico	United States
Labour force (millions) 1995	15	34	132
Labour force growth 1984-95	16%	48%	17%
Labour force participation rate 1995	64.8%	60%	67%
Female participation rate 1995	58%	37%	59%
Male participation rate 1995	73%	84%	75%
Youth participation rate (15-24 yrs) 1995	17%	29%	14%
Older workers participation rate (55-64 yrs) 1995	48%	53%	57%
Official unemployment rate, average annual, 1990-95	10.2%	2.8%	6.3%
Official unemployment rate , average annual, 1984-89	9.3%	3.2%	6.5%
Self-employed: % of workforce 1995	9.0%	26%	6.6%
Multiple job holders: % of workforce 1995	4.9%	6.9%	5.9%
Part-time workers: % of workforce	18.6%	26.6%	14.9%
Involuntary part-time workers: % of workforce 1995	5.9%	5.1%	3.6%
Temporary workers: % of workforce 1995	9.0% (1994)	4.7%	4.9%
Hourly compensation (production workers) average annual, change 1990-96	1.0%	-2.5%	-0.8%
Labour productivity: average annual, 1990-96	2.2%	7.5%	3.0%
Hourly compensation (production workers), average annual, 1985-90	0.0%	-11.7%	+0.3%
Labour productivity: average annual, 1985-90	0.8%	4.9%	2.8%
Household income : top quintile, share of after tax (1994)	41% (1993)	54.2%	47%
Average top quintile income as multiple of average bottom quintile income (1994)	7.3 times (1993)	13 times	13 times
Average real household income (% growth 1984-94)	0	26%	9.5%
Manufacturing Employment (% change, 1989-96)	-12.8%	-0.1%	-3.8%

Sources:

North American Commission for Labour Cooperation, Secretariat, North American labour Markets: A Comparative Profile, 1997. Statistics Canada Employment Earnings & Hours, United States, Department of Labor, Bureau of Labor Statistics.

per capita GDP grew 20% during the 1980-90 and 6.2% during 1990-95. That growth, as we shall see later, has been more unevenly distributed.

EMPLOYMENT AND UNEMPLOYMENT

In 1995, the US accounted for 73% of the North American labour force, with Mexico holding 19% and Canada 8%. The Mexican labour force grew 48%, almost three times as fast as the US and Canada labour force during 1984-95, the result of higher population growth in previous decades, as well as the faster entry of women into the labour force.

The US and Canada had similar labour force participation in 1995 (66.7% and 64.8%, respectively), while Mexico's was lower (59.6%) due to the lower Mexican female participation rate (37%) compared to the Canadian (58%) and US (59%) participation rates. Mexico had a higher male participation rate (84%) than either Canada (73%) or the US (75%), and the male participation rate increased during 1984-95 compared to the US and Canada, whose rates dropped.

Mexico had proportionally almost twice as many youth (15-24 years) participating in the labour force (29%) as either the US (14%) or Canada (17%) in 1995. The US had the highest participation rate of older workers (55-64 years) in the work force: 57% in 1995, up from 54% in 1984. Mexico's rate was 53%, up from 41% in 1984. Canada had the lowest older worker participation at 48%, down from 52% in 1984. This reflects the greater need to work longer due to insufficient retirement income in the US, and especially in Mexico. The Canadian rate reflects higher and growing early retirement, driven in part by fewer job opportunities.

Mexico has a large informal employment sector, estimated at 44% of total employment in 1995. The informal sector is a subsistence sector characterized by very low earnings, no benefits, and a high degree of precariousness. It includes household domestic work, employees, employers, and piece-workers in establishments with fewer than five workers (excluding formal sector self-employed as well as professional and unpaid workers). It has grown steadily as job opportunities in the formal economy have been unable to absorb the rapidly growing labour force.

The need to survive makes unemployment an unaffordable luxury for most.

The high proportion of employment in the primary sector also distinguishes the Mexican economy from the US and Canadian economies: 24% compared to 3% and 4%, respectively. The service sector in Mexico is proportionately smaller, accounting for 54% of employment, compared with 74% in both Canada and the US.

The vast majority of employment growth in all three countries during 1984-95 was in the services sector—96% in Canada, 98% in the US, 91% in Mexico (1991-95). Manufacturing accounted for a similar share of employment in all countries in 1995: 15.3% in Canada, 15.8% in Mexico, and 16.4% in the US.

Non-standard work—part-time, temporary, self- employment and multiple job holding—has grown steadily in all three countries during 1984-95, despite some cyclical fluctuation. The proportion of part-time workers has grown in all three countries; up in Canada from 14.8% to 18.6% of the employed work force during 1984-95; up in the US from 17.6% to 18.5%; and up in Mexico from 25.6% to 26.6% (1991-95). The involuntary part-time work force grew fastest in Canada and actually fell in the United States, reflecting the lower US unemployment rate.

In Canada and the US, the share of part-time female workers has remained the same, but has grown among men. In Mexico the female share of part-time workers has grown. A greater share of women hold part-time jobs involuntarily in all three countries, although the difference is most pronounced in Canada.

Self-employment is the main form of non-standard work in Mexico at 26% of the labour force, down slightly from 1991. In Canada the figure is 9%, and in the US 6.6.%. In all countries, most of this work is in the service sector, although Mexico also has a significant share in agriculture. There is a small but growing share of multiple job holders in all three countries, reaching 5.9% in the US, 4.9% in Canada, and 6.9% in Mexico in 1995.

Temporary work is hardest to compare because of data limitations and methodological differences (see NAALC, 1997, 42-43). The share of temporary workers in Canada grew from 3.5% to 9.0% during 1984-94. In Mexico, temporary workers made up 4.7% of the work-force in 1995.

In the US, temporary workers made up 2.2% of employment in 1995 (although the figure rises to 4.9% using a broader definition of temporary employment.) The US has the highest incidence of short- tenure jobs. In 1991, 29% of all jobs lasted less than one year, compared with 22% in Canada and 25% in Mexico (1993).

Education levels of workers in all three countries have grown. Higher educated, higher skilled workers in all three countries tend to have more stable, better-paying jobs. Less skilled, less educated workers have higher unemployment and underemployment rates, and less access to training. In 1994, 43% of the employed work force in the US and Canada, and 81% in Mexico, had high school education or less. The proportion of workers with at least some post-secondary education was 57% in Canada, up from 38% in 1984; and 56% in the US, up from 44% in 1984.

The official unemployment rate in Canada has been high and, despite some cyclical fluctuation, has grown throughout the 1980s and 1990s, averaging 10.2% during 1990-95, up from 9.3% during the 1980s. US unemployment declined through the 1990s to 5.3% in 1996. Unemployment averaged 6.3% during the first half of the decade, lower than the 1980s. The gap between Canadian and US unemployment, which tracked the US rate very closely from 1950 to 1980, opened up a two-point gap after the 1980s recession. It widened again to 4 points in the 1990s. Mexico's open unemployment has been low throughout, averaging 2.8% during 1990-95, but doubling in 1995 and 1996.

Unemployment rates were higher for less-educated workers in both the US and Canada, although in Mexico unemployment for workers with less than six years of education was less than for those with some high school or post-secondary education. This probably reflects the "unaffordability" of unemployment.

In all three countries, young workers have had much higher unemployment rates (more than double) than the general rate, and a much higher share of jobs lasting less than a year. During the 1990s, Canadian and US unemployment rates for men were higher than for women. In Mexico they were slightly higher for women.

Earnings, productivity, and income distribution

During 1990-96, real hourly earnings (wages and benefits) of production workers rose 1% in Canada annually, while declining 0.8% annually in the United States and falling 2.5% annually in Mexico. By contrast, labour productivity during 1990-96 grew 2.2% per year in Canada, 3% in the US, and 7.5% annually in Mexico. During 1985-90, hourly earnings of production workers in Canada did not grow at all, fell 11.7% per year in Mexico, and barely increased at the rate of 0.3% per year in the US. Productivity, on the other hand, grew 0.8% annually in Canada, 2.8% in the US, and 4.9% per year in Mexico.

In US dollars, Canadian average weekly earnings for all employees rose until 1991, closing the gap with US average earnings. Thereafter, they fell largely because of the Canadian dollar decline, widening the gap again to 13% below the US level. [In US dollar terms, Mexico's average weekly earnings for wage and salaried workers in the private formal sector in 1994 were 14% of US levels and 15% of Canadian levels. In 1995 they were even further behind at 13% of US levels.

Throughout the region, higher earnings were associated with higher levels of education. And gender differences in earnings narrowed at higher levels of education. In 1994, Canadian median weekly earnings of full-time male workers with eight years of education or less were 43% less than those of workers with a university degree. The gender wage gap narrowed from 64% of male earnings in the first category to 79% of male earnings in the universally educated category.

In 1995, median earnings for US workers with less than high school were 55% less than of those with a university degree. Women in the first category had earnings 25% less than men in that category. The gap narrowed to 15% in the high education category. Earnings of high education workers in both the US and Canada grew at a higher rate than did those at the low end. This was more marked in the US, where earnings at the low end grew 2.3% per year during 1984-91 whereas at the high end they grew 4.6% per year.

During the 1980s and 1990s, income inequality after taxes and transfers increased in both Mexico and the US; and it remained stable in Canada until the early 1990s, but has since 1996 shown signs of widening, largely as a result of cuts to social transfers.

The gap between the top and the bottom quintile in Canada narrowed slightly, but increased in relation to the middle three quintiles. In both the US and Mexico, the top quintile increased relative to the bottom four quintiles. In Canada (1993), the top quintile received 41% of household income. Average income in the top quintile was 7.3 times the average in the lowest quintile. In Mexico (1994), the top quintile received 54.2% of aggregate household income. The average income in the top quintile was 13 times the average income in the bottom quintile. In the US (1994), the top quintile received 47% of total income and the average income in the top quintile was 13 times the average income in the bottom quintile.

In both the US and Canada, taxes and transfers increased the share of income for the bottom three quintiles and reduced it for the top quintile, with transfers in both countries having a greater impact in lowering inequality than taxes. Inequality in Canada (1993) as measured by gini coefficient was reduced 30% by taxes and transfers—taxes reducing inequality by 9.5% and transfers by 22%. In the US, inequality was reduced 15.6%—4.5% from taxes and 11% from transfers.

During 1984-94, real average household income in Canada was unchanged (though it dropped 4.8% during 1989-95). In Mexico it grew 2.9% per year because, despite the decrease in earnings, the number of earners per household rose. The ratio of the average income in the top quintile to the bottom quintile in Mexico increased from 10 times to 13 times. Average US household income increased 9.5% during 1984-94, and the average income gap between the top quintile and the bottom quintile rose from 12 times to 13 times.

If real wages were either flat or declining throughout the 1980s and 1990s and GDP and productivity were growing, one group that was benefiting in all three countries was the one comprising senior corporate executives. We track the relationship between CEO compensation (a proxy for senior executives as a group) and the earnings of average workers.

The gap in the United States between CEO compensation and average worker wages widened from 60 times in 1978 to 122 times in 1989, and to 173 times in 1995 (Pearl, Meyer and Partners Inc. & Wall St. Journal, cited Mishel et. al. 1997:227). During 1989-95, average hourly wages grew 0.7% while executive compensation (inflation-adjusted) increased almost 13 times faster (38%). [Mishel 1997: 134 and 227.] During the 1980s, executive compensation grew at a slightly faster rate, but annual wages increases were almost twice as fast as in the 1990s. (ibid)

The inequality in the average compensation of CEOs of US companies compared to average wages is much higher than in Canada. According to our calculations, the CEO-average wage gap in 1994 was 36 times in Canada. Comparisons over time are not possible, since only recently have Canadian CEOs been obliged by law to reveal their compensation. Nevertheless, executive compensation surveys indicate that average increases in the 1990s have been at least as fast and probably faster than their US counterparts.

For example, a KPMG survey found average executive compensation increased 32% during 1992-95 (cited *Financial Post*. 25.9.96) Meanwhile, real average hourly wages increased only 1.4% during the entire period 1989-95. Thus, it is safe to assume that the gap in Canada between CEO and average earnings, although much lower, is growing at least as fast as the US gap.

Even less information is available on Mexican CEOs. A 1994 Towers Perrin Inc. international comparison of CEO compensation showed Mexico ranked fourth (the US was at the top). Mexico moved into first place when adjusted for taxes, social security contributions and cost of living. Given that average formal sector compensation in Mexico is currently 13% of the US average, and that it has been falling in real terms, it is safe to say that the Mexican CEO-average earnings gap, regardless of the methodology used, is far higher than is the United States differential.

TNC Restructuring under CUFTA/NAFTA

The bulk of trade in the NAFTA region is conducted by a small number of large, mostly transnational, corporations. According to Rugman (1995), just 50 large corporations, most of them US-owned, account for 70% of US-Canada trade. According to Heredia (cited Grieder, 1997: 273),

300 corporations account for 85% of its exports and imports, although we suspect that it is now more concentrated.[12]

There is a small number of Canadian-owned transnationals with investments in all three countries. Large Mexican companies are national in the sense that, while they may export to the US or Canada, they have little direct investments in either country.

There is also a growing number of East Asian and European transnationals operating in all three countries.

US transnationals at the beginning of the 1990s owned two-thirds of the stock of FDI in both Canada and Mexico (Eden,1994:195). Five years later, they had maintained their share of FDI in Canada ($82 billion), though in Mexico their share ($18 billion) had dropped to 60% of the Mexican FDI stock, reflecting the influx of Asian and European transnationals. (SECOFE cited US ITC, 1997, 3-37.)

Canadian FDI in the US has grown rapidly in the last 15 years, accounting for 8.2% of the US FDI stock in 1995 (ITC,1997,3-53). Canadian-owned transnationals' direct investment in Mexico, though small, is also growing. Its share of Mexico's FDI stock grew from 1.4% to 2.5% of the total stock in 1995 (see Gutierrez in this volume).

Transnational corporations pursue strategies which combine company-specific advantages with country-specific advantages. Transnationals make direct foreign investments in plant, equipment, etc., to gain access to the domestic market, and, in a NAFTA-type setting, both to rationalize production to gain from scale economies and specialization, and to exploit cost differences within the region—labour, energy, taxes, government incentives, interest rates, infrastructure, transportation, etc.

Before Mexico deregulated its foreign investment rules in the 1980s, only the maquiladora sector was open to majority foreign ownership and thus to the significant cross-border integration of production. TNCs entered Mexico in minority-owned arrangements, licensing or contract relationships with Mexican firms for the purpose of gaining access to the domestic market. With trade and investment deregulation, direct investment in majority-owned affiliates and trade between affiliate and parent (intra-firm) has grown in tandem. TNC subcontracting or outsourcing to Mexican firms has also grown.

About 45% of US-Canada trade is intra-firm, though the ratio is substantially higher in manufacturing. Mexico-US intra-firm exports are now 55%, up from 44% of total exports prior to NAFTA (Heredia, cited Grieder op. cit., 1997:273), with intra-firm manufacturing trade close to 100%.

In pre-CUFTA Canada, part of the manufacturing sector (one-half of which is foreign-owned) was organized on a continent-wide basis (excluding Mexico). The automotive sector, operating under the rules of the 1965 Canada-US Auto Pact (a managed trade arrangement), was the most important integrated sector with almost all of its trade being intra-firm. Another part of manufacturing (roughly one-third) was so-called branch-plant operations—affiliates producing almost exclusively for the domestic market.

CUFTA triggered a major restructuring in this latter sector, with some branch plants converting to continental production and many just closing down and consolidating production south of the border in the US or Mexico, leaving just warehouse and distribution facilities in Canada. Also, there is much evidence of affiliates moving back administrative functions and even R&D to the parent company.

Cost considerations are key determinants of company location decisions. According to a 1996 KPMG Inc. study comparing business costs in 13 Canadian and 10 United States cities across seven manufacturing sectors, labour costs are by far the most important cost factor, accounting for an average 65% of location-sensitive costs and between 19% and 32% of total operating costs, depending on the sector. [3,16][13]

TNCs simultaneously pursue both high innovation and low-cost strategies. Investment in technology, the life-blood of the company, is concentrated close to the parent and costs are spread out across as many markets as possible to recoup the heavy investment cost. This technology has become highly transferable and its ownership, when protected as it is under NAFTA, can be diffused in accordance with country-specific or region-specific cost advantages. The Mexican combination of high productivity and low wages has become very attractive for transnationals.

Let us now look at changes over time in manufacturing labour costs among the three countries, as they might be viewed through the eyes of transnational corporate investors making continental or global investment location decisions. (US Bureau of Labour Statistics, June 1997.) Hourly compensation trends for production workers in manufacturing between 1980 and 1996 show that Canadian costs rose from 88% of US costs to exceed US costs during the early 1990s, settling back to 94% in 1996 as the Canadian dollar fell, the same ratio as it was in 1975.[14]

In 1980, Mexican manufacturing labour costs were 22% of US costs, and foreign direct investment outside the maquiladora was limited by law. Costs in Asian exporting countries such as Korea, Hong Kong, Taiwan and Singapore were one-half or less of Mexican labour costs. Five years later, in the wake of the 1982 crisis and the early stages of investment and trade deregulation, labour costs had fallen to 12% of US costs, roughly on par with the Asian exporters.

Mexican labour costs rose slightly from 1986 to 1994, then again fell sharply in the wake of the 1995 financial crisis. In 1996, with investment and trade deregulation consolidated in NAFTA, Mexican hourly manufacturing labour costs were just 8% of US costs and 8.5% of Canadian costs. Mexican manufacturing labour costs had fallen to between one-quarter and one-sixth of its low-cost Asian competitors. The declining Mexican labour costs throughout this period correlates very highly with the rise of TNC investment in the maquiladora and related export sectors. Recalling that maquiladora wages have been roughly one-half of wages in the domestic manufacturing sector, the Mexican advantage becomes even more pronounced.[15]

Labour productivity in Canadian manufacturing grew at a lower rate (0.8% annually) than compensation growth (4.6%) during 1984-91, resulting in a yearly rise in unit labour costs of 3.8%. Between 1991 and 1995, the situation reversed, with labour productivity increasing at 2.8% per year, above the annual compensation growth of 1.6%, resulting in a decline in unit labour costs of 1.2% per year. (NAALC, 1997.)

In Mexico, labour productivity at large manufacturing firms grew at 6.3% annually during 1986-94, while compensation costs grew at 4% per year, resulting in a drop in unit labour costs of 2% annually. In the US, labour productivity grew at 2.7% annually during 1984-91, slightly less than compensation costs. During 1991-95, labour productivity increased to an average 3.4% annually, above the annual growth of compensation of 2.3%, reducing unit labour costs by 1.1% per year.

The common perception is that large wage differentials between Mexico and its NAFTA partners reflect the fact that productivity in Mexico is much lower. While this is true for the economy as a whole, it is not true for the manufacturing export sector.

Harley Shaiken, author of several important studies of work organization and technology transfer in the Mexican auto and electronics sector, provides the following examples of Mexican ability to handle the most technologically sophisticated manufacturing operations. (Shaiken, 1993.)

- A Big Three auto engine plant in Mexico achieved productivity levels at 85% of US performance in less than two years and in some machining lines surpassed US performance. Quality exceeded its US counterpart in four of the six years for which data are available, by 32% in the most recent year. The company is investing in a $500 million expansion with the capacity to produce 500,000 engines a year.
- The Ford assembly plant (Hermosillo) had the fifth highest quality rating out of 46 assembly plants in North America.
- The Sony television assembly plant (Tijuana) has won Sony's worldwide quality award for several years running, and its productivity is identical to its counterpart in San Diego.
- Samsung (Tijuana) opened in 1996 a picture tube, television and VCR assembly plant which, by 2000, will produce 3 million televisions per year, mainly for export to the US and Canada. (Shaiken 1997:3)

The decline of Mexican manufacturing wages for the last 17 years has occurred while manufacturing productivity grew steadily. During 1980-92, average manufacturing labour productivity grew 41% (INEGI, cited Shaiken, 1993) and another 18% to 1995 (INEGI, cited International Metal Workers Federation, 1996:25). Meanwhile, real hourly wages fell 30% during 1980-94, then tumbled another 25% by mid-1996 (Shaiken,1997:3). During 1980-96, average manufacturing labour costs fell 64% against US and almost as much against Canadian labour costs. (BLS, 1997 op cit.)

Corporate surveys confirm not only that NAFTA was the major factor influencing corporate strategies, but also the attractiveness of Mexico as an investment location. For example, a 1992 survey by the American Management Association of 200 of its member companies with investments in all three countries (three-quarters in manufacturing), found that they planned to expand employment in their Mexican operations by on average 13.7% over the next three years, by 3.3% in their US operations, and by 0.7% in their Canadian affiliates. (Companies with large Canadian subsidiaries planned to reduce their Canadian work force by 2%).

The survey also found that manufacturing TNCs planned to increase investment spending in Mexico over the next three years by an average of 15.5%, by 3.7% in the United States, and by less than 1% in Canada.

The assessment of US financial analyst Louis Nevaer exemplifies the importance of NAFTA to US corporate interests. NAFTA opened great opportunities for US business and prevented any possibility of a return of Mexico's state-led inward-looking development model. "NAFTA is the surrender of economic sovereignty, implying political sovereignty as well". (Nevaer, 1996, xv)... "The speed with which corporate America is extending into all areas of the Mexican market astounds in its completeness." [13]

According to Navaer, "the tumultuous first year of NAFTA with its armed insurrection, political assassinations, and financial collapse were to be expected—"inevitable consequences of transformation and integration of the Mexican economy with those of the US and Canada."

North American restructuring: the record of 11 TNCs [16]

We have compiled statistical profiles for a sample of 11 transnationals in order to obtain a more focused picture of corporate restructuring during the "free trade" era, 1990-96 (see Appendix.) These companies are among the small group of companies that account for the large majority of North American manufactures trade.

We were surprised to find how little of information on individual corporations is publicly accessible, and how difficult it is to piece together even very basic profiles. The ability of transnational corporations to mask their activities is yet another manifestation of the enormous power they wield.

The statistical portraits include: employment, revenues, assets, profits, average wages, and CEO compensation—broken down where possible into US, Canada, Mexican maquiladora, and worldwide operations. They were put together using various sources: 10-K reports to the US Securities and Exchange Commission, reports to the Ontario Securities Commission, newspaper reports and company annual reports. The data on company activities in the maquiladora were obtained from Solunet Inc.(El Paso, TX.), a company which monitors corporate activity in the border region, covering the majority, though not all, of their operations in Mexico.

Our corporate profiles provide a useful, if incomplete picture (see appendix) of corporate restructuring under CUFTA/NAFTA. Ten companies are US-owned. One, a telecommunications transnational, Northern Telecom, is Canadian-owned.[17] Most of the companies are in the two most important maquila sectors—automotive and electrical/electronic.

The auto sector companies are: the Big Three—General Motors, Ford and Chrysler—and parts makers United Technologies and Allied Signal. From the electronics sector are General Electric, IBM, Northern Telecom and Rockwell. Chemical giant Dupont and chemical/automotive/consumer products conglomerate 3M complete our sample.

Employment

Although the trend varies somewhat from company to company, there are clear patterns. Canada tended to be hardest hit in terms of employment, the bulk of that coming during the first, or CUFTA phase (1990-93), compared to the second, or NAFTA phase (1994-96). (In many cases, the size of the Canadian work-force has become smaller than the maquiladora work force.) Usually, the Canadian cuts were deeper than the US cuts, which in turn were usually less severe than worldwide cuts.

Even where companies were growing worldwide, their Canadian operations were cut in most cases. There were, however, notable exceptions such as Dupont, where the Canadian operations were less severely cut than the US operations. Only one company (IBM) expanded its Canadian work-force. Only three expanded their US work-force. Without exception, maquila employment expanded greatly, reflecting the rapid rise in maquila employment described earlier; however, there is some evidence of cyclical fluctuations in maquila employment.

General Electric cut its Canadian work force by more than 3,000 or 35% during the entire six-year period, compared to 15% in the US (and 20% worldwide). It expanded its maquiladora work force by 25%, surpassing its Canadian work force by more than 2,000 in 1996.

General Motors cut its Canadian work force by almost 10,000 or 25%, most of it in the NAFTA phase (1993-96), contrary to the usual trend, and by 10% (49,000) in the US. (This compares with a 14% reduction in its worldwide work- force.) It compressed its maquila work-force by 28% in phase one, but then undertook a massive 170% expansion in the NAFTA phase. Employment since 1990 rose by more than 21,000, reaching 43,000 by 1996. (Remember that maquila employment represents only a portion of total Mexican employment. GM has a total of 70,000 employees in Mexico.)

Ford's Canadian work force fell 22% in phase one (1990-93), but recovered much of that loss in the NAFTA phase, with employment for the whole period still down 8%, a loss of 2,200 jobs. Ford's US workforce grew steadily, increasing almost 34,000 (22%) during 1990-96. Worldwide employment grew 12% during this period. Ford's maquila work- force more than doubled, from 11,000 to 23,000 during the period, most of the increase coming after 1993.

Chrysler's Canadian work-force remained stable at around 14,000, while its maquila work-force almost tripled, reaching 14,000 in 1996. The US work-force grew 10% during the NAFTA phase. Employment worldwide remained stable during the period under examination.

Allied Signal cut its Canadian work-force by 24% during phase one, recovering slightly during the NAFTA phase, but still down overall by 21%. US employment figures were not available but the company cut its global work-force by 28%. Maquiladora employment jumped almost six-fold to 5,950 in 1996, more than twice the size of its Canadian workforce. The bulk of the increase came in the NAFTA phase.

United Technologies cut its US work-force steadily throughout the period, by 29%. This compares with a global employment cutback of only

6%. Its Canadian subsidiary Pratt-Whitney shrunk by 15%, although in the NAFTA phase it increased its work-force significantly. The company almost doubled its maquila employment to 14,200 in 1996, with the bulk of the increase in the NAFTA phase.

IBM, despite cutting its Canadian employment by almost one-third during phase one, expanded its work force by 5% for the entire period. US employment increased steadily throughout the entire period, by more than 20%. Worldwide employment fell during the period by 30%. Though starting from a small base, IBM tripled its maquila employment to 1,500, the large majority of it in the NAFTA phase.

Rockwell cut its Canadian operation by 13% during the entire free trade period, though in the first phase employment was cut 26%, with one-half of the loss being made up in the second phase. Not sufficient information was available to determine the employment trend of the US parent, but worldwide employment dropped 5% (1991-95). Maquila employment more than doubled, though from a small base, with most of that coming in the NAFTA phase.

3M reduced its Canadian work-force by 11.3% during 1990-96, while expanding its maquiladora work-force by 169% over the same period. US employment figures for 3M are not available, but the company's worldwide work-force increased 6.5% during 1992-96.

Dupont cut its Canadian work-force steadily throughout the free trade period, by 18%. The US parent cut 40% of its work-force (1992-96). Worldwide staff cuts were almost as severe at 32% during 1990-96. Maquiladora employment expanded fourfold, though from a very small base, mostly in the NAFTA phase.

Canadian-owned Northern Telecom expanded its worldwide work-force 18% to 67,584 (1991-96). Major restructuring in the early 1990s saw cuts of 4,000 to its Canadian work-force, but it has since expanded employment to 21,000 in 1996. Canadian sales were 14% of worldwide sales in 1995, while US sales were 54%. Both have been falling as a share of the total as European and Asian sales experienced large gains. Northern's maquila plant tripled its work-force to 1,500 in 1996. Northern's domestic Mexican work-force has also grown on the strength of a $330 million contract to upgrade the telephone system.

Wages/Productivity/Profit

Using sales per employee as a surrogate for labour productivity and using available data, we are able to provide an approximate picture of these relationships in Canada and the United States.[18] We then looked at how those productivity gains were distributed among workers, CEOs (the proxy for senior executives) and worldwide profits. For the US-owned companies the comparison is with average US wages in the sector. For Northern Telecom the comparison is with the average Canadian sector wage.

The findings confirm that this sample of transnationals has had major productivity gains during the 1990s. However, the lion's share of these gains has been appropriated by profits and, more dramatically, by senior executive compensation. Average worker wages have been modest, in some cases barely keeping pace with inflation. These trends reflect broader industry trends (though more accentuated) and the growing inequality in both countries.

General Electric increased the productivity of its Canadian operation by 112% and that of its US operation by 37%. Comparing gains in CEO compensation with nominal wage gains for the average production worker in the sector (SIC 36), CEO compensation rose more than 500% during 1991-96 to $32.6 million in 1996, while worker wages in the sector increased a modest 16% to $26,284 in 1996, roughly the same as their Canadian counterparts.

Thus the CEO-average wage ratio widened from 224 times to 1,240 times. Worldwide profits, which averaged $3.9 billion during 1991-93, jumped to an annual average $6.3 billion during 1994-96. [We do not have senior executive compensation for the Canadian subsidiary of GE because, like the other Canadian subsidiaries of the companies in our sample, their compensation is well down the ladder of executive compensation. Their compensation does not register on lists of the highest-paid Canadian CEOs.]

The labour productivity of GM's Canadian operation increased 88%, while the productivity of its US parent rose 51%. CEO compensation rose 247% to $5.9 million. Average wages in the US auto sector (SIC

371) increased 24%. Wages in the Canadian auto sector (SIC 323) increased 33%. The ratio of US CEO compensation to the average US sectoral wage widened from 50 times in 1991 to 143 times in 1996. Meanwhile, worldwide losses averaging $8.5 billion during 1990-93 turned into $4.6 billion annual profits during 1994-96.

Productivity at Ford Canada jumped 88%, while productivity at the US parent rose 54%. CEO compensation rose 645%, while sectoral wages rose 24% (33% in the Canadian sector). The CEO-average wage ratio widened from 34 times to 198 times during 1991-96. Worldwide profits which were negative, $2.4 billion during 1991-93, jumped to a yearly average $4.6 billion during 1994-96.

At Chrysler Canada, productivity jumped 93%, while at the US parent productivity rose 28% (1993-96). CEO compensation rose more than 1,000% to $12.6 million during 1991-96, while average US sectoral wages increased 24%, (33% at their Canadian counterparts), with a consequent widening of the gap from 33 times to 305 times. Worldwide profit at Chrysler averaged $1.8 billion during 1991-93, increasing to $3.1 billion during 1994-96.

Productivity at Allied Signal's Canadian affiliate increased 28%. While US figures are not available, worldwide productivity jumped 52%. CEO compensation rose 550% to $13 million, while average sectoral wages increased 24%, widening the gap from 59 times to 319 times. The information available on profits was not sufficient to make a comparison.

Productivity at Pratt Whitney Canada increased 35%, and by 32% at its parent United Technologies. CEO compensation soared 415% to $6.7 million in 1996, while average sectoral wages increased 22%. Global profits increased from an average $270 million during 1991-93 to $750 million during 1994-96.

IBM's Canadian productivity level rose 14% during 1991-96 (although during 1990-91 it jumped 74%). It is not possible to calculate a figure for the US parent, but worldwide productivity jumped 68%. CEO compensation jumped fourfold to $10.5 million while average sectoral wages increased 16% (15% in Canada), resulting in a widening of the CEO-average wage gap from 80 times to 343 times. Meanwhile worldwide profits, which averaged a negative $-5.4 billion during 1991-93, rose to $2.2 billion during 1994-96.

Rockwell's Canada's productivity rose 75%, while worldwide productivity rose 28%. CEO compensation increased a relatively modest 133% compared to the average sectoral wage increase of 23%, widening the CEO-average wage gap from 44 times to 89 times. Global profits averaged $549 million during 1991-93, rising to $649 million during 1994-96.

The productivity of 3M's Canadian affiliate rose 38% while productivity world-wide rose 24% (1996-96). CEO compensation increased 100% while sectoral average wages in the US (and Canada) increased 14%, widening the CEO-wage discrepancy from 74 to 131 times. Global profits averaged $1.24 billion during 1992-93 and $1.27 billion during 1994-96.

Dupont Canada's labour productivity jumped 63% during 1991-96 while increasing 55% at its US parent. CEO compensation increased 75% while the average sectoral wage increased just 16% (14% in Canada), widening the gap from 52 times to 78 times. Global profit averaged $771 million during 1992-93, jumping to $3.2 billion during 1994-96.

Northern Telecom's worldwide sales revenue grew 57%, much faster than its labour force, reflecting a 33% gain in labour productivity. Profits averaged $185 million during 1991-93, including a major loss of $878 million in the latter year. Profits recovered thereafter, averaging $501 million during 1994-96. Average wages increased 16% in both US and the Canadian electronics sectors. We do not have figures on CEO compensation before 1993, but increases are much more modest than for the US-owned companies in our sample. Consequently, the CEO-average wage gap is smaller, fluctuating between 54 and 108 times during 1993-96.

ENDNOTES

1   Cited in David Crane, Toronto Star, May 3, 1997, p. c3. Neoliberal thought attributes problems of unemployment, inflation, economic stagnation, etc., to post-war interference by governments and other actors such as unions in constraining and distorting self-regulating markets, and espouses all forms of market decontrol including trade and investment, labour market, privatization and public sector downsizing as the solution to these problems.

2   This policy package later came to be known as the Washington consensus, denoting the like-minded thinking of the US policy establishment, and officials from Washington-based international financial institutions and private banks.

3   *Canada 2005: Global Challenges and Opportunities,* Privy Council Office Feb. 25, 1997: cited D. Crane Toronto Star, May 4, 1997: C2.

4   The Washington Post, reporting a speech by the US Treasury Secretary Robert Rubin, said "Rubin warned that because Mexico has been regarded as the star pupil of free market development, its collapse might have prompted officials throughout the developing world to repudiate the liberal approach US policy-makers and academic economists have been promoting so zealously for the last two decades." cited Doug Henwood, *Left Business Observer*, March 1995.

5   The value of high unemployment as an investment incentive is illustrated in a September 1997 study from an affiliate of Prudential Relocation Inc. pitched to US companies considering relocating to Canada (The company describes itself as the leading provider of relocation, real estate, human resources and related consulting services to the global business community.) Company Vice- President Charles Galloway is quoted in the press release as saying: "Canada offers a highly educated work force....with a considerable discount off the US dollar for labor costs, and a *much higher unemployment rate.*"—italics added]

6   Hinojosa, 1996,34, see figure 3.11 showing the parallel increase in intermediate imports and manufactured exports.

7   (Note that under NAFTA to date the average tariff level has dropped from 12% to 5%, a less dramatic change.)

8   By comparison, Canadian manufacturing employment during 1981-88, a period of major restructuring and deep recession, fell by 0.9%.

9   A Canadian External Affairs Department Staff Paper found that for 1991 a billion Cdn. dollars of exports supported 12,016 jobs overall, with a billion dollars to the US supporting a slightly lower 11,039 jobs, and an even lower ratio in key sectors like autos and electronics. The US Department of Commerce estimated that a billion dollars US of exports in 1992 supported 16,532 jobs (see Larudee). Moreover, 14% of the value of US exports was imported inputs, while 26% of the value of Canadian exports was imported inputs.

10   This is based largely on data compiled by the NAALC Secretariat and published in June 1997 as *North American Labour Markets: A Comparative Profile.*

11   It is noteworthy that Canada and US GDP were at parity in 1990 at the outset of NAFTA negotiations. The Canadian deterioration can be explained by poorer economic performance and the depreciation of the Canadian dollar.

12   US-owned corporations conduct about two-thirds of the trade in the region. According to Mersereau [Statistics Canada, 1992, 4.1-4.15], 37 of the 50 largest Canadian importers were US-owned.

13   This study treated manufacturing labour productivity as equivalent in both countries, based on the slight differences as measured by the US Bureau of Labour Statistics manufacturing output index, 1988-94. If Mexico were included, one would expect an adjustment for productivity.

14   The KPMG study found that location-sensitive costs (which make up approximately 40% of operating costs) were on average 16% lower in Canada. In the seven sectors examined, where labour costs make up between 60-70% of location sensitive costs, average labour costs in the Canadian cities were 17% to 30% lower in every sector.

15   The data on individual sectors are only available up to 1994. They show, however, that for electrical/electronic and transportation equipment sectors—the two largest maquila sectors—manufacturing costs closely paralleled the manufacturing average. Other sectors also showed little deviation from the average. (Source: US Dept. of Labour, Bureau of Labour Statistics, June 1996, unpublished data hourly, compensation costs for 40 manufacturing industries, 31 countries.)

16   The data for this section was compiled by Arun Purkayastha, a student research assistant with the Canadian Centre for Policy Alternatives during the Summer of 1997.

17   Information was gathered on two Japanese transnationals: Sony and Honda, but the information was not complete enough to be included in the sample. In the case of Honda, we can say that the Canadian work-force has remained stable since 1990 at about 2,300, while their maquila workforce grew from 408 in 1990 to 2,800 in 1996. (US employment figures are not available). Sony has 1,250 Canadian employees, and its maquila workforce doubled from 4,239 to 8,600 during 1990-96. (US employment figures are not available.). We also lack data to compare CEO-average wage compensation for these companies but we do know that, on average, Japanese CEOs' compensation is a much smaller multiple of average employee earnings than that of their US counterparts.

18   Though we lack sufficient information to make detailed comparisons with Mexico, recall that average Mexican manufacturing production worker wages fell from 11% to 8% of the average US manufacturing wage during 1991-96, the reference period for our comparison; and as well the huge gap between CEO and average wages discussed earlier.

BIBLIOGRAPHY

Alberto-Semerena, J. (1997, February) *Growing Inequality and Productive Restructuring: Productivity and Performance of the Mexican Economy, 1970-96.* Paper prepared for NAALC, Seminar on Incomes and Productivity, Dallas.

Appleton, B. (1994) N*avigating NAFTA, A Concise User's Guide to the North American Free Trade Agreement,* Carswell.

Banco de Mexico

Bolle, M.J. (1997, September) *NAFTA Labor Side Agreement: Lessons for Worker Rights and Fast Track Debate.* U.S. Congressional Research Service, Economics Division, Washington DC.

Bronfenbrenner, K. (1996, September) The Effects of *Plant   Closing or Threat of Plant Closing on the Right of Workers to Organize.* Paper prepared for the North American Commission for Labor Cooperation, Secretariat, Dallas.

Cameron, D., and Watkins, M. (eds) (1993) Canada Under Free Trade, Lorimer.

Campbell, B. (1993) Free Trade, Destroyer of J*obs: AnExamination of Canadian Job Loss Under the FTA and NAFTA,* Canadian Centre for Policy Alternatives, Ottawa.

Campbell, B. (1994) "Trade and Investment Policy Under NAFTA: As If Jobs Mattered," *Canadian Foreign Policy,* Vol. 2, No. 1 (Spring) 147-67.

Canadian Labour Congress (1996) Social Dimensions of North American Economic Integration, report for the Canadian Government, Department of Human Resources Development.

Castaneda, J. (1995, July) "Ferocious Differences," Atlantic Mo*nthly,* 63-76.

Castenada, J.G. (1996) "Mexico's Circle of Misery," *Foreign   Affairs,* July/August. 92-105.

CCPA/CHO!CES (1997) *Alternative Federal Budget Papers, 1997,* Canadian Centre for Policy Alternatives.

Commission for Labour Cooperation (NAALC) (1997) *Plant Closings and Labour Rights.*

Compa, L. (1997) "NAFTA's Labour Side Accord: A Three-Year Accounting" *NAFTA: Law and Business Review of the Americas,* Summer 1997, 6-23.

Dillon, J. (1997) *Turning the Tide: Confronting the Money Traders,* Canadian Centre for Policy Alternatives.

Economic Policy Council-U.S. United Nations Association (1992) *The Social Implications of a North American Free Trade Agreement,* New York.

Economic Policy Institute et. al. (1997, June) *The Failed Experiment: NAFTA at Three Years*.

Eden, L. (ed) (1994) *Multinationals in North America,* University of Calgary Press.

Grieder, W. (1997) *One World, Ready or Not: The Manic Logic of Global Capitalism,* Simon and Schuster.

Grinspun, R. and Kreklewitch, R. (1994), "Consolidating Neoliberal Reforms: Free Trade as a Conditioning Framework," *Studies in Political Economy.* 43, Spring, 33-61.

Herzenberg, S. (1997) *Switching Tracks: Using NAFTA"s Labour Agreement to Move to the High Road. Interhemispheric Resource Centre,* Alberquerque, NM, Border Briefing #2.

Hinojosa Ojeda, R. et. al. (1996, December) North American Integration, *Three Years After NAFTA: A Framework for Tracking, Modelling and Internet Accessing the National and Regional Labour Market Impacts,* UCLA Los Angeles, School of Public Policy and Social Research. website: naid.sppsr.ucla.edu.

Instituto Nacional de Estadistica, Geographica y Informatica (INEGI) Encuesta Industrial mensual.

International Labour Organization (1994) *Defending Values, Promoting Change: Social Justice in a Global Economy,* Report of the Director General. (pp. 90, 94)

International Labour Organization (ILO) (1997) *World Employment Report.*

International Monetary Fund, *Balance of Payments Statistics*, various years.

International Monetary Fund, *Direction of Trade Statistics*, various years.

Jenkins, B. (1992) *The Paradox of Continental Production: National Investment Policies in North America.*

Kopinak, K. (1997) *Desert Capitalism,* Black Rose Books.

KPMG Inc. (1996) *The Competitive Alternative: A Comparison of Business Costs in Canada and the United States.*

Levinson, J. (1996, November) *NAFTA's Labour Side Agreement: Lessons From the First Three Years,* Institute for Policy Studies, International Labour Rights Fund, Washington DC.

Lipsey, R. and Meller, P. (eds) (1997) *Western Hemisphere Trade Integration: A Canada-Latin American Dialogue,* MacMillan Press.

Lustig, N (1997) NAF*TA: Setting the Record Straight,* Brookings Institution, Policy Brief, 20.

Lustig, N. (1992) Mexico, *The Remaking of an Economy,* Brookings Institution, Washington DC.

Maschino, D. and Griego, E. (1997) "L'Accord nord-américain de coopération dans le domaine du travail: Bilan et perspectives," Le *Marché du Travail,* Avril, Gouvernement du Québec.

Mersereau, B. (1992, August) "Characteristics of Importing Firms: 1978-86," *Canadian Economic Observer,* Statistics Canada, 4.1-4.15.

Mishel, L. et. al. (1997) *The State of Working America, 1996-97,* Economic Policy Institute, M.E. Sharpe.

Morales, I. (1997) "The Mexican Crisis and the Weakness of the NAFTA Consensus, "*The Annals of the American Academy of Political and Social Science,* 550, March, 130-52.

Nevaer, L.E.V. (1995) *Strategies for Business in Mexico: Free Trade and the Emergence of North America, Inc.,* Quorum Books.

North American Commission for Labour Cooperation (1997) Secretariat: *Plant Closings and Labour Rights: A Report to the Council of Ministers.*

North American Commission for Labour Cooperation Secretariat (1997) *North American Labour Markets: A Comparative Profile,* North American Agreement on Labour Cooperation.

North American Free Trade Agreement (1992) *Final Text,* December 17, 1992, CCH International.

OECD (1997, July) Em*ployment Outlook.* Paris.

Patten, M. (1997, May) "Maquila Industry Grows Up," *Twin Plant News,* El Paso, Tx, 27-31.

Ranney, D.C. (1997, April) *NAFTA and the Devalorization of Labour Power: A U.S. Perspective.* Mimeo.

Robinson, I. (1993) *North American Trade As If Democracy Mattered*, Canadian Centre for Policy Alternatives, International Labour Rights, Education & Research Fund.

Shaiken, H. (1990) *Mexico in the Global Economy: High Technology and Work Organization in Export Industries,* Centre for U.S.-Mexico Studies, University of California, San Diego.

Shaiken, H. (1993) "Going South: Mexican Wages and U.S. Jobs After NAFTA" *The American Prospect*, Fall.

Shaiken, H. (1997, February) *The First Three Years of NAFTA,* memo to Reps. Richard Gephart and David Bonior.

Stanford J. et. al. (1993) *Social Dumping Under North American Free Trade*, Canadian Centre for Policy Alternatives.

Stanford, J. (1993) *Estimating the Effects of Northern American Free Trade: A Three-Country General Equilibrium Model with "Real World" Assumptions*. Canadian Centre for Policy Alternatives, Ottawa.

Treffler, D and Gaston, G. (1997) "The Labour Market Consequences of the Canada-U.S. Free Trade Agreement," *Canadian Journal of Economics,* February.

Treffler, D. (1997, February) *No Pain, No Gain: Lessons from the Canada-U.S. Free Trade Agreement,* Paper presented to NAALC Seminar on Income and Productivity, Dallas Tx.

U.S. Department of Labour, Bureau of Labour Statistics, Office of Productivity and Technology (1996, June) *Hourly Compensation Costs for Production Workers, 40 Manufacturing Industries, 1975-95.*

U.S. Department of Labour, Bureau of Labour Statsitics \(1997, June) *International Comparisons of Hourly Compensation Costs for Production Workers in Manufacturing, 1996.*

U.S. Office of Technology Assessment, (1993), *Pulling Together, Pulling Apart,* Washington DC.

U.S., International Trade Commission (1997, June) *The Impact of the North American Free Trade Agreement on the U.S. Economy and Industries: A Three-Year Review.* Investigation No. 332-281, Washington DC.

United Nations Development Program (1997) *Human Development Report.*

Vargas, L. (1997, March) "Behind the Boom: Which Sectors are Growing" *Twin Plant News,* El Paso Tx, 23-24.

Vernon, R. (1994) "Multinationals and Governments: Key Actors in the NAFTA," in Eden, L., *Multinationals in North America,* University of Calgary Press.

Wood, A. (1994) *North-South Trade Employment and Inequality: Changing Fortunes in a Skill-Driven World,* Oxford University Press.

World Bank (1997) *World Development Report*, 1997 Washington, DC.

APPENDIX

TABLE 5

CANADA-U.S.: CANADA-MEXICO
EXPORTS AND IMPORTS BY MANUFACTURING SECTOR 1988-96

FOOD	1988	1993	1996	1988-1993	1993-1996	1988-1996
	Millions $ Can	Millions $ Can	Millions $ Can	% Change	% Change	% Change
Imports -US	2168.1	4094.5	5315	88.9%	29.8%	145.1%
Imports- Mexico	25.1	22.7	57.3	-9.6%	152.4%	128.3%
Exports- US	2724.2	3997.6	6011.8	46.7%	50.4%	120.7%
Exports- Mexico	57.0	50.6	71.8	-11.2%	41.9%	26.0%

BEVERAGES	1988	1993	1996	1988-1993	1993-1996	1988-1996
	Millions $ Can	Millions $ Can	Millions $ Can	% Change	% Change	% Change
Imports -US	62.6	133.3	195.7	112.9%	46.8%	212.6%
Imports- Mexico	12.6	17.2	32.8	36.5%	90.7%	160.3%
Exports- US	470.0	800.8	955.3	70.4%	19.3%	103.3%
Exports- Mexico	0.5	0.1	0.2	-80.0%	100.0%	-60.0%

RUBBER PRODUCTS	1988	1993	1996	1988-1993	1993-1996	1988-1996
	Millions $ Can	Millions $ Can	Millions $ Can	% Change	% Change	% Change
Imports -US	969.9	1560.9	2164.2	60.9%	38.7%	123.1%
Imports- Mexico	1.3	5.1	15.3	292.3%	200.0%	1076.9%
Exports- US	875.0	1641.9	2309.2	87.6%	40.6%	163.9%
Exports- Mexico	3.3	2.2	8.5	-33.3%	286.4%	157.6%

PLASTIC PRODUCTS	1988	1993	1996	1988-1993	1993-1996	1988-1996
	Millions $ Can	Millions $ Can	Millions $ Can	% Change	% Change	% Change
Imports -US	1430.5	2112.3	2946.6	47.7%	39.5%	106.0%
Imports- Mexico	1.5	10.6	27.8	606.7%	162.3%	1753.3%
Exports- US	837.8	1469	2623.8	75.3%	78.6%	213.2%
Exports- Mexico	1.1	0.9	4.1	-18.2%	355.6%	272.7%

LEATHER &	1988	1993	1996	1988-1993	1993-1996	1988-1996
ALLIED PRODUCTS	Millions $ Can	Millions $ Can	Millions $ Can	% Change	% Change	% Change
Imports -US	141.4	214.1	225.3	51.4%	5.2%	59.3%
Imports- Mexico	4.2	8.9	29.9	111.9%	236.0%	611.9%
Exports- US	122.6	141.5	221.7	15.4%	56.7%	80.8%
Exports- Mexico	0.0	0.2	0.02	1611.4%	-90.0%	71.1%

TABLE 5 (CONT'D)

CANADA-U.S.: CANADA-MEXICO
EXPORTS AND IMPORTS BY MANUFACTURING SECTOR 1988-96

PRIMARY TEXTILES	1988	1993	1996	1988-1993	1993-1996	1988-1996
	Millions $ Can	Millions $ Can	Millions $ Can	% Change	% Change	% Change
Imports -US	733.3	1168.9	1677.2	59.4%	43.5%	128.7%
Imports- Mexico	24.6	14.3	35.5	-41.9%	148.3%	44.3%
Exports- US	225.7	681.7	1249.6	202.0%	83.3%	453.7%
Exports- Mexico	5.6	3.5	4.3	-37.5%	22.9%	-23.2%

	1988	1993	1996	1988-1993	1993-1996	1988-1996
TEXTILE PRODUCTS	Millions $ Can	Millions $ Can	Millions $ Can	% Change	% Change	% Change
Imports -US	455.3	957.1	1311.3	110.2%	37.0%	188.0%
Imports- Mexico	8.2	22.8	42.4	178.0%	86.0%	417.1%
Exports- US	231.1	315.9	588.9	36.7%	86.4%	154.8%
Exports- Mexico	0.5	1.1	0.9	120.0%	-18.2%	80.0%

	1988	1993	1996	1988-1993	1993-1996	1988-1996
CLOTHING	Millions $ Can	Millions $ Can	Millions $ Can	% Change	% Change	% Change
Imports -US	132.3	492.3	634.6	272.1%	28.9%	379.7%
Imports- Mexico	4.9	19.1	66.7	289.8%	249.2%	1261.2%
Exports- US	355.1	704.1	1470	98.3%	108.8%	314.0%
Exports- Mexico	0.5	1.1	3.2	120.0%	190.9%	540.0%

	1988	1993	1996	1988-1993	1993-1996	1988-1996
WOOD	Millions $ Can	Millions $ Can	Millions $ Can	% Change	% Change	% Change
Imports -US	838.5	1058.5	1219	26.2%	15.2%	45.4%
Imports- Mexico	0.5	2.5	2.9	400.0%	16.0%	480.0%
Exports- US	4652.5	8381.1	12254	80.1%	46.2%	163.4%
Exports- Mexico	0.3	0.4	0.2	33.3%	-50.0%	-33.3%

	1988	1993	1996	1988-1993	1993-1996	1988-1996
FURNITURE & FIXTURES	Millions $ Can	Millions $ Can	Millions $ Can	% Change	% Change	% Change
Imports -US	490	1055.5	1043.8	115.4%	-1.1%	113.0%
Imports- Mexico	7	7.2	14.3	2.9%	98.6%	104.3%
Exports- US	1131.2	1935.2	3511.9	71.1%	81.5%	210.5%
Exports- Mexico	0.7	2.5	1.3	257.1%	-48.0%	85.7%

PAPER &	1988	1993	1996	1988-1993	1993-1996	1988-1996
ALLIED PRODUCTS	Millions $ Can	Millions $ Can	Millions $ Can	% Change	% Change	% Change
Imports -US	1403.3	2355.2	3620.6	67.8%	53.7%	158.0%
Imports- Mexico	4.3	7.8	8.8	81.4%	12.8%	104.7%
Exports- US	10303.3	10546.1	15070.5	2.4%	42.9%	46.3%
Exports- Mexico	45.4	52.3	28.2	15.2%	-46.1%	-37.9%

TABLE 5 (CONT'D)

CANADA-U.S.: CANADA-MEXICO
EXPORTS AND IMPORTS BY MANUFACTURING SECTOR 1988-96

PRINTING, PUBLISHING	1988	1993	1996	1988-1993	1993-1996	1988-1996
& ALLIED IND.	Millions $ Can	Millions $ Can	Millions $ Can	% Change	% Change	% Change
Imports -US	1419.9	2238.5	2688.9	57.7%	20.1%	89.4%
Imports- Mexico	0.1	0.8	2.3	700.0%	187.5%	2200.0%
Exports- US	562.9	696.8	1067.2	23.8%	53.2%	89.6%
Exports- Mexico	0.3	1.1	1.1	266.7%	0.0%	266.7%
	1988	1993	1996	1988-1993	1993-1996	1988-1996
PRIMARY METALS	Millions $ Can	Millions $ Can	Millions $ Can	% Change	% Change	% Change
Imports -US	2551.2	3241.1	4821.7	27.0%	48.8%	89.0%
Imports- Mexico	31.1	15.3	54.7	-50.8%	257.5%	75.9%
Exports- US	8192.1	9450.1	13918	15.4%	47.3%	69.9%
Exports- Mexico	49.7	70.6	29.4	42.1%	-58.4%	-40.8%
FABRICATED METAL	1988	1993	1996	1988-1993	1993-1996	1988-1996
PRODUCTS	Millions $ Can	Millions $ Can	Millions $ Can	% Change	% Change	% Change
Imports -US	2942.7	4357.2	6114	48.1%	40.3%	107.8%
Imports- Mexico	10.6	20	71.44	88.7%	257.2%	574.0%
Exports- US	2107.0	2718	5230.6	29.0%	92.4%	148.2%
Exports- Mexico	4.7	14.6	15.2	210.6%	4.1%	223.4%
MACHINERY (EX.	1988	1993	1996	1988-1993	1993-1996	1988-1996
ELECT. MACH.)	Millions $ Can	Millions $ Can	Millions $ Can	% Change	% Change	% Change
Imports -US	9442.7	10791.3	14564.4	14.3%	35.0%	54.2%
Imports- Mexico	56.2	150.8	178.1	168.3%	18.1%	216.9%
Exports- US	3770.8	4393.7	7855	16.5%	78.8%	108.3%
Exports- Mexico	19.5	39.1	59.5	100.5%	52.2%	205.1%
TRANSPORTATION	1988	1993	1996	1988-1993	1993-1996	1988-1996
EQUIPMENT	Millions $ Can	Millions $ Can	Millions $ Can	% Change	% Change	% Change
Imports -US	31687.2	35818.7	49130.8	13.0%	37.2%	55.0%
Imports- Mexico	551.2	2257.7	3230.8	309.6%	43.1%	486.1%
Exports- US	36898.7	49437.7	67340.3	34.0%	36.2%	82.5%
Exports- Mexico	81.6	182.7	290.5	123.9%	59.0%	256.0%

TABLE 5 (CONT'D)

CANADA-U.S.: CANADA-MEXICO
EXPORTS AND IMPORTS BY MANUFACTURING SECTOR 1988-96

ELECTRICAL & ELECTRONIC	1988	1993	1996	1988-1993	1993-1996	1988-1996
PRODUCTS	Millions $ Can	Millions $ Can	Millions $ Can	% Change	% Change	% Change
Imports -US	10730.4	15145.7	22879.4	41.1%	51.1%	113.2%
Imports- Mexico	234.1	578.5	1319.9	147.1%	128.2%	463.8%
Exports- US	5790.1	9568.9	16122.8	65.3%	68.5%	178.5%
Exports- Mexico	36.0	90.6	138.4	151.7%	52.8%	284.4%

NON-METALLIC MINERAL	1988	1993	1996	1988-1993	1993-1996	1988-1996
PRODUCTS	Millions $ Can	Millions $ Can	Millions $ Can	% Change	% Change	% Change
Imports -US	1217.9	1656.7	1990.1	36.00%	20.1%	63.40%
Imports- Mexico	22.4	58.2	75.2	159.80%	29.2%	235.70%
Exports- US	1063.4	1242.3	2125.1	16.80%	71.1%	99.80%
Exports- Mexico	2	5.4	4.2	170.00%	-22.2%	110.00%

REFINED PETROLEUM	1988	1993	1996	1988-1993	1993-1996	1988-1996
& COAL PRODUCTS	Millions $ Can	Millions $ Can	Millions $ Can	% Change	% Change	% Change
Imports -US	760.1	955.4	1420	25.7%	48.6%	86.8%
Imports- Mexico	4.4	13.7	33.1	211.4%	141.6%	652.3%
Exports- US	2373.7	3587	6196.7	51.1%	72.8%	161.1%
Exports- Mexico	0.1	0.1	0.06	0.0%	-40.0%	-40.0%

CHEMICAL &	1988	1993	1996	1988-1993	1993-1996	1988-1996
CHEMICAL PRODUCTS	Millions $ Can	Millions $ Can	Millions $ Can	% Change	% Change	% Change
Imports -US	5333.9	9347.7	13689.5	75.3%	46.4%	156.7%
Imports- Mexico	15.4	28.7	107.3	86.4%	273.9%	596.8%
Exports- US	3887.6	5930.4	9991.4	52.5%	68.5%	157.0%
Exports- Mexico	12.7	16	69	26.0%	331.3%	443.3%

OTHER MANUFACTURING	1988	1993	1996	1988-1993	1993-1996	1988-1996
INDUSTRIES	Millions $ Can	Millions $ Can	Millions $ Can	% Change	% Change	% Change
Imports -US	3965.9	6455.5	8310.2	62.8%	28.7%	109.5%
Imports- Mexico	17.4	79.2	161.4	355.2%	103.8%	827.6%
Exports- US	1566.8	2717.8	4668.6	73.5%	71.8%	198.0%
Exports- Mexico	4.6	12.6	31.9	173.9%	153.2%	593.5%

Corporate Statistical Profile: Allied Signal

Allied Signal - Canada

	1990	1991	1992	1993	1994	1995	1996
Employment	3,288	3,284	2,500	2,500	2,203	2,000	2,600
Sales ($'000s CND)	435,697	446,533	386,586	354,840	368,977	422,894	444,210
Assets ($'000s CND)	299,844	308,409	226,942	224,362	239,543	268,624	364,141
Employee/sales ratio	132,511	135,972	154,634	141,936	167,488	211,447	170,850
Net Income ($'000s CND)	16,565	18,696	31,385	30,034	25,787	28,824	49,841
Yearly Wage 323 ($ CND)	41,930	43,783	47,005	50,658	55,025	55,938	n.a.

Allied Signal - U.S.

	1991	1992	1993	1994	1995	1996
Sales (millions $ US)	8,908	8,978	9,220	9,739	10,734	10,774
Assets (millions $ US)	8,273	8,677	9,045	8,907	9,378	9,880
CEO Compensation ($'000s US)	1,974	9,598	9,544	4,753	9,741	13,224
Yearly Wage 371 ($ US)	33,500	34,064	37,088	40,712	40,486	41,443
CEO/Ave. wage ratio	58.93	281.76	257.33	116.75	240.60	319.09

Allied Signal - Maquiladora

	1988	1990	1993	1996
# of facilities	2	4	4	8
# of employees	1,000	1,150	2,250	5,950

Allied Signal - Worldwide

	1990	1991	1992	1993	1994	1995	1996
Employment	105,800	98,300	89,300	86,400	87,500	88,500	76,600
Sales (millions $ US)	11,831	12,042	11,827	12,817	14,346	13,971	n.a.
Net Income (millions $ US)	759	875	1,020	n.a.	n.a.	n.a.	n.a.
Employee/sales ratio ($ US)	n.a.	120,356	134,849	136,887	146,480	162,102	182,389

CORPORATE STATISTICAL PROFILE: CHRYSLER

Chrysler - Canada

	1990	1991	1992	1993	1994	1995	1996
Employment	14,000	13,200	13,800	14,200	13,600	14,000	14,000
Sales ($'000s CND)	7,067,000	8,337,400	9,453,800	13,594,800	15,722,100	13,619,000	17,060,000
Assets ($'000s CND)	2,845,000	3,125,000	3,141,700	4,095,100	4,317,800	4,875,000	5,854,000
Employee/sales ratio	504,786	631,621	685,058	957,380	1,156,037	972,786	1,218,571
Net Income ($'000s CND)	16,100	34,200	48,600	262,600	201,700	83,000	152,000
Average Wage 323	41,930	43,783	47,005	50,658	55,025	55,938	n.a.

Chrysler - U.S.

	1991	1992	1993	1994	1995	1996
Employment	n.a.	n.a.	91,000	97,000	100,000	100,000
Sales ($ millions US)	24,537	31,529	37,847	45,655	47,289	53,171
Assets ($ millions US)	37,136	35,137	37,625	42,752	46,794	47,843
Employee/sales ratio	n.a.	n.a.	415,901	470,670	472,890	531,710
CEO Compensation ($'000s US)	1,094	1,960	9,260	6,205	4,171	12,625
Yearly Wage 37 1 ($ US)	33,500	34,064	37,088	40,712	40,486	41,443
CEO/Ave. wage ratio	32.66	57.54	249.68	152.41	103.02	304.64

Chrysler - Maquiladora

	1988	1990	1993	1996
# of facilities	4	6	7	7
# of employees	2,500	5,669	8,938	14,000

Chrysler - Worldwide

	1991	1992	1993	1994	1995	1996
Employment	124000	128000	128000	121000	126000	126000
Sales ($ millions US)	29370	36897	43600	52235	53195	61397
Employee/sales ratio	236855	288258	340625	431694	422183	487278
Net Earnings($ millions US)	-810	934	3838	3713	2025	3529

CORPORATE STATISTICAL PROFILE: DUPONT

Dupont - Canada

	1990	1991	1992	1993	1994	1995	1996
Employment	4,275	4,162	4,143	3,997	3,707	3,650	3,520
Sales ($'000s CND)	1,411,389	1,325,315	1,416,642	1,570,188	1,676,386	1,832,009	1,827,437
Assets ($'000s CND)	1,015,912	1,065,719	1,166,431	1,220,752	1,353,943	1,503,266	1,597,191
Employee/sales ratio	330,149	318,432	341,936	392,842	452,222	501,920	519,158
Net Income ($'000s CND)	62,433	56,165	81,779	65,632	155,243	181,554	200,012
Average Wage 37 ($ CND)	36,642	37,929	39,964	41,185	42,272	41,887	n.a.

Dupont - U.S.

	1991	1992	1993	1994	1995	1996
Employment	n.a.	91,808	81,587	73,507	71,121	67,119
Sales ($ millions US)	21,609	20,331	20,342	20,769	21,534	22,969
Assets ($ millions US)	19,345	19,197	17,117	17,479	17,387	17,230
Employee/sales ratio	n.a.	221,451	249,329	282,545	302,780	342,213
CEO Compensation ($'000s US)	1,628	2,649	2,684	3,744	2,080	2,816
Yearly Wage 28 ($ US)	31,321	32,520	33,214	33,988	35,089	36,324
CEO/Ave. wage ratio	51.98	81.46	80.81	110.16	59.28	77.52

Dupont - Maquiladora

	1990	1993	1996
# of facilities	1	1	1
# of employees	200	310	810

Dupont - Worldwide

	1990	1991	1992	1993	1994	1995	1996
Employment	144,000	133,000	125,000	114,000	107,000	105,000	97,000
Sales ($ millions US)	n.a.	38,695	37,799	37,098	39,333	42,163	43,810
Net Income ($ millions US)	n.a.	n.a.	975	566	2,727	3,293	3,636
Employee/sales ratio	n.a.	290,940	302,392	325,421	367,598	401,552	451,649

CORPORATE STATISTICAL PROFILE: FORD

Ford - Canada

	1990	1991	1992	1993	1994	1995	1996
Employment	28,000	23,100	21,800	21,800	14,000	22,500	25,818
Sales ($'000s CND)	13,706,200	12,174,000	14,443,100	15,918,400	20,100,600	21,254,800	25,536,617
Assets ($'000s CND)	3,564,200	3,446,100	3,881,900	4,216,100	5,029,000	6,001,300	8,805,958
Employee/sales ratio	489,507	527,013	662,528	730,202	1,435,757	944,658	989,101
Net Income ($'000s CND)	(57,100)	(208,900)	(363,800)	(246,700)	(34,900)	212,700	423,645
Average Wage 323 ($ CND)	41,930	43,783	47,005	50,658	55,025	55,938	n.a.

Ford - U.S.

	1991	1992	1993	1994	1995	1996
Employment	156,079	158,377	166,943	180,861	186,387	189,718
Sales ($ millions US)	40,627	51,918	61,559	73,759	73,870	76,048
Assets ($ millions US)	26,728	34,334	39,666	45,889	45,841	51,681
Employee/sales ratio	260,298	327,813	368,743	407,821	396,326	400,848
CEO Compensation ($'000s US)	1,141	1,196	3,701	7,823	7,630	8,198
Yearly Wage 371 ($ US)	33,500	34,064	37,088	40,712	40,486	41,443
CEO/Ave. wage ratio	34.06	35.11	99.79	192.16	188.46	197.81

Ford - Maquiladora

	1988	1990	1993	1996
# of facilities	8	9	11	15
# of employees	10,000	11,312	14,064	23,000

Ford - Worldwide

	1991	1992	1993	1994	1995	1996
Employment	331,977	325,333	321,925	337,728	346,989	371,702
Sales ($ millions US)	n.a.	n.a.	n.a.	n.a.	n.a.	n.a.
Net Income ($ millions US)	(2,258)	(7,385)	2,529	5,308	4,139	4,446

CORPORATE STATISTICAL PROFILE: GENERAL ELECTRIC

General Electric - Canada

	1990	1991	1992	1993	1994	1995	1996
Employment	9,257	7,870	6,932	6,565	6,200	6,100	6,238
Sales ($'000s CND)	1,580,965	1,360,747	1,439,423	1,467,155	1,638,912	1,949,599	2,277,932
Assets ($'000s CND)	1,050,490	1,126,053	1,065,265	1,113,072	1,264,558	1,574,519	2,182,356
Employee/sales ratio	170,786	172,903	207,649	223,481	264,341	319,606	365,170
Net Income ($'000s CND)	48,054	13,065	23,121	6,366	31,322	57,687	99,076
Average Wage 33 ($ CND)	33,600	35,156	37,856	38,727	39,319	38,555	n.a.

General Electric - U.S.

	1990	1991	1992	1993	1994	1995	1996
Employment	183,000	173,000	168,000	157,000	156,000	150,000	155,000
Sales ($ millions US)	n.a.	47,277	48,710	52,039	49,005	52,935	58,110
Assets ($ millions US)	n.a.	147,648	168,797	219,903	142,710	158,884	189,593
Employee/sales ratio	n.a.	273,277	289,940	331,459	314,135	352,900	374,903
CEO Compensation ($'000s US)	n.a.	5,101	10,390	7,285	8,628	13,997	32,598
Yearly Wage 36 ($ US)	n.a.	22,645	23,566	24,431	25,236	25,288	26,284
CEO/Ave. wage ratio	n.a.	225.25	440.88	298.18	341.9	553.51	1240.2

General Electric - Maquiladora

	1988	1990	1993	1996
# of facilities	6	6	6	6
# of employees	5,000	6,534	7,200	8,300

General Electric - Worldwide

	1990	1991	1992	1993	1994	1995	1996
Employment	298,000	284,000	268,000	222,000	221,000	222,000	239,000
Sales ($ millions US)	n.a.	51,283	53,051	55,701	60,109	70,028	79,179
Net Income ($ millions US)	n.a.	2,636	4,725	4,315	4,726	6,573	7,280
employment/sales ratio		180,574	197,951	250,905	271,986	315,441	331,293

CORPORATE STATISTICAL PROFILE: GENERAL MOTORS

General Motors - Canada

	1990	1991	1992	1993	1994	1995	1996
Employment	42,555	42,251	41,318	40,572	37,519	35,000	32,701
Sales ($'000s CND)	18,458,171	19,303,908	18,347,173	21,777,209	24,919,421	30,775,542	28,079,058
Assets ($'000s CND)	5,960,991	6,227,781	6,230,929	6,570,210	8,050,837	10,994,498	n.a.
Employee/sales ratio	433,749	456,886	444,048	536,755	664,181	879,301	858,661
Net Income ($'000s CND)	45,526	323,310	72,032	327,730	1,026,380	1,390,907	679,334
Average Wage 323 ($ CND)	41,930	43,783	47,005	50,658	55,025	55,938	n.a.

General Motors - U.S.

	1991	1992	1993	1994	1995	1996
Employment	486,000	478,000	448,000	437,000	437,000	n.a.
Sales ($ millions US)	84,025	90,243	99,573	106,262	113,994	113,069
Assets ($ millions US)	142,958	148,378	151,344	151,058	161,606	166,724
Employee/sales ratio	172,891	188,793	222,261	243,162	260,856	n.a.
CEO Compensation ($'000s US)	1,675	1,328	1,441	5,215	4,837	5,939
Yearly Wage 371 ($ US)	33,500	34,064	37,088	40,712	40,486	41,443
CEO/Ave. wage ratio	50	38.99	38.85	128.1	119.47	143.31

General Motors - Maquiladora

	1988	1990	1993	1996
# of facilities	17	23	26	35
# of employees	16,018	22,500	16,018	43,336

General Motors - Worldwide

	1991	1992	1993	1994	1995	1996
Employment	756,000	750,000	711,000	728,000	745,000	647,000
Sales ($ millions US)	n.a.	127,378	132,991	148,499	160,272	164,069
Net Income ($ millions US)	(4,453)	(23,498)	2,466	4,901	6,881	4,963
Employee/sales ratio	n.a.	169,837	187,048	203,982	215,130	253,584

Corporate Statistical Profile: IBM

IBM - Canada

	1990	1991	1992	1993	1994	1995	1996
Employment	12,741	10,000	9,985	8,633	9,139	12,300	13,323
Sales ($'000s CND)	4,578,000	6,255,000	6,760,000	6,698,000	8,449,000	10,310,000	9,500,000
Assets ($'000s CND)	3,170,000	3,386,000	3,110,000	2,922,000	n.a.	n.a.	n.a.
Employee/sales ratio	359,312	625,500	677,016	775,860	924,499	838,211	713,053
Net Income ($'000s CND)	316,000	(17,000)	800	(130,000)	155,000	n.a.	n.a.
Average Wage 33 ($ CND)	33,600	35,156	37,856	38,727	39,319	38,555	n.a.

IBM - U.S.

	1991	1992	1993	1994	1995	1996
Sales ($ millions US)	24,427	24,633	25,703	24,118	26,789	29,395
Assets ($ millions US)	43,417	42,109	38,333	37,156	38,584	39,724
CEO Compensation ($'000s US)	2,096	7,000	7,710	12,355	6,321	10,460
Yearly Wage 35 ($ US)	26,346	27,232	28,464	29,541	29,880	30,458
CEO/Ave. wage ratio	79.56	257.05	270.87	418.23	211.54	343.42

IBM - Maquiladora

	1988	1990	1993	1996
# of facilities	1	1	1	2
# of employees	200	300	500	1,500

IBM - Worldwide

	1991	1992	1993	1994	1995	1996
Employment	344,553	301,542	256,207	219,839	225,347	240,615
Sales ($ millions US)	64,766	64,523	62,716	64,052	71,940	75,947
Net Income ($ millions US)	(2,861)	(4,965)	(8,101)	3,021	4,178	5,429
Employee/sales ratio	187,971	213,977	244,786	291,359	319,241	315,637

CORPORATE STATISTICAL PROFILE: NORTHERN TELECOM

Northern Telecom - Canada

	1991	1992	1993	1994	1995	1996
Employment	n.a.	n.a.	n.a.	22,000	22,000	21,000
Sales ($ millions US)	2,304	2,237	1,780	1,476	1,461	1,489
Assets ($ millions US)	2,228	2,637	2,432	2,040	2,052	2,274
Employee/sales ratio	n.a.	n.a.	n.a.	67,091	66,409	70,905
Average Wage 33 ($ CND)	35,156	37,856	38,727	39,319	38,555	n.a.

Northern Telecom - US

	1991	1992	1993	1994	1995	1996
Employment	n.a.	n.a.	n.a.	n.a.	n.a.	24,300
Sales ($ millions US)	4,336	4,500	4,431	5,437	5,812	7,401
Assets ($ millions US)	3,893	3,944	4,020	3,485	3,482	4,213
Employee/sales ratio	n.a.	n.a.	n.a.	n.a.	n.a.	304,568
CEO Compensation ($ millions CND)	n.a.	n.a.	1.3	2.7	2.2	2.7
Average Wage 36 ($ US)	22,645	23,566	24,431	25,236	25,288	26,284
CEO/Ave. wage ratio	n.a.	n.a.	54	108	88	104

Northern Telecom - Maquiladora

	1990	1993	1996
# of facilities	1	1	1
# of employees	500	750	1,500

Northern Telecom - Worldwide

	1991	1992	1993	1994	1995	1996
Employment	57,059	57,955	60,293	57,054	63,715	67,584
Sales ($ millions US)	8,183	8,409	8,148	8,874	10,672	12,847
Net Income ($ millions US)	515	548	-878	408	473	623
employee/sales ratio	143,413	145,095	135,140	155,537	167,496	190,089
Assets ($ millions US)	9,534	9,423	9,543	8,797	9,480	10,903

CORPORATE STATISTICAL PROFILE: ROCKWELL

Rockwell - Canada

	1990	1991	1992	1993	1994	1995	1996
Employment	2,286	n.a.	1,700	1,650	1,894	2,000	2,000
Sales ($'000s CND)	470,383	357,907	377,341	427,102	562,449	694,072	719,848
Assets ($'000s CND)	479,400	524,597	571,746	632,890	760,428	916,129	1,004,000
Employee/sales ratio	205,767	n.a.	221,965	258,850	296,964	347,036	359,924
Net Income ($'000s CND)	37,635	55,258	40,360	48,622	84,826	78,477	39,802
Average Wage 32 ($ CND)	35,686	37,498	39,476	41,699	43,854	44,095	n.a.

Rockwell - U.S.

	1991	1992	1993	1994	1995	1996
Employment	n.a.	n.a.	n.a.	52,978	61,880	n.a.
Sales ($ millions US)	n.a.	8,869	8,824	8,918	10,266	n.a.
Assets ($ millions US)	n.a.	6,158	5,999	6,220	8,734	n.a.
Employee/sales ratio	n.a.	n.a.	n.a.	168,334	165,902	n.a.
CEO Compensation ($'000s US)	n.a.	1,453	5,355	2,198	3,055	3,511
Yearly Wage 37 ($ US)	32,138	33,039	35,329	38,032	38,127	39,354
CEO/Ave. wage ratio	n.a.	43.98	151.58	57.79	80.13	89.22

Rockwell - Maquiladora

	1988	1990	1993	1996
# of facilities	1	2	2	2
# of employees	200	550	700	1,200

Rockwell - Worldwide

	1991	1992	1993	1994	1995
Employment	87,004	78,685	77,028	71,891	82,671
Sales ($ millions US)	11,282	10,728	10,637	10,933	12,970
Net Income ($ millions US)	601	483	562	634	742
Employee/sales ratio	129,672	136,341	138,093	152,077	156,887

Corporate Statistical Profile: 3M

3M - Canada

	1990	1991	1992	1993	1994	1995	1996
Employment	2,089	n.a.	2,060	2,071	2,114	2,140	1,853
Sales ($'000s CND)	567,120	n.a.	584,682	648,165	707,892	764,183	731,537
Assets ($'000s CND)	366,672	n.a.	393,410	399,336	401,700	412,949	449,014
Employee/sales ratio	175,525	n.a.	190,976	192,823	190,019	192,967	242,317
Net Income ($'000s CND)	53,264	n.a.	32,268	22,420	30,411	n.a.	n.a.
Average Wage 35 ($ CND)	32,788	34,361	36,144	36,312	36,544	37,391	n.a.

3M - U.S.

	1992	1993	1994	1995	1996
Sales ($ millions US)	6,922	5,531	5,944	6,207	6,655
Assets ($ millions US)	5,634	5,795	6,462	7,337	7,825
CEO Compensation ($'000s US)	1,895	1,628	2,615	2,268	3,787
Yearly Wage 32 ($ US)	25,455	26,312	27,375	27,749	28,866
CEO/Ave. wage ratio	74.44	61.87	95.53	81.73	131.19

3M - Maquiladora

	1988	1990	1993	1996
# of facilities	1	1	1	3
# of employees	600	650	891	1,748

3M - Worldwide

	1992	1993	1994	1995	1996
Employment	69,732	69,715	69,843	70,687	74,289
Sales ($ millions US)	10,817	11,053	12,148	13,460	14,236
Net Income ($ millions US)	1,233	1,263	1,322	976	1,526
Employee/sales ratio	155,122	158,546	173,933	190,417	191,630

CORPORATE STATISTICAL PROFILE: UNITED TECHNOLOGIES

Pratt & Whitney - Canada

	1990	1991	1992	1993	1994	1995	1996
Employment	9,447	8,611	7,802	7,100	7,018	7,329	8,005
Sales ($'000s CND)	1,583,589	1,501,576	1,426,582	1,436,317	1,551,043	1,776,563	1,882,507
Assets ($'000s CND)	1,031,122	1,076,831	1,088,528	1,082,513	1,259,260	1,424,378	1,481,441
Employee/sales ratio	167,629	174,379	182,848	202,298	221,009	242,402	235,166
Net Income ($'000s CND)	n.a.	n.a.	n.a.	n.a.	n.a.	n.a.	n.a.
Average Wage 32 ($ CND)	35,686	37,498	39,476	41,699	43,854	44,095	n.a.

United Technologies- US

	1991	1992	1993	1994	1995	1996
Employment	98,000	91,400	81,700	75,900	70,900	69,800
Sales ($ millions US)	14,201	14,403	13,818	13,088	13,434	13,415
Assets ($ millions US)	8,959	8,200	7,934	7,912	7,110	7,252
Employee/sales ratio	144,908	157,582	169,131	172,437	189,478	192,192
CEO Compensation ($'000s US)	1,313	2,090	2,440	2,746	2,333	6,721
Yearly Wage 37 ($ US)	32,138	33,039	35,329	38,032	38,127	39,354
CEO/Ave. wage ratio	40.86	63.26	69.07	72.2	61.19	170.78

United Technologies - Maquiladora

	1988	1990	1993	1996
# of facilities	12	16	18	19
# of employees	7,090	8,593	9,406	14,200

United Technologies - Worldwide

	1991	1992	1993	1994	1995	1996
Employment	185,100	178,000	168,600	171,500	170,600	173,800
Sales ($ millions US)	20,840	21,641	20,736	20,801	22,624	23,273
Net Income ($ millions US)	(1,021)	(287)	487	585	750	906
Employee/sales ratio	112,588	121,579	122,989	121,289	132,614	133,907

Impact of the Canada-US Free Trade Agreement (FTA) and the North American Free Trade Agreement (NAFTA) on Canadian Labour Markets

by Andrew Jackson

Introduction

Economic Integration and Labour and Social Standards

Prevailing economic orthodoxy holds that liberalization of trade and investment may create short-term transitional problems for some groups of workers, sectors and communities, but has long-term positive impacts on efficiency and growth. Liberalization results in a reallocation of labour and capital to areas of comparative advantage, raising productivity and potential growth. This in turn provides the basis for improvement in wages, working conditions and social standards.

This is held to be true even in the case of closer economic integration between relatively high wage, high social standard countries such as Canada, and lower wage, developing countries. For example, the International Monetary Fund[1] argues on the basis of a survey of the mainstream literature that increased North-South trade and investment flows have not been a significant driving force behind deindustrialization, the erosion of the relative position of unskilled workers and increased wage and social inequality in the advanced industrial countries.

Other, more balanced accounts, such as that in the ILO World Employment Outlook of 1996/1997, find some evidence that increased North-South trade has had negative impacts on relatively unskilled workers, but lay more emphasis on macro-economic and institutional factors in terms of explaining increased inequality and declining labour market and social standards in the advanced industrial countries.

The ILO has laid particular emphasis on the role of contractionary macro-economic policy in raising unemployment and inequality in the advanced industrial countries, and has also consistently drawn attention to the linkages between declining rates of unionization and labour market deregulation, and increasing inequality among workers and in the wider society.

However, the linkages between trade and investment liberalization and institutional changes in the labour market is left unexplored in this broad overview of trends in employment in the advanced countries. These linkages are explored in this paper.

The dominant neo-classical theory of gains from liberalized trade (and most econometric models based on this theory) rest upon assumptions which abstract from reality in a number of key respects. Perhaps most importantly, the theory assumes full employment—workers displaced from some jobs move to others. But this assumption is clearly unrealistic in the context of the high and rising rates of unemployment which have existed in most advanced countries, including Canada, for at least the past two decades.

High unemployment may be the result of macro-economic policy, but it is nonetheless the context in which liberalization of trade and investment has taken place. Further, there is a key linkage between liberalization of trade and investment and macro-economic policy in that it is more difficult to pursue expansionary policies in a context of globalized financial and product markets. The possibility of capital flight limits the scope for expansionary monetary policy, while leakages to imports limit the scope for expansionary fiscal measures.

Theory also assumes that capital flows from declining to expanding sectors, creating new jobs to replace those lost to imports as an economy is restructured through greater exposure to external market forces. But this assumption may be unrealistic, given the increased integration of national capital markets and the real possibility of capital flight. Today's "free trade" agreements—including the FTA and NAFTA—are explicitly intended to reduce barriers, not just to the flow of goods and services, but also to direct investment capital flows between countries. It is by no means certain that direct investment inflows will balance outflows.

Finally, theory assumes that trade will be balanced by compensating movements in the exchange rate which reduce trade deficits or decrease surpluses. But, in the real world, shifts in the exchange rate do not necessarily balance trade, at least in the short term, and balance of trade deficits financed through foreign borrowing can and do persist for long periods of time. The assumption of mutual gains from trade through balancing movements in exports and imports cannot be assumed.

Anwar Sheikh[2] has argued with others that the real world is increasingly one in which *absolute* advantage rather than *comparative* advantage holds sway. As in an integrated national economy, in countries integrated through trade and investment agreements, production, investment and jobs will tend to shift to those locales which are most cost competitive in the sense that they provide the best combination of wage and other costs in relation to productivity.

Countries with the lowest unit labour costs will tend to have growing and dynamic export sectors, while countries with high unit labour costs will tend to suffer slower growth or recession and severe adjustment problems in the form of rising unemployment and declining labour market and social conditions as a result of lack of competitiveness. Of course, the constraints of cost competitiveness can, to some degree, be lessened through specialization in high quality and innovative products and services, as opposed to commodities and commodity like goods, but this requires a shaping of competitive advantage through strategic investments in plant, innovation and skills which cannot simply be assumed to arise from "free markets."

The key point is that, in the real world as opposed to the world of the neo-classical models, it cannot simply be assumed that there will be mutual gains from increased trade. There is the possibility of significant loss of jobs and production for any one country. And this possibility makes it even more likely that the "losers" from integration driven adjustments will not be compensated from overall increases in economic efficiency.

Shaikh argues that economic integration is likely to be much less disruptive between countries with broadly comparable levels of productivity and wages. Many labour market economists have also recognized that the impact of economic integration will be different if labour and social standards differ between countries. If competition in integrated product and capital markets tends to shift jobs, investment and production to regions where labour and social costs are low in relation to productivity, then there will be downward pressures on such standards in relatively high standard jurisdictions. As leading Canadian industrial relations academic M. Gunderson argues:

"The economic forces of free trade, global competition and capital mobility put pressure on countries to harmonize their labour regulations, and these pressures tend to be in the direction of harmonizing downwards towards the lower common denominator. The pressure is especially great for measures that are the most interventionist and involve the protection of rents. They are also substantial, unfortunately—for regulations that serve an equity role if they conflict with efficiency."[3]

In short, economic integration and institutional factors at work in the labour market are not separate and distinct, but are rather closely connected.

THE BACKGROUND TO ECONOMIC INTEGRATION BETWEEN CANADA AND THE US

Labour and Social Standards in Canada

The impact of growing economic integration between Canada and the US offers an interesting example of the impacts of economic integration on labour markets, social standards and national distinctiveness.

Canada has traditionally had a modestly lower level of income than the US, reflecting in part lower levels of productivity. Measured in terms of purchasing power parity, disposable income per capita in Canada was 77% of the US level in 1985, but this had fallen to 68% in 1995.[4] The widening of the income gap reflects both macro-economic and structural developments related to economic integration, as explored below.

Notwithstanding lower incomes, labour market and social standards have, since at least the 1970s, been higher in Canada. Certainly, there have been and remain key differences in terms of rates of unionization. Overall union density in Canada has been more or less steady at about one in three workers in the 1980s and into the 1990s, but the US unionization rate has fallen by half, from 23% to about 12% over the same period.

While this difference partly reflects high rates of unionization in a larger Canadian public sector, private sector unionization in Canada has been and has remained much higher, at 20% to 25% in the 1980s and into the 1990s, compared to a fall from 15% to 10% in the US. Union density in US manufacturing has been about 10% since the early 1980s, compared to about 35% in Canada.[5] Minimum wages and employment standards have also played a more significant role in Canada.

Canadian labour markets thus have been and remain significantly more regulated by unions and by governments than those in the US. The generosity of income support programs for workers has also been significantly greater. In the 1980s, roughly twice the proportion of unemployed workers qualified for Unemployment Insurance benefits in Canada compared to the US, and the Canadian program generally covered the vast majority of the unemployed. Social welfare programs in Canada in the 1980s covered all unemployed workers who did not qualify for unemployment benefits, while US welfare programs have typically been much more limited.

The tax/transfer system has equalized incomes to a much greater extent than in the US. Strikingly, in the 1980s, a family at the mid-point of the income distribution was better off in Canada than in the US, notwithstanding higher average incomes in the US, because of greater equality in the distribution of income.

A final major difference lies in the fact that Canada has had public Medicare since the late 1960s.

These differences in labour market institutions and social programs bearing on labour reflect many factors, but certainly have been shaped by the relatively much stronger social democratic tradition in Canada. Put simply, Canada has weaker unions and welfare state programs than is typical of European countries, but has been much closer to the European social market economy model than the US.

A major National Bureau of Economic Research-funded study of the impact of these differences in the 1980s by US labour economists David Card and Richard Freeman, tellingly titled *Small Differences that Matter*, found that:

"Labour market institutions have resulted in less income inequality and poverty in Canada than in the US. The United States chose to give relatively free play to market forces during the 1980s, whereas Canada pursued a more activist strategy of providing broader social safety nets and labour regulations that were more favourable to trade unionism. The American policies generated substantial employment growth, but did little to mitigate the redistribution of income towards higher income workers and families. Canada's programs produced comparable employment growth, but also eased the forces that tended to promote inequality and poverty. Taken together, these studies show that subtle differences in unemployment compensation, unionization, immigration policies and income maintenance programs have significantly affected the levels of poverty, unemployment and income inequality in the two countries."[6]

Empirical work confirmed that transfer programs markedly lowered Canadian poverty rates compared to those in the US in the 1980s, while the rise in earnings inequality in Canada was much less than that in the US, in part because of the relative strength of Canadian unions.

Labour economists—as opposed to orthodox neo-classical economists—have tended to see Canadian distinctiveness in terms of labour market institutions as subject to erosion by competitive pressures in an integrated economic environment. For example, Gunderson argues that—

"the threat of capital mobility and plant location decisions will put pressure on different jurisdictions to harmonize their labour law and regu-

lations. This will be true between Canada and the US, especially under free trade. It is also the case that harmonization will be towards the lowest common denominator since jurisdictions with more costly regulations will be subject to pressures from investment flight and business relocations. In essence, the legislative authorities will be under more political pressure to pay attention to the concerns of employers over regulatory costs, including those emanating from the labour market. They will be under more pressure to compete with other jurisdictions to attract and retain business and the jobs that are involved."[7]

Chaykowski and Slotsve have argued that private sector union density in Canada is likely to decline under the competitive pressures of free trade, unless the union wage premium declines or productivity gains in the more heavily unionized Canadian environment outpace those in the US.[8] Increased competitive pressure will not necessarily lead to deunionization, but it will undermine the bargaining power of labour vis-à-vis capital and make employers more resistant to unionization.

Of course, it is possible for unions to help raise productivity to offset these pressures, but while unionization tends to be associated with higher than average productivity growth, unions will rightly insist that the gains be shared. High productivity does not necessarily translate into high rates of return on capital.[9]

While labour laws and regulations and income support programs which strengthen the bargaining power of workers, notably Unemployment Insurance, are subject to downward pressures in an integrated economy, other social programs have more mixed effects. Canada's Medicare system has given Canadian employers an important competitive advantage vis-à-vis US employers, or at least those US employers who contribute significantly to employee medical costs. Medicare also has given a significant cost advantage to auto production in Canada.

The same could be argued of higher levels of Canadian public investment in transportation, education and other services. However, taxation on business to finance such public services is clearly subject to some competitive pressures, not least because corporations operating in both Canada and the US can allocate taxable profits to one jurisdiction or the other through transfer pricing.

The Economic Role of the State

Canada has also been highly distinct from the US with respect to the role played by the state in economic development. Close trade and investment ties with the US began to displace those with Britain from the 1920s, with Canadian resource exports flowing to the US in return for US manufactured goods, and with US corporations establishing Canadian branch plants to produce behind the then high Canadian tariff wall.

Canada and the US were already significantly integrated in terms of trade flows in the 1950s, and two-way trade grew strongly as tariffs were successively lowered through GATT rounds. By the 1970s, US direct investment in Canada accounted for a large—often majority—stake in the resource and manufacturing sectors. In brief, long before the FTA and NAFTA, Canada and the US were already highly integrated economies.

But the nature of Canada-US economic integration was significantly shaped by government policies until well into the 1980s. The broad purpose of such policies was to broaden the industrial and employment base from resources and resource-based products to more advanced products and services, and to capture more resource rents. In the 1980s, tariffs were quite low for most products, but trade in the large integrated auto sector was managed through the Auto Pact with the US which guaranteed production in Canada broadly equivalent to market share.

Public ownership was significant even in commercial, non-regulated sectors such as energy, and foreign direct investment was subject to review and approval, conditional upon Canadian employment and other benefits. Canadian-based producers were given preferential access to Canadian resources, notably energy in the National Energy Program. Regulation gave US companies limited access to several key sectors, including transportation, communications, cultural industries and the financial sector. In short, regulation, public investment and a wide range of industrial and regional development policies shaped and managed a close economic relationship integration with the US.

The negotiation of the Canada-US Free Trade Agreement— concluded in 1988— was very much part of a wider federal government agenda of deregulation and privatization and "structural reform" consciously intended to give wider sway to market forces. The FTA was, of course, liberalizing in the sense that it eliminated, or phased out, remaining tariff barriers. Prior to the agreement, one-third of Canadian industrial production was protected by meaningful tariffs of 7.5% or higher, with tariff protection being particularly significant in some labour-intensive sectors such as clothing, textiles and footwear, as well as in food and beverages, rubber and plastics.

But it was more deeply liberalizing in the sense that it prohibited or limited traditional tools of economic policy such as conditional access to resources, two price systems for resources, regulated market access as in the Auto Pact, foreign investment review, "discrimination" by governments and Crown corporations, and use of public procurement, among others.

The NAFTA went beyond the FTA in some respects, further liberalizing trade in some services and further limiting regulation of investment. It also, of course, added Mexico to the FTA region, but this was of modest direct significance for Canada, given that direct trade and investment ties with Mexico were and remain of minor importance (with the partial exception of trade in auto and electronic products). However, close integration with the US clearly means that NAFTA impacts on the US arising from the integration of Mexico can have significant repercussions in Canada.

It should be underlined that the FTA/NAFTA is much more than a "free trade" agreement and goes well beyond tariff elimination to limit government actions which can be seen as affecting the evolution of markets. The agreement is, in essence, a declaration that Canadian and US corporations have the right (subject still to certain limits) to ship products and sell services across the border and to invest in the other country and to be treated by governments in a non-discriminatory fashion.

The key message to Canadian and US corporations is that the locale of production and investment and jobs can be determined on the basis of the logic of profit maximization rather than political criteria, and that henceforth the US and Canada should be seen as a single market. It is worth noting that, unlike the EC, the FTA/NAFTA is almost completely a liberalizing agreement designed to break down "barriers" and prevent government "discrimination" and does not create new institutions which pool sovereignty. It deregulates the market by limiting the scope for national government intervention without creating new international institutions. The environmental and labour commissions created by NAFTA stand as minor, weak exceptions.

THE CANADIAN POLICY DEBATE

There were four major strands to the Canadian economic policy and political debate over the FTA and then NAFTA.

The first had to do with whether the FTA secured one of its ostensible key purposes—namely, secure access to the US market and protection for Canadian exports against recurrent US protectionism. The FTA did not exempt Canada from US countervail and anti-dumping laws, though it did establish a dispute settlement process to determine if US law has been fairly applied. (This may have resulted in some modest benefits over and above GATT/WTO tribunals, but the US has, post-FTA, continued to periodically limit Canadian exports of lumber, steel, agricultural and other sensitive products.)

The second strand had to do with limits on the role of government in the economy. Nationalist, labour and other critics of the FTA argued that tools of policy sacrificed under the agreement were needed to build productive capacity and to broaden Canada's narrow advanced industrial base, while supporters argued that market access and free markets would narrow the productivity gap with the US and lead to more and better jobs in sophisticated industries. It was recognized on both sides that Canadian industry was less advanced and competitive than US industries, particularly in technologically sophisticated sectors.

Third, critics argued that restructuring driven by the agreement would lead to significant job losses and adjustment problems, while supporters said that adjustment would be modest and that there would be net gains from reallocation of production of investment. Critics expected that companies which had traditionally operated production facilities on both sides of the border (mainly US companies which had operated "branch plants" in Canada to avoid tariffs and comply with Canadian content requirements) would shift production to larger US plants, while supporters expected that better access to the US would encourage modernization and expansion of Canadian plants. There was evidence for both positions in the evolution of the Canadian industrial structure in the 1980s.

Finally, critics said that economic integration and the competitive pressures to which it gave rise would lead to downward harmonization of labour and social standards to the lower levels prevailing in the US. This process would result not just from the more competitive environment created by tariff reduction, but also through the wider deregulation of the economy driven by the FTA .

The key assessment of the FTA released by the Department of Finance in 1988[10] argued that the FTA would provide secure and enhanced access to the US market and would lead to a *"more efficient and lower cost economy"* via economies of scale, higher productivity, and higher rates of innovation. The lower consumer prices driven by tariff cuts and the productivity gains from comparative advantage and economies of scale in production specialization were expected to result in a long-term real income gain of at least 2.5%. More intangible results were expected in the form of *"increased flexibility and dynamism."*

"The economic benefits from the Free Trade Agreement will start to be realized shortly after the implementation of the Agreement on January 1, 1989. Prices for a wide range of consumer goods will begin to decline, expanding the purchasing power of Canadian households. Investment in plant and equipment will expand as Canadian firms move to take advantage of their enhanced access to the huge US marketplace. Increased consumer and investment spending will lead to stronger economic growth and more job creation. Department of Finance estimates of the impacts of the Agreement on employment over the government's medium-term fiscal planning horizon indicate that 120,000 net new jobs will be created by 1993, only five years into the agreement."

The government-funded Economic Council of Canada study[11] estimated the stimulus to consumption and investment which would come from price reductions flowing from lower Canadian tariffs, and the impacts of trade-driven rationalization and specialization on the manufacturing sector. It forecast a 2.5% gain in real GDP over 10 years. This result was heavily dependent upon an assumed productivity increase as a result of rationalization and economies of scale. The Council forecast modest 2-3% job losses in heavily protected sectors as a result of tariff reduction, and calculated that there would be net job losses if only tariff changes were considered. However, the adjustment problem was viewed as very small.

Both of these major studies argued that there would be modest but positive benefits, mainly because of an expected increase in productivity. Tariff-driven changes to employment were seen as small and manageable. Neither study saw any threat at all to labour and social standards or to Canadian distinctiveness vis-à-vis the US.

In his foreword to the Department of Finance report, the Minister wrote: *"A stronger and more productive economy will allow us to better support our social programs and further advance our cultural identity."* The Economic Council argued that *"there is no reason to think that free trade can be used to alter or undermine Canada's Unemployment Insurance, Medicare or other programs fundamental to the social safety net. Rather, by strengthening economic growth and employment in Canada, the free-trade agreement will increase government revenues and improve the ability of governments to address social issues."*

Neither the Department of Finance nor the Economic Council study looked at Canada-US wage and productivity differences or at the implications of different labour market institutions in the two countries in a more integrated environment.

The Department of Finance study, *NAFTA: An Economic Assessment (November 1992)*[12] similarly dismissed the "downward harmonization" argument, with specific reference to Mexico. The basic argument—which was not disaggregated by sector or even to the traded goods sector alone—was that the huge Canada-Mexico wage gap was more than paid for by higher productivity. It forecast tiny income gains from trade and investment liberalization.

Critics of the FTA forecast significant job losses as manufacturing industries in Canada were restructured and rationalized and two-way trade and investment flows increased as a result of tariff reduction and more secure rights for foreign investors.[13] While there was concern over job displacement from tariff reduction, the leading concern was loss of the economic tools needed to advance an interventionist Canadian industrial policy.

Economists opposed to the FTA were highly skeptical of the view that market forces alone would lead to industrial diversification and the growth of more sophisticated industries in Canada, and feared that the US would continue to dominate such sectors as Canada became even more reliant on resources. In short, much of the debate was less about "free trade" per se, than over the role of the state in economic development and job creation.

Critics also forecast a process of downward harmonization of labour and social standards. In its brief to the House of Commons Committee on International Trade, the Canadian Labour Congress, the largest trade union organization, argued that *"if this deal is consummated, we can count on business on both side of the border to threaten not to invest in Canada if they think costs and conditions are out of line with those in the US. That way, we get a further endless round of harmonization through the market that could erode everything, from Medicare and environmental protection to the corporate income tax and workers' rights to organize and bargain collectively."*

Similarly, the CLC submission to the government on NAFTA argued that the extension of the FTA to include Mexico would *"pose the very real threat of further job losses, wage cuts and erosion of labour, social and environmental standards as the international competitiveness threshold to which Canadians are directly exposed is dramatically lowered."*

The debate over NAFTA in Canada, as in the US, centred around fears of downward harmonization, with many Canadians arguing that the inclusion of Mexico in NAFTA would increase pressures that had already become clear under the FTA. The basic argument was that NAFTA would increase both capital mobility and competition, leading employers to attempt to lower wages in relation to productivity.

Contrary to the assumption of neo-classical economists that wages reflect relative productivity, it was argued that in the US and, even more dramatically, in Mexico, productivity and wages had become delinked. Examples of high productivity, low-wage production in Mexico—as in the auto engine industry studied in detail by Shaiken—made it clear that labour market institutions as well as macro-economic conditions are key intervening variables.

With the option of relocation to a lower wage, lower labour stand-ard jurisdiction with little or no loss of quality or productivity, employers will be placed in a position to successfully push workers for wage conces-sions and to better resist unionization.[14]

IMPACTS OF FTA AND NAFTA

Canada in the 1990s

By almost any measure, the post-FTA period of 1989 through 1996 has been one of the most dismal in Canadian history. Leading economist Pierre Fortin has characterized this period as "the great Canadian slump"— the longest period of below potential growth since the Great Depression.

Growth

As shown in Table 1, the recession of the early 1990s was deeper and more prolonged in Canada than in the US, and the recovery more tentative. Prior to 1997—a year in which the economy has finally begun to grow at or above 3%—1994 was the only year of growth above 2.4%. The contrast to the pre-FTA recovery period of the mid- to late 1980s is marked. Economic growth averaged 3.2%, 1980-88, compared to 1.4% 1989-1996.

These periods are both ones of recession and recovery. Canada grew significantly faster than the US, 1980 to 1988 (notwithstanding la-bour market institutions and social programs which were stronger than in the US, and a more regulated economy). However, growth in the post-FTA period has been significantly slower than in the US, averaging just 1.4% compared to 2.0%. Because of slower growth, Canadian incomes have fallen significantly behind those in the US. Given population growth, there has been almost no growth in real living standards in Canada since 1988.

Major Labour Market Trends

The national unemployment rate soared from a low of 7.5% in 1989 to more than 11% in the early 1990s, and remained well above 9%. The average duration of unemployment is approximately six months, so the unemployment rate indicates that at least one in five Canadian workers have been unemployed each year in the 1990s. Regionally, unemployment has been highest in Quebec and the Atlantic provinces, and lowest in Western Canada. However, the recession was deepest in heavily industrialized Ontario and Quebec. The more resource industry based Western provinces were less directly impacted by the FTA.

TABLE 1

CANADA AND THE USA — MAJOR INDICATORS

YEAR	REAL G.D.P.		UNEMPLOYMENT RATE	
	CANADA	USA	CANADA	USA
1980	1.5	-0.3	7.5	7.2
1981	3.7	2.5	7.6	7.6
1982	-3.2	-2.1	11.0	9.7
1983	3.2	4.0	11.9	9.6
1984	6.3	6.8	11.3	7.5
1985	4.8	3.7	10.5	7.2
1986	3.3	3.0	9.6	7.0
1987	4.2	2.9	8.8	6.2
1988	5.0	3.8	7.8	5.5
1989	2.4	3.4	7.5	5.3
1990	-0.2	1.3	8.1	5.6
1991	-1.8	-1.0	10.4	6.8
1992	0.8	2.7	11.3	7.5
1993	2.2	2.3	11.2	6.9
1994	4.1	3.5	10.4	6.1
1995	2.3	2.0	9.5	5.6
1996	1.5	2.4	9.6	5.4
Av. 1980-1988	3.2	2.7	9.6	7.5
Av. 1989-1996	1.4	2.0	9.7	6.1

Source: OECD Economic Outlook December 1996

An historically unprecedented gap has emerged between unemployment rates in Canada and the US, largely because of much slower job growth in Canada. The absolute number of full-time jobs recorded in 1990 was not regained until 1997, reflecting the severity of the recession and the concentration of job growth for women in part-time employment. The participation rate has fallen steadily from 67.5% in 1989 to below 65% today, with most of the decline concentrated among young people.

Were it not for the fall in the participation rate since 1989, the unemployment rate in 1996 would have been above 13%. The unemployment rate among young people aged 15 to 24 has been close to 20% through the 1990s, and this is on the basis of an extremely steep fall in the participation rate since 1989 (10% for young men and 7% for young women).[15] The incidence of part-time employment among young people has also increased sharply, from 36% in 1988 to more than 50% today.

The incidence of part-time work has increased from 20% to 25% among adult women since 1989, and this is almost entirely explained by the increased incidence of involuntary part-time employment. The trend towards part-time jobs for women has also been somewhat disguised by the growth of multiple job holding—about one in four jobs are now part-time, though only one in five workers work part-time because a growing number work full-time hours by combining jobs.

Part-time workers—overwhelmingly women—earn just two-thirds the wage of equivalent full-time workers, and less than 20% receive benefits from their employer. Increasingly, part-time work has become more and more casual, with hours in sectors such as retail trade, restaurants and hotels being highly variable from one week to the next.

The casualization of employment in the 1990s is also revealed in the rapid growth of temporary work, which increased from 5.0% to 11.6% of total employment between 1991 and 1996, according to the Statistics Canada Survey of Work Arrangements. Self-employment, meanwhile, grew by 15% between 1991 and 1995, and has contributed about one-half of all "job" growth in the 1990s.

While there is a layer of skilled professionals in high demand among the ranks of the self-employed, the growth of casual and self-employment is driven above all by the unwillingness of employers to hire workers into regular jobs, and by their ability to meet their needs on this basis in a very high unemployment economy.

The phenomenal growth of self-employment has not been extensively analyzed, but it is clear that earnings generally average well below those of paid workers with comparable skills. Measures of income from self-employment in the National Accounts show little growth, indicating that the average incomes of the self-employed are falling.[16]

The very marked casualization of employment in the 1990s, particularly among women, young people and other disadvantaged groups in the labour market, has been much greater than in the 1980s, and undoubtedly reflects very weak demand for workers and high unemployment, combined with major cuts to income support programs. It is driven by employer competitiveness strategies of contracting-out and out-sourcing work, and making the hours of work highly variable in order to minimize the fixed costs of permanent, full-time workers who usually have access to benefits such as pensions, and are frequently unionized.

Hours worked in full-time jobs increased in the 1980s, and the rate of increase has picked up in the 1990s. The proportion of adult men working more than 41 hours per week rose from 18.0% in 1980 to 21.4% in 1989 and to 24.3% in 1995. (The comparable data for adult women are 5.6%, 7.3% and 8.6%). The proportion of adult men in the goods sector working more than 41 hours per week rose from 15.8% in 1989 to 19.4% in 1989, and to 24.6% in 1995.[17]

Long and increasing hours tend to be worked by professionals—both women and men—and by male production workers in manufacturing and the resource sector. Average weekly overtime hours for hourly paid workers have averaged 3.2 hours 1994-96, significantly higher than the previous cyclical high of 2.2 hours in 1988.[18]

Measured solely in terms of hours worked, there has been a significant intensification of work for many workers in blue collar occupations, as well as in the public sector (where overtime is frequently unpaid.) High levels of overtime result from the high costs of training new hires, and from the fact that a significant proportion of wage costs for workers with pension and other benefits coverage are fixed.

Work has also been greatly intensified in most workplaces by delayering and "downsizing," and by the widespread adoption of "lean production" techniques, both in industrial and non-industrial settings. The intensification of work has gathered pace in the 1990s.[19]

Table 2 shows wage increases for all workers and for unionized workers in the business sector, and the increase in the Consumer Price Index. Over the eight-year period 1989-96, there was a very modest 6% increase in the broadest wage measure (which covers salaried as well as hourly-paid workers) while wage settlements for unionized workers in the business sector basically just matched inflation. Wage settlements for public sector workers averaged well under those in the private sector because of wage freezes and legislated controls.

Real annual earnings fell for virtually all adult male workers between 1989 and 1993. As shown in Table 3, real earnings of the bottom decile of adult men fell 31.2% between 1989 and 1993, and those of the second decile fell by 20.2%. Real annual earnings of the top two deciles of men fell by just 2%. There has thus been continuing polarization in earnings of men, though this trend has been driven more by a decrease in time worked as a result of high unemployment than by polarization of wages.

Nonetheless, the proportion of adult male workers earning less than $8.80 per hour (in 1993 dollars) rose from 7.9% in 1989 to 8.9% in 1993, while the proportion of such workers earning more than $27.60 per hour rose from 9.3% to 11.6%. Inequality of hourly earnings has increased, but the rate of increase has not accelerated since the early 1980s.

The real annual earnings of the bottom 50% of adult women fell between 1989 and 1992, again because of changes in hours worked. Annual earnings fell by 10.8% for women in the bottom decile and by 5.9% for women in the second decile. The proportion of women in very low wage jobs did not increase, and hourly earnings among women have not polarized in the same way as those of men. However, women are heavily concentrated in the lowest pay categories—19.9% of women earned less than $8.80 per hour in 1993 compared to 8.9% of men, and just 5.4% of women earned more than $27.60 per hour compared to 11.6% of men.[20]

TABLE 2

EARNINGS

YEAR	CHANGE IN AVERAGE HOURLY EARNINGS	MAJOR WAGE SETTLEMENTS BUSINESS SECTOR	CONSUMER PRICES
1984	4.5	3.4	4.3
1985	4.0	3.6	4.0
1986	3.6	3.1	4.2
1987	3.7	3.8	4.4
1988	3.9	4.7	4.0
1989	5.4	5.0	5.0
1990	5.6	5.7	4.8
1991	5.1	4.0	5.6
1992	3.7	2.6	1.5
1993	1.8	0.9	1.8
1994	1.6	1.2	0.2
1995	2.3	1.3	2.2
1996	2.6	1.6	1.6
1989-1996	31%	24%	25%

Source: Statistics Canada. Canadian Economic Observer Historical Statistical Supplement. Hourly earnings are fixed weighted.

TABLE 3

EARNINGS TRENDS 1989-1993
CHANGE IN REAL ANNUAL EARNINGS

DECILE	ADULT MEN	ADULT WOMEN
Decile 1	-31.2%	-10.8%
Decile 2	-20.2%	-5.9%
Decile 9	-2.1%	+5.2%
Decile 10	-1.8%	+5.4%

Source: Statistics Canada data

The negative impact on incomes of working people and families of increased unemployment and the erosion of earnings, particularly for the low paid, has not been offset by income transfers to the same extent as in the 1980s. Three major rounds of cuts to the national Unemployment Insurance program since 1988 cut benefit entitlement periods drastically— often in half—and raised the qualification period to 26 weeks of work for full-time workers.

In 1989, 85% of unemployed workers qualified for UI benefits, but less than 50% qualified in 1997, and the proportion has fallen to one-third in Ontario. The benefit rate as a proportion of prior earnings has also been reduced. The Department of Finance estimates that the effect of these cuts has been to eliminate the impact of the major improvements to the system made in the 1970s. The program is certainly very substantially smaller than it was in 1988.

Income support from social assistance grew rapidly in the recession and the early recovery, but benefits have been significantly cut in most provinces since 1992, and it has become more difficult to claim benefits. Thus, despite continuing very high rates of unemployment, transfer income has been shrinking relative to employment income. The inevitable result has been a sharp increase in poverty, particularly among families with children. The incidence of low income for families with children has risen from 15.3% in 1989, to 21.0% in 1995.[21]

Macro-Economic Policy and Economic Integration

Most economists — certainly Department of Finance, the Bank of Canada, the OECD and business economists—would argue that Canada's dismal recent history is largely unrelated to the FTA. Indeed, most would argue that increased exports to the US flowing from the FTA have led growth in the recovery. The argument would be that economic performance has been weak and unemployment very high because of the impacts of monetary and fiscal policy. Extremely high interest rates and exchange rate overvaluation lie behind the recession of the early 1990s, while subsequent recovery has been held back by stringent fiscal policy as governments have sharply cut spending to deal with a growing debt load.

It would also be argued that major structural adjustments to "globalization" were inevitable, notwithstanding the FTA and NAFTA (an argument which glosses over the fact that continental economic integration is precisely the form that "globalization" has taken in Canada.)[22]

There can be no doubt that macro-economic policy has been the major cause of the Canadian slump and labour market trends. In particular, blame has to be placed primarily on monetary policy. From the low 70 cents US level of the mid- 1980s, the Canada-US exchange rate rose by more than 20% to at or above 86 cents US in 1989 through 1991, before falling back to the low 70 cent level. In 1990, short-term interest rates were 5% higher than in the US, compared to a normal average of about 2%, and this fuelled the sharp exchange rate appreciation which came almost coincidentally with the introduction of the FTA in 1989.

The traditionally large Canadian merchandise trade surplus with the US (needed to finance the usually still larger deficit on trade in services and dividend flows) fell in the 1989-to-1991 period, when the manufacturing and much of the resource sector contracted sharply. Extraordinarily high real interest rates put the domestic economy into deep recession.

As prominent Canadian macro-economist Pierre Fortin and others have argued, it was the contractionary monetary policy of the late 1980s which led to the very severely contractionary fiscal policy of the 1990s. Government debt loads soared in the recession because of the combination of high interest rates on accumulated debt, and high unemployment and sluggish revenues.

The significant Canadian debt problem was caused by monetary policy, rather than by "excessive" spending. Program spending had been cut in the 1980s as a share of the economy, and has been cut sharply in the 1990s.[23] Fiscal retrenchment in the 1990s has been, according to the OECD, the most severe in any major country in the post-war era. Real federal government spending on programs has fallen by more than 20% since 1993, cutting real growth rates by well over 1% per year in the recovery. There have been massive job cuts to public services, directly and, via cuts in federal transfers, to provincial and local services and to health and education.

While the fiscal tightening has been rooted in monetary policy, it is not unrelated to economic integration in that the drive for international competitiveness has taken priority over stimulation of internal demand. For example, cuts to Unemployment Insurance have been justified in terms of perceived negative impacts on the labour market, and the traditional countercyclical role of the program has been consciously scaled back.

Further, tax increases, particularly tax increases on business, have been rejected as an alternative to social program and public service cuts because of the perceived negative impacts on competitiveness. As in other countries, much of government's role has been reconstrued to be the enhancement of business competitiveness via domestic policies of austerity, a trend which has been accelerated by the fact that more and more domestic demand is now met through imports, so fiscal stimulus in less effective.

Critics of monetary policy rightly lay much of the blame on the determination of the Bank of Canada to achieve an explicitly stated "zero inflation" objective under Governor John Crow. Notwithstanding a rather low peak rate of inflation of 5% in 1989, the monetary brakes were tightened to a much greater extent than in the US. Many prominent economists, including Paul Krugman, have argued that the Bank of Canada has pursued a much more stringent anti-inflation objective than even the US Federal Reserve, and that the Canadian case stands as an example of the large costs of adopting too low an inflation target.

There, is, however, much more to the shift in monetary policy than an error in macro-economic judgment. The Bank of Canada was responding not so much to higher consumer price inflation than in the US as to the perceived loss of Canadian cost competitiveness vis-à-vis the US in the 1980s. As shown in Table 2, inflation in 1989 was 5.0%, only 0.2% higher than in the US, and wage increases were broadly in line with price increases even at the end of the expansion and were not out of line with productivity growth.

Put bluntly, the Bank deliberately increased unemployment in order to discipline Canadian workers in a more integrated economic environment. From the perspective of business and many economists in the 1980s, a key Canadian problem was eroding cost competitiveness with the US in manufacturing and the traded goods sector generally. The expansion of the 1980s saw a sharp increase in unit labour costs and an erosion of Canada's cost competitive position which was offset only by continued exchange rate depreciation.

The crux of the problem was that productivity was growing more slowly than in the US, while wages were growing somewhat more rapidly in relation to productivity than in the US.[24] The problem was not "excessive" wage growth in Canada, per se—real wage increases were barely increasing and were more than justified by productivity—but rather the potent competitive threat posed by the particularly sharp delinking of wages from productivity growth in the largely deunionized US.

Beginning from at least the mid-1980s, business interests in Canada expressed growing concern about loss of competitiveness. While much of the blame could be placed on corporate under-investment in innovation and research and skills, it was argued that Canadian labour was "too strong" in the new, more competitive, more integrated economic environment which flowed from the overall process of deregulation, tariff reduction and looming free trade.

Put in more technical terms, it was argued by the Bank of Canada, the Department of Finance and the OECD that Canada had a higher "natural rate" of unemployment or NAIRU than the US, in large part because of stronger unions and more "generous" social programs.[25] "Natural rate" theory was the justification for the sharp tightening of monetary policy in the late 1980s and the successive rounds of cuts to UI made in the late 1980s and 1990s.

To summarize, monetary tightening and the consequent squeeze in fiscal policy were not unrelated to the context of much closer economic integration with the US. Inflation per se was not a problem in the late 1980s. What was a problem was the perceived higher propensity of the Canadian economy to inflation than the US. This difference was seen as rooted primarily in labour market institutions. High unemployment was used deliberately to promote long-term competitiveness with the US, even at the cost of a short-run deterioration in relative costs.

It can be added that there is some evidence that the FTA would not have been approved by the US Congress if an exchange rate appreciation had not been anticipated. Indeed, a member of the federal cabinet that negotiated the FTA, Sinclair Stevens, has said that there was a "secret deal" to placate hostile members of Congress.

THE FTA, TRADE AND DIRECT EMPLOYMENT IMPACTS

Analysts basically agree that the FTA and NAFTA have had a significant impact on Canadian trade patterns. Both exports and imports have risen sharply as a share of GDP, and trade has become even more geographically concentrated. Exports have risen from 26% of (nominal) GDP in 1988 to 38% in 1996, matched by an almost equally large increase in the import share of GDP from 26% to 35%. The Canadian merchandise trade surplus with the US moved in a narrow range between 1988 and 1992, in the early FTA period, and then rose very rapidly, from $15 billion to $40 billion. (The growth of the merchandise trade surplus accounted for about 25% of economic growth, 1992-1996). Exports to the US rose from 75% to 81% of total exports over the same period, while imports from the US rose from 69% to 75% of the total.

Measured in nominal dollars, both exports and imports of goods and services have about doubled in the post FTA period. This expansion of both exports and imports was much more rapid than in the 1980s or in the 1970s. In short, the Canadian and US economies have indeed become much more integrated in trade terms at a rapid pace. The extent of integration is now remarkable. A greater share of Canadian manufacturing production is now exported to the US than is consumed in Canada, and Canadian manufacturers supply less than half of the Canadian market for manufactured goods.

It should be noted that a very high portion of Canada-US trade— 40%—is intra-company trade, particularly in the highly integrated automotive sector. Trade is made up of inputs to cross-border production chains as much as resources and finished goods.

There have been some changes in the broad structure of Canada-US trade under the FTA and NAFTA. Resource-based goods as a share of Canadian merchandise exports have diminished slightly in importance, from 34% to 31% of the total, while the share of machinery and equipment in exports has risen from 16% to 23%, 1988 to 1996. This has been driven by exports of telecommunications equipment, a traditional area of Canadian strength, and by growing exports of office machinery and software.

Canada's small "high technology" sector has been the major beneficiary of the FTA. However, Canada remains a very large net importer of machinery and equipment, exporting 80% of the value of imports in 1996. The export to import ratio would likely fall if depressed Canadian industrial investment recovered strongly.

A detailed analysis of changes in the pattern of trade by Schwanen[26] shows that the growth of trade has been particularly strong in sectors liberalized by the agreement, and that the growth of trade with the US has been greater than would have been expected, given slower growth in the US than in other markets, and the greater depreciation of the Canadian dollar against other currencies.

While overall exports to the US grew by 99%, 1988 to 1995, exports in liberalized sectors grew by 139%. As a result of the FTA, the US market share in Canada increased significantly in sectors liberalized by the agreement, notably clothing, furniture, processed foods, steel and chemicals. Canadian exports to the US have grown particularly strongly in liberalized sectors also. A US Congressional Research Service Report[27] similarly concludes that the FTA has had an important independent impact on trade flows. If anything, the impact of the FTA on trade has probably exceeded expectations, indicating that corporations reconsidered production strategies in a new light after the agreement was concluded, rather than making marginal adjustments.

Shifts in trade in response to the FTA, in combination with exchange rate movements and domestic economic conditions, resulted in a major restructuring of the manufacturing sector. There was a massive wave of plant closures and mass layoffs in industrial Canada, particularly Ontario and Quebec, in 1989 through 1992. Over this short period, about one in five manufacturing jobs were lost. Since 1992 there has been a modest recovery in payroll employment in manufacturing. Job losses were often in US (or, more rarely, Canadian) companies which operated production facilities in the US and decided to rationalize higher cost operations in Canada. Other jobs were directly lost to competition from imports.

As shown in Table 4, there have been significant job losses in those industries which enjoyed significant tariff protection before the FTA—notably clothing and food. Strikingly, jobs have also been lost in significant numbers in sectors where exports have expanded, notably machinery and electrical and electronic products (though employment in some sub-sectors producing telecommunications and office equipment has grown.)

University of Toronto economist Daniel Trefler has calculated that employment in sectors with tariff protection of more than 10% (about one-third of manufacturing employment) fell by 17% 1988 to 1996 and that 138,000 of 290,000 manufacturing jobs lost between 1988 and 1996 can be attributed directly to the FTA rather than to other factors. He finds that these protected sectors, such as clothing and textiles, have restructured mainly by shrinkage—there have been limited productivity but not jobs gains even in the smaller sector which has survived. Conversely, there was rapid growth of output and productivity in sectors which had more modest tariff protection before the FTA.[28]

Between 1988 and 1995, there was a very sharp 18.7% fall in the number of manufacturing establishments in Canada. Some 7,544 establishments closed, with the most severe declines in clothing (1,094 establishments, 39% of the 1988 total) furniture (612 establishments or 31.4% of the 1988 total), printing and publishing (1,190 establishments or 21% of the 1988 total). The fact that the number of establishments shrank more than the fall in employment indicates that restructuring resulted in increased concentration of production. This appears to have taken place mainly in medium-sized plants, since the number of large (more than 500 worker) manufacturing establishments fell from 436 to 365.[29]

Under the FTA, cross-border trade in services with the US has also grown, though less rapidly than merchandise trade. Such trade—travel, transportation and commercial services—accounts for only 14% of the value of merchandise trade. Canada's traditional deficit in the trade of services with the US widened from $4.6 billion in 1988 to a high of $10.7 billion in 1992, and has since gradually shrunk to $9 billion. Canada currently exports $2 of services to the US for every $3 which is exported.

TABLE 4

EMPLOYMENT IN MANUFACTURING 000 s

SECTOR	1988	1993	JAN. 1997
Total	1,992	1,667	1,719
Food	208	180	175
Clothing	121	85	85
Primary Metals	103	80	80
Fabricated Metal Products	174	135	155
Machinery (Non Electrical)	85	65	91
Electrical & Electrical Products	157	116	117
Transportation Equipment (Auto & Aerospace)	224	197	223

Source: Statistics Canada Employment Earnings and Hours

There have been significant FTA and NAFTA related impacts on Canadian transportation industries, notably cross-border trucking. Competitive pressures have greatly increased in all transportation industries.

Under NAFTA, direct Canada-Mexico trade has about doubled in volume but continues to be modest, amounting to only about 3% of the value of Canada-US trade. This may be underestimated in that US goods assembled in Mexico may be counted as US goods. There has been a large and growing imbalance in direct Canada-Mexico trade, driven by the shift of auto industry parts sourcing to Mexico and by the slump in Mexican imports following the peso crisis. In 1996, Canadian imports from Mexico were five times greater than exports ($6 billion vs $1.2 billion) and this large imbalance has grown.

In the first five months of 1997, Canadian imports from Mexico were six times greater than Canadian exports to Mexico. While still modest in dollar terms, the trade deficit undoubtedly has translated into direct job losses. Several Canadian auto parts producers (e.g., Magna, Ford) and electronic equipment producers (e.g., Northern Telecom) have established production facilities in Mexico. In these sectors, the threat—real or potential—of relocation has been used in collective bargaining.

THE FTA AND ECONOMIC PERFORMANCE

As noted above, proponents argued that the FTA would lead to a revitalization of the manufacturing sector based on higher productivity and new investment. Performance in this respect has been disappointing. As shown in Table 5, labour productivity growth in manufacturing (output per hour) averaged 2.0% 1989 to 1995, down from 2.3% 1981 to 1988. Productivity growth was just above 1% in 1995 and 1996 (based on preliminary data for 1996). The productivity gap with the US has not been closed and has in fact recently widened. Labour productivity growth in US manufacturing has been rising at above 3% since 1993, and averaged 2.6%, 1989-95. The same trend is equally apparent with respect to total factor productivity in manufacturing.[30]

While poor Canadian productivity performance undoubtedly reflects depressed domestic conditions, it has been low considering the closure of many low productivity firms (which should have raised growth through a concentration effect) and considering that free trade gave Canadian manufacturers access to a faster growing market. The 1996 OECD Country Review of Canada expresses surprise and concern that the expected impacts of structural reform, including free trade, have yet to appear, and the same tone of puzzlement is present in the recent Conference Board of Canada report on Canadian Economic Performance. Comments are made on the negative effects of the rapidity of needed adjustments— begging the question of whether more gradual liberalization would have resulted in better performance.

Poor productivity performance likely reflects relatively poor levels of manufacturing investment. Measured in nominal dollars, investment in construction of new manufacturing facilities was more than $4 billion in 1989 and 1990 but, after a sharp fall, has been consistently below $3 billion per year, even in the 1992-to-1996 recovery.

Investment in manufacturing plant and equipment has been stronger, but only regained the nominal dollar level of 1989 in 1996. Measured as a share of GDP, non-residential investment has fallen from 12% in the late 1980s to the 10% level in the 1990s, with much of the investment effort focused in the trade and financial sectors. Canadian manufacturers' historically poor record of investment in research and development and in skills has not appreciably increased.

While there is no doubt that exports—and manufacturing exports in particular—have led the weak recovery, there is very limited evidence that free trade has produced a structurally stronger manufacturing sector. To be sure, some sectors have invested significantly and have grown on the basis of exports—auto, aerospace, telecommunications equipment, software—but the overall competitive position of the manufacturing sector vis-à-vis the US has been maintained only through depreciation of the exchange rate.

The Conference Board of Canada has calculated that 80% of the improvement in Canada's competitive position in the US in the recovery has been based on exchange rate depreciation, with the remainder coming from slower nominal wage growth than in the US. (See Table 5).

The FTA and NAFTA have not resulted in a significant inflow of net new foreign direct investment into Canada. Overall, foreign direct investment inflows from the US have about matched outflows since 1989. US FDI in Canada increased by $47 billion or 61%, 1988 to 1996, while Canadian FDI in the US increased by $42 billion or 82%.

Most of the inward flow to Canada represents reinvestment of earnings in the modernization of plant and equipment, while outflows represent new investments by Canadian companies in the US or elsewhere. While there has not been FDI disinvestment in net dollar terms, the ratio of Canadian FDI in the US to US FDI in Canada has risen from .67 to .75.

The US has been a more attractive locale for new Canadian corporate investment than Canada has been for US corporations. There have been very few new "greenfield" manufacturing investments in Canada by US corporations under the FTA and NAFTA, but many major Canadian manufacturing corporations have established new facilities in the US and, increasingly, in Mexico. Canadian FDI in Mexico doubled between 1993 and 1994 to $1 billion, and rose to $1.3 billion in 1996.

It is worth noting that the US-controlled share of operating revenues of Canadian corporations grew from 17.3% in 1988 to 20.1% in 1995, even though the US share of assets grew only from 11.8% to 11.4%. This reflects the fact that export growth has been strongest in areas where

TABLE 5

GROWTH OF HOURLY WAGES
AND HOURLY LABOUR PRODUCTIVITY IN MANUFACTURING —
CANADA VERSUS THE USA

YEAR	PRODUCTIVITY		HOURLY WAGES (REAL)			
	CANADA	USA	CANADA		USA	
1981	4.9	1.3	15.1	(2.7)	9.9	(-0.4)
1982	-4.5	4.7	10.6	(-0.2)	9.6	(3.5)
1983	7.3	3.8	6.1	(0.3)	2.7	(-0.5)
1984	8.5	2.9	4.7	(0.4)	3.5	(-0.8)
1985	2.9	3.7	5.2	(1.2)	5.5	(2.0)
1986	-1.6	4.5	3.9	(-0.3)	4.5	(2.6)
1987	0.9	2.7	3.0	(-1.4)	2.8	(-0.9)
1988	0.4	1.3	4.4	(0.4)	3.9	(-0.2)
1989	0.4	1.8	3.8	(-1.2)	3.3	(-1.5)
1990	1.7	1.8	5.6	(0.8)	4.8	(-0.6)
1991	0.4	2.5	6.4	(0.8)	5.2	(1.0)
1992	3.9	3.6	3.0	(1.5)	4.5	(1.5)
1993	1.7	2.1	0.1	(-1.7)	2.4	(-0.6)
1994	4.4	3.1	2.0	(1.8)	2.7	(0.1)
1995	1.2	3.4	1.8	(-0.4)	3.7	(0.9)
1996	1.1	3.8	4.4	(2.8)	3.5	(0.6)
Av. 1981-1988	2.3	3.1	6.6	(0.4)	5.3	(0.7)
Av. 1989-1995	2.0	2.6	3.2	(0.2)	3.8	(0.1)

Source: Statistics Canada. The Daily. June 5. 1997. The 1996 data is preliminary.

US transnationals are dominant players—notably auto, aerospace, electrical and electronic products, chemicals and wood and paper.[31]

ASSESSING THE BROADER FTA IMPACT ON LABOUR MARKETS

Aside from the direct impact on jobs, critics forecast that the FTA and NAFTA would increase the bargaining power of capital vis-à-vis labour, resulting in slower growth of wages, possible deunionization, and a downward harmonization of standards. There is mounting evidence that this has indeed been the case, and that the FTA and NAFTA are, therefore, contributing to the dismal overall labour market trends described above.

As detailed in Table 6, wages have grown significantly more slowly in relation to productivity in the manufacturing sector than in the business sector as a whole. Between 1989 and 1995, real wages in manufacturing rose by an average of just 0.2% in both manufacturing and the business sector as a whole, even though productivity growth in manufacturing averaged 2% per year compared to 0.8% in the business sector as a whole.

This suggests that competition from the US and now Mexico has a significant impact upon the growth of wages in relation to productivity, since the manufacturing sector is much more directly exposed to competitive pressure from the US and Mexico than is the business sector as a whole. There is some evidence of a growing gap between productivity and real wage growth in manufacturing which could be attributed to the FTA and NAFTA.

Real wage growth as a proportion of real productivity growth in manufacturing has clearly fallen, though this has also been true for the business sector. It is difficult to determine trends in that workers are highly resistant to wage cuts, and concessions made in collective bargaining have taken the form of rollbacks on other issues such as benefits and work rules. This has shown up in the increased work-time noted above.

The data in Table 6 indicate the intense downward competitive pressures on wages to which Canadian workers have been subjected by US competition. Despite reasonably strong productivity growth in US manufacturing, real wages of US manufacturing workers have barely increased in the 1990s.

Strikingly, workers in those manufacturing sectors identified as "winners" under free trade have not benefitted in the form of higher wages. Trefler found "no link" between wage growth and export or productivity growth in different manufacturing sectors, and Schwanen found no link to more rapid wage growth in sectors with fast growing exports. Between 1988 and 1997 (January), average hourly earnings of hourly paid workers increased quite uniformly across the manufacturing sector, and rose no higher in the fast-growing electrical machinery sector (30% in nominal terms) than in manufacturing as a whole (33%).[32] Again, this suggests that competitive pressures have eroded the bargaining power of labour.

Erosion of worker bargaining power has resulted in a redistribution of income from labour to capital. In the post FTA-period, corporate profits plunged in the recession, and then recovered strongly. Profits as a share of GDP have still not recovered to pre-recession levels, but this reflects the still depressed domestic economy. Statistics Canada has reported that profitability for large corporations has returned to the peak levels of the 1980s and rates of return are very high in auto, electrical machinery and equipment, pulp and paper, and other winning sectors.[33] In short, the income gains from the growing export sector have mainly been appropriated by shareholders.

Between 1988 and 1995, production worker wages as a share of value added in direct manufacturing activity fell from 31.2% to 27.2%, and total salaries and wages in manufacturing as a share of value-added also fell, from 43.0% to 37.4%. The decline in labour's share of value-

TABLE 6

ANNUAL GROWTH OF REAL HOURLY WAGES AND HOURLY PRODUCTIVITY –
CANADA AND THE USA

1.   BUSINESS SECTOR

	PRODUCTIVITY		REAL WAGES	
	CANADA	USA	CANADA	USA
Av. 1981–1988	1.6	1.5	0.5	0.9
Av. 1989–1995	0.8	0.9	0.2	0.0

2.   MANUFACTURING

	PRODUCTIVITY		REAL WAGES	
	CANADA	USA	CANADA	USA
Av. 1981–1988	2.3	3.1	0.4	0.7
Av. 1989–1995	2.0	2.6	0.2	0.1

Source: Calculated from Tables in Statistics Canada. The Daily. June 5, 1997. Wages (total compensation per hour) have been deflated by the Consumer Price Index for each country.

added has not been as significant in successful and profitable export sectors, such as transportation equipment, as in the manufacturing sector as a whole, as indicated in Table 7.

The overall unionization rate has remained stable at 32% (as measured by the CALURA survey) and unionization in the private sector has also remained stable. However, the unionization rate in manufacturing fell from 35.0% in 1988 to 33.4% in 1992. This may reflect the fact that heavily unionized industries have suffered disproportionately high job losses, perhaps in part due to the growth of contracting out to non-union firms.[34]

Leading Canadian industrial relations analysts Meltz and Verma have summarized the impacts of the FTA on Canadian unions as follows:

"Some degree of union avoidance has always characterized Canadian management practices. What gives them a new flavor is the growing ability of employers to stay non-union in greenfield sites. But perhaps the strongest weapon that employers have used with success against unions and workers in the 1980s is the threat of closure. In response to increasing competition as a result of the Free Trade Agreement (FTA) with the United States and lower tariffs in general, a number of employers (especially, but not only, the US manufacturing companies) began to wind up their branch plant operations in Canada. Even as these plants closed, other employers have missed no opportunity to point to these cases to win concessions or to defeat organizing campaigns.

Despite management resistance, the Canadian labour movement as a whole is far from weakened in the way that the US labour movement found itself circa 1980."[35]

Canadian employers have extensively used the argument of international competitiveness vis-à-vis the US and Mexico to press governments for changes in labour laws and regulations and social programs. For example, the Canadian Manufacturers' Association has proposed that all policies should be subject to a "competitiveness test":

"Government now plays a more pervasive role in the economy than ever before. Tax rates and their coverage; tax expenditures and support programs; public spending for social programs and public infrastructure;

TABLE 7

PRODUCTION WORKER WAGES AS % VALUE-ADDED
IN MANUFACTURING ACTIVITY IN SELECTED INDUSTRIES

Industry	1988	1995
All Manufacturing	31.2	27.2
Food	28.0	27.1
Rubber	41.4	39.4
Clothing	47.8	38.2
Paper & Allied	25.4	20.1
Primary Metals	30.0	29.7
Machinery	35.2	30.8
Transportation Equipment	37.3	30.5
Electrical & Electronic Products	29.7	25.5

Source: Statistics Canada Cat. 31–203 Manufacturing Industries of Canada

regulation and administrative measures of many kinds all have a significant impact on the economic system of the country.

*"Governments in other countries do the same thing, and every nation
has its own unique mix of public and private programmes and public and
private cost. While national sovereignty makes any such mixture possible, the realities of international competition and economic interdepend-
ence reduce the range of choices which are feasible in practice.*

*"Now more than ever, governments must recognize that their choices
about taxation, spending and regulation cannot be made in isolation.
Companies make decisions every day about where to invest, produce and
employ. Selecting new locations around the world is becoming easier as
time goes by. The government cost and regulatory burden is part of the
environment which firms evaluate in making these choices. In this context, governments do compete, at all levels, for business, for jobs and for
the tax revenues that support and strengthen our social fabric."*[36]

While labour laws and employment standards have tilted in both
directions since the FTA came into effect, the recent trend—notably in
Ontario, Alberta and Manitoba—has been to severely limit the effective
right of workers to organize, and to roll back even basic employment
standards. While employer acceptance of the legitimacy of collective

bargaining and employment standards has always been tenuous, the depth of opposition to unionization has grown and this reflects, at least in part, the greatly increased pressures of international competition.

The shift against the bargaining power of organized labour attributable in part to the FTA is a major factor behind the overall labour market trends described above, notably casualization of work and increased polarization of incomes and working-time.

CONCLUSIONS

Advocates of the FTA and NAFTA drew on the neo-classical theory of mutual gains from free trade to argue their case. By contrast, it was argued above that integration of trade and investment in a context of high unemployment and international capital mobility opens the possibility of significant losses, particularly to workers, as a result of intensified international competition. In such a context, it was argued that bargaining power in the labour market will shift in favour of capital.

The above analysis detailed dismal developments in the Canadian labour market and wider society in the post-FTA era —high unemployment, increased inequality and insecurity, and erosion of the social safety net. It was argued that macro-economic policy underlay many of these developments, but links between economic integration and contractionary macro-policy were also noted.

It was also argued that there are direct and demonstratable links between the FTA and NAFTA and job losses, stagnation of real wages relative to productivity, the erosion of union bargaining power, and the downward harmonization of the Canadian social safety net relative to that in the US.

Finally, it was noted that the expected efficiency gains of the FTA and NAFTA have not materialized— undercutting the possibility of providing assistance to "losers" from the adjustment process.

For workers, closer continental integration has meant job losses, and little or no real wage growth, even in "winning" sectors. Meanwhile, some sectors of business have done well under conditions of continental economic integration after a major process of readjustment.

The major policy issue that arises from this analysis is how to ensure that the possible gains from closer trade and investment ties are equitably shared. This requires that labour's bargaining power not be diminished through the integration process. For working Canadians, this is a particularly key issue since labour market and welfare state institutions have been generally superior to those in the US and Mexico.

Unfortunately, the erosion of labour's position in Canada has not been offset in any significant way through the development of new regulatory instruments and institutions at the NAFTA level, since the FTA/NAFTA integration process has been almost exclusively one of deregulation.

In recent years, the Canadian labour movement has pressed strongly for "social clauses" to promote and protect labour rights in all trade and investment agreements, including the WTO and the proposed Free Trade Agreement of the Americas (FTAA). At the same time, the movement has remained strongly critical of purely liberalizing agreements.

The Canadian dilemma is that economic integration in North America has undercut national labour and social standards, but has provided little or no basis for reconstituting those standards at a regional level (not least given political realities in the US.). Regional integration in the Americas will continue to be much more unbalanced than in Europe.

ENDNOTES

1.   International Monetary Fund. *World Economic Outlook*, May 1997, Chapter III

2.   Anwar Shaikh. *Free Trade, Unemployment and Economic Policy* in John Eatwell (Ed.) *Global Unemployment: Loss of Jobs in the '90s*. M. E. Sharpe, London, 1996

3.   M. Gunderson. *Efficient Instruments for Labour Market Regulation*. School of Policy Studies. Queen's University. 1993.

4.   Conference Board of Canada. *Performance and Potential: Assessing Canada's Social and Economic Performance*. 1995.

5.   See R. Chaykowski and G. Slotsve *Union Wage Premiums and Union Density in Canada and the United States in Canadian Business Economics*. Spring, 1996 and

Pradeep Kumar. *Organized Labour In Canada and the US: Similarities and Differences*. Queen's University Industrial Relations Centre. 1987.

6. David Card and Richard Freeman (Eds.) *Small Differences that Matter: Labor Markets and Income Maintenance in Canada and the US*. The University of Chicago Press. 1993.

7. Gunderson. (1993) P.18

8. Chaykowski and Slotsve (1996)

9. See Andrew Jackson. *Unions, Competitiveness and Productivity*. Industrial Relations Centre. Queen's University. 1993

10. Department of Finance. *The Canada US Free Trade Agreement: An Economic Assessment. 1988*

11. Economic Council of Canada. *Venturing Forth: An Assessment of the Canada-US FTA*. 1988

12. Department of Finance. *NAFTA: An Economic Assessment*. 1992

13. See Duncan Cameron (Ed.) *The Free Trade Deal*. Toronto. Lorimer. 1988

14. See Ian Robinson *How will NAFTA Affect Workers Rights in North America* in M. Cook and H. Katz (Eds.) *Regional Integration and Industrial Relations in North America*. New York State School of Industrial and Labor Relations Cornell University, 1994 and James Stanford *Social Structures, Labour Costs and North American Economic Integration*. PhD thesis. New School for Social Research. 1995.

15. Unless otherwise indicated, labour force data is from Statistics Canada's *Labour Force Survey*.

16. On the casualization of employment see the report of labour representative Alexandra Dagg in the *Report of the Advisory Committee on the Changing Work lace*. Department of Human Resources Development. 1997.

17. *The Changing Work Week* in Statistics Canada *The Labour Force Survey*, June, 1996

18. Statistics Canada *Employment, Earnings and Hours*.

19. See Alexandra Dagg (1997) and Chris Schenk and John Anderson (Eds.) *Re Shaping Work*. Ontario Federation of Labour Technology Adjustment Research Program. 1995.

20. See Garnet Picot. *Working Time, Wages and Earnings Inequality Among Men and Women in Canada, 1981 — 1993*. Analytical Studies Branch. Statistics Canada. 1996. Data in Table 3 calculated from the Appendix to this study. This is the most recent published data on wage inequality.

21. Statistics Canada. *Income Distributions By Size.* 1995.

22. See Richard Lipsey. *The Case for the FTA and NAFTA.* Canadian Business Economics. Winter, 1995

23. Lars Osberg and Pierre Fortin, (Eds.) *Unnecessary Debts.* Toronto. Lorimer. 1996.

24. See the Economic Council of Canada. *Pulling Together: Productivity, Innovation and Trade.* 1992.

25. See eg. *The 1996 OECD Country Review of Canada* and the Department of Finance *Agenda: Growth and Jobs. 1995.* See also Andrew Jackson: *"The Future of Jobs".* CLC Research Paper #4.

26. Daniel Schwanen. *Trading Up.* C.D. Howe Institute. 1996

27. Arlene Wilson. *Canada-US Trade and Investment under the FTA and NAFTA.* November, 1996

28. Daniel Trefler. *No Pain, No Gain: Lessons from the Canada-US Free Trade Agreement.* Paper presented to the North American Labor Commission. 1997.

29. Statistics Canada. *Manufacturing Industries of Canada*

30. See Conference Board of Canada (1995). Chapter 5.

31. Statistics Canada. *CALURA*

32. Data from Statistics Canada. *Employment, Earnings and Hours.*

33. Statistics Canada. *The Daily.* October 30, 1996.

34. Noel Gaston and Daniel Trefler. *The Labour Market Consequences of the Canada-US Free Trade Agreement.* Canadian Journal of Economics. February, 1997.

35. Noah Meltz and April Verma: *"Developments in Industrial Relations"* in R. Locke, T. Kochan and M. Piore (Eds) *Employment Relations in a Changing World Economy.*

36. Canadian Manufacturers' Association. *"The Aggressive Economy". 1992*

NAFTA's Impact on U.S. Labour Markets, 1994-1997

by Mehrene Larudee

INTRODUCTION

The backdrop against which we hope to assess NAFTA's effects on US output, trade, employment and wages is that of a decline more than two decades long in labour's share of productivity gains. Real hourly compensation in the US has stagnated since 1978, and income inequality in the US notably worsened during the 1980s and much of the 1990s. Workers at lower skill levels have been particularly hard hit, as the wage penalty for the lack of a college education has grown[1] (Wood 1995). At the same time, in 1995 after-tax profits for US manufacturing corporations reached 16.1% as a percentage of stockholder's equity, their highest level since 1988 (ERP 1997: Table B-92.).

While there is dispute over the size and nature of the role that trade (or the relocation of production that gives rise to trade) has played in reducing labour's bargaining power in the US, it is clear that it has played some role. The world labour market has become more competitive, and it is harder than before for US manufacturing workers to maintain their wages and working conditions, despite the fact that the value of their output has continued to grow. The expansion of production in China alone has led to massive US imports from that country of clothing, toys, tools, household furnishings and other goods, produced at wages with which US workers cannot possibly compete.

The debate among economists over the main causes of increasing wage inequality between more- and less-educated workers in the US during the 1980s and 1990s has been (inappropriately) narrowed to two possible causes: "technology" and "trade." By "technology" is meant skill-biased technical change, which increases the demand for skilled labour relatively to less-skilled labour. By "trade" is meant import penetration which forces domestic low-skilled labour to compete with low-skilled, low-wage labour in other countries; this includes outsourcing by US-based multinational firms.

Wood (1995), Freeman (1995) and Richardson (1995) provide useful surveys of the issues; among these, Wood is particularly persuasive that the evidence is best interpreted as implying a large role for trade in causing trends in wage inequality in the US and other developed countries.

But labour market institutions, and in particular the long-term decline in the real value of the US minimum wage, surely also play a role. More generally, the advance of the neoliberal program—even apart from NAFTA—is central. Globalization, in other words, is not simply technologically driven, or outside the political decision-making process. On the contrary: a series of changes in laws and institutions, under the broad rubric of market-oriented reforms, has contributed to the weakness of labour's bargaining power, more so in the US than in other industrialized countries.

For example, it has been suggested that the overall long-term decline in the value of the US real minimum wage is one factor undermining the average real wage: expressed in 1995 dollars, the minimum wage peaked at $5.97 in 1979 and steadily declined to $4.12 in 1989; several increases since then have raised its value, but only to just over $5.00 an hour. While there is dispute over the main cause of the decline in the real wage in the US, in countries with stronger labour institutions the trend in the real wage has been more favourable to labour (see, e.g., OECD 1993:166).

Some other factors accounting for labour's weakness are the erosion of eligibility for unemployment benefits during the 1980s; the rise of part-time and temporary work that undermines organizing efforts; the determination of the Federal Reserve throughout much of this period not to allow the unemployment rate to fall "too low"; and the steady decline in the percentage of the workforce represented by unions, from 24% in 1979 to just 15% in 1994 (Mishel et al. 1997).

Meanwhile, national and local governments have tried to increase the advantages of capital, by removing regulations on capital movements, and granting tax concessions to firms, on the premise that this will make them more competitive and lead to greater prosperity. This process of advantaging capital includes various rules written into NAFTA, but it also includes the Uruguay Round of the GATT and the creation of the World Trade Organization (WTO), and it includes the Multilateral Agreement on Investment being drawn up by the OECD, and in the US Congress, the Republican agenda of deregulation and tax breaks for business.

NAFTA, then, is just a piece of a much larger picture. But because of the fierce debate over its passage, and the extravagant claims made both for and against it, as well as the mobilization against it by labour, environmentalists and community groups, it has in a sense come to represent globalization itself. This is surely because it was and is one of the few ways that the public can get a handle on globalization and exercise some control over its advance. Globalization as such will never be put to a democratic vote; but NAFTA was a concrete proposal that was to be voted up or down by the US Congress, and related proposals such as fast-track legislation have the same status. Hence, in the public and legislative eye, the question of whether NAFTA has had devastating effects is a crucial one.

Based on the best estimates available, NAFTA's effects on labour in the US overall appear to have been negative, moderate in size, and harsh in some sectors and regions. For example, job losses have been substantial in the apparel sector, in El Paso, Texas, and in some small communities heavily dependent on factories which shut down and moved to Mexico. These effects should not be minimized, and the workers affected ought to have received full compensation for their losses, but did not.

Overall, however, the fact that NAFTA's first three years occurred during a business cycle upswing in the US cushioned its effects. Some of its effects have therefore been a reduction in the rate of creation of new jobs, rather than an increase in actual layoffs. In a growing economy, the duration of unemployment for those affected has also been shorter than it would have been in a declining economy. The question suggests itself whether the US business cycle upswing was itself accelerated or facilitated by NAFTA; existing studies differ on whether there is any evidence that this is so, but the most detailed study, by the US International Trade Commission (ITC 1997), finds no significant statistical evidence of a net change in GDP due to NAFTA during 1994-1996.

This paper mainly considers impact on employment, with brief consideration given to impact on wages and on labour rights later in the paper.

The employment impact may be thought of in two conceptually different ways, which are often confused in public discussion. One is the *net* employment impact: the difference between the number of jobs which actually existed (say, at the end of 1996), given that NAFTA was implemented, and the number of jobs which would have existed if NAFTA had never been implemented. It is this kind of number that was predicted by some studies of employment impact done before 1994[2]. It includes three things: jobs created due to NAFTA, jobs actually eliminated due to NAFTA, and jobs which failed to be created due to NAFTA (but which in the absence of NAFTA would have been created).

The second concept is the *gross* employment impact, perhaps better described as the number of displaced workers. This concept includes only the middle of the three categories that make up the net employment impact, that is, jobs actually eliminated.

Of course, the number of jobs affected is not only a consequence of NAFTA but of labour's response. In some cases, by making concessions to employers over wages and working conditions, workers have managed to keep jobs in the US, at least for some period, so that the impact of NAFTA is felt in labour incomes and working conditions rather than in job losses per se. Likewise, displaced workers may be displaced for shorter periods if they are willing to accept lower-wage jobs, and in that case the impact is more on incomes than on employment.

Thus, strictly speaking, employment impact makes most sense if calculated in a situation in which real hourly compensation is constant. Some pre-NAFTA studies made predictions of employment impact in exactly this way. However, no post-NAFTA assessments of employment impact have been conducted in this way or have attempted to calculate the *income* impact of displacement of workers. In what follows I try to distinguish clearly between net and gross employment impact; the whole issue is discussed in greater detail later in the paper.

Among the studies to be reviewed here, the best estimates available indicate that NAFTA to date has brought a nearly zero net gain in output in the United States, probably together with a small percentage overall loss to US labour income and a gain of a comparable dollar amount to property incomes. While the December 1994 peso crisis brought in its wake a severe worsening of the US trade balance with Mexico, implying a significant negative impact on US employment creation, in the context of a much larger expanding US economy this impact has fortunately not been devastating.

This is not to say that the usual mechanisms creating "gains from trade" have been absent. Rather, gains from trade are typically thought of in the context of an assumption of full employment before and after trade opens up—or, in practice, of the same level of employment (apart from growth of the labour force) before and after trade liberalization. But I will argue that NAFTA brought with it a set of political pressures which led to an exceptionally severe currency crisis in Mexico, and thus the macroeconomic difficulties it helped to create partially offset the gains from trade over the few years NAFTA has been in existence.

Assessments of NAFTA released in late 1996 or during 1997 range from defining it largely as a success (USTR 1997) to defining it as a clear failure (EPI et al. 1997). Between these two polar views, several extensive studies find that, though NAFTA has had significant effects on trade, it has had remarkably small net effects on output and employment, except in a few sectors (Hinojosa et al. 1996; ITC 1997).

The study by Weintraub (1997) takes a somewhat different tack. Weintraub washes his hands of the debate over employment effects almost entirely, arguing that different criteria should be used to assess NAFTA, such as the increase in total trade and investment, the increase in the rate of growth of productivity and wages, effects on the environment, and the extent to which the institutions of economic integration are developed. Though he expresses the usual concern for compensation and retraining of displaced workers, he argues that bilateral trade balances, typically used as the basis for calculation of employment effects, fluctuate for all sorts of reasons and are not a sound basis for evaluating NAFTA's effects.

While his observations are important, insufficiently precise data are available on many of the criteria he suggests (productivity, wages) to make an adequate assessment at this time; or, to put it another way, there is no statistically significant evidence of overall productivity or wage increases or decreases due to NAFTA, according to ITC (1997). And the increases, say, in total trade—for which data *are* available—hardly seem an appropriate category for a definitive assessment of NAFTA's success.

We proceed by briefly summarizing theory and previous studies on the effects of trade liberalization, and then turn to a detailed discussion of the recent NAFTA studies.

PRE-1994 PREDICTIONS OF NAFTA'S EFFECTS

It is a common public misconception that neoclassical theory holds that, always and everywhere, free trade is good for everyone. Nothing could be further from the truth. While the public cannot be blamed for drawing this conclusion from hearing the repeated refrain, "win, win win," the NAFTA debate did not in fact provide an accurate representation of what trade theory says.

Trade theory contains many different models, with different sets of assumptions. Among them, the most basic textbook model (the Heckscher-Ohlin) says clearly that, when a high-wage country opens up trade with a low-wage country, workers in the high-wage country will suffer a fall in their real wages. In models which categorize workers into at least two skill levels, low-skilled workers in the high-wage, high-skill country may experience a decline in wages relative to workers with higher skill levels.

It may be surprising, then, that in the early 1990s studies predicting NAFTA's effects sometimes found that hardly any category of the population would lose. One reason for this result is that these studies typically assumed that capital flows as well as trade effects would occur: there would be a substantial increase in the inflow of investment into North America from outside the continent, and this often was the main source of the beneficial effects.

It was not just the free trade among NAFTA countries, but the protectionism against non-NAFTA countries, that would create this tariff-jumping investment. Firms would switch production from some Asian countries to Mexico because Mexico offered similarly low wages, but without the necessity of paying a tariff on goods entering the US. To some extent this has occurred in practice; for example, ITC (1997:6-58) reports that about 80 German auto parts firms have established Mexican production in recent years to enable Volkswagen to meet NAFTA's rules of origin requirements for exemption from tariff. However, the size of the contribution to North American income depends in part on what fraction of profits are repatriated to non-NAFTA countries.

Another reason for optimistic projections was the assumption in some studies of substantial scale economies. In an econometric analysis of data on Mexican production, Tybout and Westbrook (1995) have challenged this assumption, however, at least for Mexico.

Studies predicting NAFTA's effects typically found that the effects of tariff liberalization alone were likely to be small for several reasons. For Canada, of course, a free trade agreement already had been implemented beginning in 1988. For Mexico, the maquiladora program, in existence in various forms since 1965, permitted US firms to locate assembly production south of the Mexican border and be exempted from Mexican tariffs on intermediate and capital goods entering Mexico for use in those plants; later the same opportunity was provided throughout Mexico.

About one-third of the value of US imports from Mexico entered duty-free before NAFTA. The majority (about one-half the value of about 45% of US imports from Mexico in 1989) entered under the production-sharing provisions of the US tariff code, HTS 9802, which allows US firms to assemble goods abroad from US components and re-import them into the US, paying tariff only on the value added abroad (ITC 1991:1-5; ITC 1997). A smaller share (about 9% in 1989) entered duty-free under the Generalized System of Preferences (ITC 1991:1-5). In addition, of course, NAFTA was expected to have a larger impact on Mexico's economy than on the US because of their relative sizes.

RECENT ASSESSMENTS OF NAFTA

In late 1996 and in 1997, a number of studies were released which attempted to assess NAFTA's effects during its first three years or so. Among relatively substantial studies, the most positive assessment has been by the office of the US Trade Representative (USTR 1997), whose study was endorsed by President Clinton and submitted as his required report to the US Congress on the first three years of NAFTA's operation.

The USTR report draws heavily on other, more detailed studies, such as the voluminous report by the US International Trade Commission (ITC 1997), to some extent on the preliminary report by Hinojosa et al. (1996), and on several other studies much more limited in scope, such as DRI (1997), Kouparitsas (1997) and Gould (1996).

At the opposite pole, a study by the Economic Policy Institute (EPI et al. 1997, hereafter "EPI 1997") asserts that NAFTA is a failure, because it has failed to promote high and rising living standards for the great majority of the population. While it recognizes that NAFTA has not been the primary cause of declining living standards in North America, it asserts that NAFTA has made matters worse. My assessment is that their analysis is largely correct. Moreover, in actuality little or nothing in EPI's assessment conflicts with the data or even many of the conclusions (if carefully understood) which are presented in other studies.

Between these two opposing views, several substantial studies argue that the net effect of NAFTA on output and employment has been very small, some say effectively zero. Apart from a nearly zero net effect, these studies do recognize that some gross job displacement has occurred in the US ITC (1997) summarizes its findings by saying that in general

NAFTA had positive but modest effects on the US economy. This conclusion is puzzling, since for the US it finds no effects on GDP or its growth rate, no aggregate employment or earnings effects, and no effects on aggregate investment, and the study notes that it was unable directly to analyze productivity effects.

It is unclear, then, what are the positive effects which it finds "in general"—perhaps the reference is to increased trade or to the "improvement in the business climate" or other effects it describes as not easily quantified or observed. Hinojosa et al. (1996) find that there has been a very small net positive effect on US employment from the changes in trade which occurred during 1994-96.

In addition, we consider a few other studies whose analyses are far more limited (Gould 1996; Kouparitsas 1997; DRI 1997), but which need to be discussed since they are cited in USTR (1997) as evidence of NAFTA's positive effects. Essentially, I judge that none of the conclusions of these limited studies is reliable, either because of errors in statistical methods, or because the data series used were too short and yielded results with a low level of statistical significance, or because the model was conceptually flawed.

The finding of DRI (1997) that NAFTA, apart from the peso devaluation, had a small positive effect on US exports to Mexico (and possibly a smaller positive effect on US imports from Mexico) must be understood in the context of the study's assumption that NAFTA and the peso crisis were completely independent events. The main problem with these studies is that, as I believe, the effects of the peso crisis are partially attributable to NAFTA and the political process set in motion by the NAFTA debate, and these authors instead treat NAFTA as completely separable from the peso crisis.

The study by Weintraub (1997) is of a different nature, sidestepping the dispute over short-term effects on output and employment, and arguing that these are essentially irrelevant. Weintraub urges that NAFTA be judged by outcomes such as the amount of trade created (from which should be subtracted trade diversion from outside North America), the amount of new investment created, the degree of further specialization achieved, the increase in productivity and competitiveness and real wages.

In addition, he says the effect on the environment should be considered—
but not the number of jobs displaced which, although a concern, according to Weintraub, should not be central to the debate.

CHANGES IN TRADE, OUTPUT, AND EMPLOYMENT: AGGREGATE AND SECTORAL TRENDS

US total trade with Canada and Mexico has been growing rapidly,
while the trade balance with both countries sharply worsened during 1994-
1996. From 1993 to 1996 US exports to Mexico grew 35.8%, from $40.3
billion to $54.7 billion, while US imports from Mexico grew 91.8%, from
$38.7 billion to $74.2 billion, as shown in Table 1. The more rapid growth
of imports was due largely to the peso devaluation in December 1994,
causing large US trade deficits with Mexico of $16.8 billion in 1995 and
$19.5 billion in 1996.

During 1993-96 US exports to Canada grew 29.7%, from $91.9
billion to $119.1 billion, while US imports from Canada grew 41.5%,
from $110.5 billion to $156.3 billion (ITC 1997). The US trade deficit
with Canada thus grew from $18.6 billion to $37.2 billion over the period.

These increases in US trade deficits with both its NAFTA partners
are the basis for the largest estimates that have been made of US job losses.
EPI (1997) estimates total US job losses (jobs eliminated, plus jobs that
failed to be created) at 420,000 as a result of the worsening trade balance.
Since not all of these represent actual jobs eliminated, the number of displaced workers is smaller.

In 1994, a NAFTA Trade Adjustment Assistance program (a program of compensation and training similar to the existing general Trade
Adjustment Assistance program) was created to assist workers displaced
by trade and investment among NAFTA countries. The number of workers certified under the NAFTA-TAA as impacted by trade with Mexico or
Canada, or relocation of production to either country, was 134,492 as of
mid-July 1997. Because the number of certifications is in some respects
an underestimate and in other respects an overestimate of those affected

specifically by NAFTA, we believe it is a good rough approximation to the number of workers actually displaced.

The issue of the effect of changes in the trade balance on employment is controversial, and will be discussed at length below. Our conclusion will be that, taking account of the ways in which various methods may overstate or understate the employment impact, the EPI estimate of the larger category is in the ball park, if likely somewhat high. However, it is important to understand the differences in the categories used in different studies to analyze employment impact, and this, too, will be clarified below.

Two sectors—auto and auto parts, and apparel—account for most of the US trade deficit with Mexico and a significant fraction of the trade deficit with Canada as well. Among sectors prominent in NAFTA trade, none is larger than the motor vehicle and vehicle parts sector. This sector accounted for approximately one-fourth of total US trade with Mexico and Canada in 1996, as shown in Table 2. In 1996 it accounted for about 20% of all US exports to NAFTA partners ($35.8 billion out of $173.8 billion in total exports to Mexico and Canada), and over 25% of all imports ($62.3 billion out of $230.5 billion in total imports from Mexico and Canada).

The predominant pattern was for parts to be exported from the US, assembled or otherwise processed, and then returned to the US as imports. In fact, some of the trade recorded as US exports of textiles, leather and electronic components, to name a few, also consists of goods destined for auto plants, as seat belts, fabric or leather for seat covers, and electronic components in autos. The US trade deficit in vehicles and vehicle parts with its two NAFTA partners was $26.5 billion in 1996, accounting for nearly half the total US trade deficit with Mexico and Canada.

The sectoral trade deficit for vehicles and parts together worsened by $12.2 billion during 1993-96, not only because of the peso devaluation, but also because a decline in Mexican demand for autos during the peso crisis caused automakers in Mexico to export a much larger share of their product than before. Among other things, this allowed them to retain workers in whom they had invested considerable time and money in training (as well, of course, as to produce the vehicles more cheaply than in the US).

Due to expansion of US domestic output in the sector in a macroeconomic boom, however, these changes did not result in a net loss of employment in the sector; rather, US employment in the two sectors combined grew from 910,000 in 1993 to 1,035,000 in 1996 (ITC 1997: 6-52-3, 6-60). At the same time, however, from 1994 through mid-1997, 9,663 US workers were certified under the NAFTA-TAA program as impacted by trade in auto and auto parts with Mexico and Canada, or relocation of production to either country (DOL 1997).

The apparel sector also accounts for a large share of trade with Mexico and Canada, and has in addition experienced a large number of job displacements due to changes in this trade, largely derived from relocation of production. These were concentrated during 1995-96, after the peso devaluation reduced Mexican labour costs sharply. As shown in Table 3, during 1993-96 US imports from both Mexico and Canada nearly doubled, while US exports to both countries grew more slowly.

In 1996, US apparel exports to Mexico were $2.0 billion while imports from Mexico were $4.5 billion. Sectoral trade with Canada was more nearly balanced, with $0.8 billion in exports and $1.2 billion in imports. The US trade balance in apparel worsened with Canada by $0.4 billion and with Mexico by $1.4 billion from 1993 to 1996. During this same period the total number of US apparel production workers fell by 130,000 to 698,000, a decline of 16% (ITC 1997: 6-22).

ITC (1997) notes that the growth in exports to Mexico consisted mostly of garment parts for assembly. Movement of apparel production to Mexico using US-formed and US-cut fabric accelerated, in part because NAFTA contained a specific expansion of US production-sharing opportunities under HTS 9802. Under this section of the US tariff code, US firms were already able to send US components abroad, have them assembled, and re-import them into the US, paying tariff only on the value added abroad. The new provision made the re-importation both duty-free and quota-free from Mexico. It also allowed processing, such as stone-washing and wrinkle-free processing, in Mexico, although if done in other countries, these would invalidate the tariff exemptions on the resulting goods when re-imported into the US.

Industry officials told the ITC that these provisions were the most important effect of NAFTA in their decision to produce in Mexico (ITC 1997: 6-25). Where the increase in US exports consisted of garment parts for processing and assembly in Mexico, and simply was the continuation of an existing supplier relationship, of course the increase in demand for these US exports was matched by a decline in domestic demand for the same goods, and implied no new job creation in the US.

From 1994 through mid-1997, 29,247 apparel workers were certified under NAFTA-TAA as displaced by trade with Mexico and Canada, or by relocation of production to either country. Some of the growth in US apparel imports, however, was due to diversion of production from Asian or Caribbean countries to Mexico. During 1993-96, Hong Kong's apparel exports to the US declined by 1%, South Korea's declined by 39%, and Taiwan's by 11%. Apparel imports from China rose by only 2% over the same period (ITC 1997:6-24).

While ITC reports an increase in the average wage in US apparel, it cautions that the 9% increase is explained by the change in composition of the workforce, that is, the exodus of lower-paying apparel assembly jobs, leaving behind the higher-skilled and higher-paying jobs in cutting.

Another major sector which accounts for a large share of NAFTA trade, and for a portion of the worsened US trade deficit with its NAFTA partners, is electronic components and equipment, for which data are given in Table 4. The US has exported an increasing quantity of electronic components to maquiladora and other enterprises in Mexico as inputs into radios and televisions, computer and peripheral equipment, communications equipment, and so forth. Net US exports of electronic components to Mexico increased by $1.7 billion from 1993 to 1996, while net imports from Mexico of computers and peripheral equipment increased by $1.4 billion, net imports from Mexico of radio and television equipment increased by $3.1 billion, and net imports from Mexico of communications equipment increased by $0.3 billion (ITC 1997).

Electronic components are also used in auto and auto parts production. While the data indicate a worsening of the US trade balance with

Mexico in these combined sectors, Hinojosa et al. (1996) note that the negative impact may be somewhat greater than it seems. This is because some of the electronic components recorded as exported from the US are actually goods that were produced in Asian countries, sent to warehouses in the US, and then re-exported to Mexico without any further processing in the US. However, although this point is noted in their text, it was not incorporated into their numerical estimates of NAFTA's employment impact. Nine sectors were identified by ITC (1997) as ones in which trade among NAFTA countries increased significantly relative to the size of the sector during 1994-96, including several not mentioned above. These sectors were vehicles, vehicle parts, apparel, textiles, women's footwear, appliances, leather, grains and cotton. The nature of these effects (whether the increase was primarily in US exports or imports), as well as the reasons for them, varied among these sectors.

THE MAIN POINTS OF AGREEMENT AND CONTENTION

Reading pro- and anti-NAFTA authors' assessments of the last three years is much like reading the six blind men's reports on the elephant—with one exception: even where they are groping the same part of the animal, one could hardly tell it from reading their accounts. Yet on closer examination, the differences among these studies are somewhat smaller than they seem. True, the reports written from the two most diametrically opposed viewpoints (USTR 1997; EPI 1997) use language that seems crafted to maximize the apparent differences. On casual reading, for instance, one would think that USTR (1997) claims creation of 90,000 to 160,000 jobs in the US over the three years of NAFTA. But contrary to appearances, the USTR report does not say this; in fact, remarkably, it does not explicitly claim *any* job creation by NAFTA. Instead it uses a category called "jobs supported by exports," which is different from "jobs created," and will be discussed below.

In contrast, EPI (1997) estimates 420,000 net jobs lost (due to worsening of the trade balance with both Mexico and Canada). However, this category includes job opportunities not created, a category which USTR (1997) does not consider at all. Thus the total number of actual layoffs that resulted from NAFTA is judged by EPI to be less than the 420,000 figure. EPI points out that the number of workers who applied for and were certified to receive NAFTA Trade Adjustment Assistance (NAFTA-TAA) is in some measure an underestimate, since some workers who were affected very likely did not apply for assistance, and some who applied were actually affected, but were not certified because of the restriction of the program to goods-producing workers, or for other reasons. The report does not, however, draw a conclusion about how many persons actually were laid off due to NAFTA, and notes that the prolonged strong business cycle upswing in the US has obscured for the present the negative effects of NAFTA on actual employment.

There are two main bones of contention between opposing views on NAFTA's effects. The most central is disagreement over whether NAFTA and the peso crisis were completely independent events, whose effects can be statistically disentangled, or whether NAFTA was a cause of the peso devaluation and crisis (as EPI (1997) and Blecker (1997) argue). The majority of studies have assumed that NAFTA had nothing to do with the peso crisis, but have typically not explained or defended this view.

These studies use statistical methods to factor out the negative effects of the peso crisis and then attribute the remaining positive effects on US employment to NAFTA (Gould 1996; DRI 1997). ITC (1997) takes a slightly different approach, defining sectoral effects as attributable to NAFTA only if in their statistical analysis the effect is significant in all three years 1994-96, and in addition is either positive in all three years, or else negative in all three years. Although a peso devaluation of some amount was unavoidable, NAFTA and the political process entwined with NAFTA turned what could have been an orderly, smaller devaluation into a major crisis; hence NAFTA is an important cause of the effects attributed to the devaluation.

The second bone of contention is how changes in US exports and imports affected employment. This controversy centres on the appropriateness of using the Department of Commerce export-jobs multiplier, particularly on whether it should be applied to imports. These issues will be discussed in detail below.

NAFTA AND THE PESO CRISIS

What causal relationship exists between NAFTA and the peso crisis? USTR (1997), DRI (1997) and several other studies assume implicitly that there is no causal relationship, and hence in essence give NAFTA credit for positive effects on US output and employment in 1994, while blaming the peso crisis for the worsening of the trade balance in 1995 and any resulting US job losses.

In contrast, NAFTA opponents tend to assume, suggest or assert that all effects that occurred after NAFTA was implemented on January 1, 1994—including the entire peso crisis—are consequences of NAFTA.

The evidence shows that NAFTA was an important cause of the peso devaluation and crisis, but not the only cause. Hence *part* of the effects of the peso crisis should be attributed to NAFTA, a fraction difficult to determine.

Mexico is no stranger to episodes of overvaluation of the peso, and eventually balance of payments crisis, followed by devaluation. Such episodes (along with other causes) led to devaluations in 1976 and 1982, and another series of devaluations occurred in 1985-1987, though each episode had somewhat different causes. The most recent overvaluation also had historically particular features.

The problems of overvaluation in the early 1990s, and the potential seriousness of its consequences, were exacerbated by several factors related to NAFTA. One was the enormous inflow of capital, particularly portfolio investment, into Mexico in 1991-93 in anticipation of gains after NAFTA was passed. This capital inflow was partly caused by Mexico's huge selloff of state enterprises to the private sector—including foreigners—but it was also a consequence of the euphoric atmosphere created by pro-NAFTA official and unofficial pronouncements.

Of course, liberalization of capital inflows, such as Mexico implemented in 1989, may cause currency appreciation with or without a NAFTA. This has happened in a number of countries in Latin America (see Agosin and Ffrench-Davis 1995). However, the capital inflow into Mexico was on an unprecedented scale, reaching in 1993 the astonishing level of $29 billion (Banco de México 1996), and the overvaluation of the peso proceeded apace. This overvaluation, among other things, improved the US trade balance with Mexico, helping lend credence to the claim by NAFTA supporters that US exports would grow under NAFTA.

Moreover, Wall Street investment firms such as Goldman, Sachs and others became deeply involved with Mexico, to the extent that in March and April 1994 they took an active role in prolonging the overvaluation of the peso and building up the financial house of cards which collapsed catastrophically in December 1994. According to a June 1994 *Wall Street Journal* report (Torres & Vogel 1994), a group of investors reacted with alarm when the assassination of the PRI Presidential candidate Colosio in March led to a sudden selloff of peso-denominated assets, forcing Mexico to use up $10 billion in foreign currency reserves to defend the value of the peso (Weintraub 1997: 55). The investment group urged the Mexican government to take several steps, including assuming much more exchange-rate risk on new debt by issuing a large quantity of securities called *tesobonos* indexed to the US dollar (Torres & Vogel 1994).

The government proceeded to do this, and as a result, in December when the peso collapsed, the burden of servicing the *tesobono* debt was far greater than it would have been to service an equal value of debt not indexed to the value of the dollar; thus the crisis was deeper than it might otherwise have been.

The hype about the marvels of economic integration probably also played a role in the motivating US bankers to extend substantial loans to private enterprises in Mexico, and many firms took on a heavy burden of dollar denominated debt (Danby 1997), which after the devaluation became far more burdensome to service, contributing to the prolongation of the crisis.

In short, the hype during the NAFTA debate, together with the role played by US investment firms, both support the argument that NAFTA, and the political and economic processes set in motion by the NAFTA proposal and debate, contributed substantially to the seriousness of the peso crisis. The fall in the value of the peso was evidently much deeper than it might have been absent NAFTA; the fragility of the debt structure caused interest rates to rise higher, and hence consumer demand and Mexican imports from the US to fall to a lower level than they might otherwise have done; and the result was a larger worsening of the US trade balance with Mexico than might have occurred in the absence of NAFTA. For these reasons, the assumption by USTR (1997) and other authors that NAFTA had no causal role in the peso crisis is indefensible.

While we cannot attribute an exact fraction of the peso crisis to NAFTA, if even half of its effects flow from NAFTA, assessments by USTR (1997) and others cited in it that NAFTA had a net positive effect on US employment would likely have to be reversed.

TRADE AND EMPLOYMENT

In addition to the controversy over the relationship between NAFTA and the peso crisis, there is a second bone of contention: how have changes in exports and imports affected US employment? Several main methods have been used to derive the employment impact, none of which is free from controversy. Before we discuss these, however, it is useful to provide a framework for analysis.

Whenever there is a change in the demand for labour, its impact may be felt either on employment levels, or on the real wage level, or else partially on employment and partially on real wages. Pre-1994 studies forecasting NAFTA's impact sometimes estimated the impact of a change in labour demand in two different ways; one was to assume the impact occurred entirely on wages, with the employment level fixed (the "full employment" assumption); the other was to assume the impact occurred entirely on employment, with wage levels fixed. The assumption was that if both employment and wages were affected, the net effects would lie within these bounds.

In the short run, the net effects are likely to be more on employment than wages, at least in a country like the US which has unemployment insurance. As many displaced workers eventually accept new jobs at lower wages, the initial employment impact is converted into a wage impact.

Apart from this, there is gross job displacement, which is typically greater than the net employment effect. Gross job displacement could easily be larger than the upper bound on net employment effect, and imposes burdens on displaced workers, as well as often on the communities in which they live.

In practice, the effects of NAFTA are overlaid onto business cycle fluctuations in output, trade, employment and wages. Since 1994-96 saw a business cycle upswing in the US, we would expect that NAFTA's net employment and wage impact would show up more as jobs that failed to be created than as jobs actually eliminated, and that the wage impact could appear as a slower rate of growth of real wages than is normal in an economic boom, rather than an actual decline. We begin by describing and assessing several methods of estimating net and gross employment impact, and then turn in a later section to the question of NAFTA's wage impact.

Several main methods have been used to derive the employment impact of NAFTA, and none is free from controversy. We consider first the positive employment impact of an increase in exports; the next section discusses the negative employment impact of an increase in imports.

How do changes in US exports affect employment?

The most widely used method of deriving the positive employment impact of an increase in exports is the US Department of Commerce export-jobs multiplier. For example, this ratio for 1992 was that a $1 billion increase in exports would create 16,532 jobs (Scott 1997). The number of jobs per billion dollars would be slightly smaller for later years, due to inflation. This multiplier, while accurate when the increase in exports truly represents an increase in demand for US products, is subject to two errors.

First, the multiplier is not based on US exports to a specific country, but on US exports overall. Thus, if US exports to a specific country, like Mexico, differ in an important way from US exports to the rest of the world, the employment multiplier could give inaccurate results. While we have no reason to think this is true in general, the Hinojosa et al. (1996) study suggests that US exports of electronic components to Mexico (valued at $4.5 billion in 1996, or 8.3% of total US merchandise exports to Mexico (ITC 1997:3-30,6-186)) may have an unusually low aggregate US domestic content.

Hinojosa et al. conducted interviews with electronic industry personnel, who explained that many of these electronic components are actually trans-shipped through the US, rather than produced in the US Asian producers set up warehouses in California to which they ship parts; these parts are then shipped to Mexican assembly plants on a just-in-time basis, and are recorded as US exports to Mexico. If such phenomena are significant in US-Mexico trade, the export-jobs multiplier would overstate how many jobs are created in the US due to increased US exports to Mexico. It is difficult to determine the extent of the problem, since US data do not distinguish between US exports which are trans-shipped goods, and US exports which have some US domestic content (Hinojosa et al. 1996).

A second and more important problem with the export-jobs multiplier is that US exports can rise for a variety of reasons, not all of them signalling an increase in US output or employment. It is sometimes the case that the increase in export demand is matched by a decline in domestic demand, because a domestic buyer has moved abroad. For instance, when an apparel maker moves from the US to Mexico, and continues to buy the same quantity of fabric from the same US supplier, made by the same workers as before, this fabric now is recorded as an increase in US exports, but has generated no new US output or employment. Instead, the increase in export demand was exactly offset by an equal decline in domestic demand, as the purchaser moved abroad. If situations of this kind account for a significant fraction of the 1994-96 increase in US exports to Mexico, then application of the export-jobs multiplier to this situation will seriously overstate the resulting creation of new jobs in the US.

There is ample reason to believe that such situations *do* account for a substantial fraction of the increase in US exports. For many sectors, the detailed sectoral analyses provided in ITC (1997) observe that trade (at least between the US and Mexico) is generated primarily by "production-sharing," that is, sending inputs from the US to assembly or processing plants in Mexico and then re-importing the finished products into the US. The same sectoral analyses also observe that in many sectors firms have relocated production to Mexico to take advantage of low wages, particularly in 1995-96 after the peso devaluation reduced wage costs initially by about half.

Moreover, the business press regularly reports relocation of production from the US to Mexico. One example is the announcement in January 1997 by the apparel maker Guess, Inc. of a decision to reduce the percentage of its jeans produced in Los Angeles from 75% to 35%, and to shift the balance to Mexico to save an estimated $1.50 to $2.00 per pair of jeans in labour costs (Scheeres 1997).

In addition, the maquiladora sector in Mexico expanded at a breakneck rate during 1995-96, with employment rising from 542,074 in 1993 to 754,858 in 1996, a 39.3% increase, after the peso devaluation reduced labour costs initially by about half; and more than 100,000 jobs have since been added (INEGI 1997). The maquila sector imports nearly all its inputs, typically from the United States, and exports its output, typically back to the US. To the extent that these plants represent production relocated from the US, then, using US-produced inputs before and after the move, the export-jobs multiplier will greatly overstate the number of new jobs created by increased US exports of inputs to these plants.

USTR (1997) sidesteps this issue by referring to the employment effect derived from the export-jobs multiplier as "jobs supported by exports" rather than "jobs created by exports." This is literally correct. However, the report does a grave disservice by failing to explain the distinction between these two concepts, and hence leaving the false impression with unwary readers (the press? the public?) that "jobs supported" *means* the same thing as "jobs created," which it assuredly does not.

"Jobs (newly) supported by exports" includes two categories: (1) jobs that already existed, but are now supported by exports (that is, they produce goods which used to be bought by domestic buyers and are now exported to those same relocated buyers), as in the hypothetical apparel-textile example above; and (2) jobs that were, in fact, newly created by an increase in exports which was not offset by a decline in domestic demand. In the example above, the unchanged number of textile jobs supplying the apparel maker are not "jobs created by exports," but they *are* jobs that are newly "supported by exports," whereas before they were supported by domestic demand. In the apparel-textile example, *no* new jobs were created.

The rub is that it is not at all clear that an increasing number of US jobs "supported by exports" is of any inherent benefit to the US labour force. In fact, just the opposite is likely to be true: buyers (such as assembly plants) that relocate to low-wage countries will presumably be more tempted than before to switch to suppliers in the low-wage country, if quality requirements can be met. Apparel makers that learn how to operate in the Mexican business environment may advise their textile suppliers how to make the move to Mexico. US "jobs supported by exports" may in such cases be the first step toward US jobs displaced.

In fact, USTR (1997) makes *no* claim that NAFTA has created any jobs at all, since the estimated 311,000 increase in the number of "jobs supported by exports" is nowhere disaggregated into "jobs newly created" and "existing jobs newly supported by exports." The report's only specific estimates of NAFTA's job creation in the US is its citation of the finding by Gould (1996) that in the absence of the peso devaluation, NAFTA *would have created* 90,000 to 160,000 jobs.

Again, the way this result is reported is misleading, obscuring the fact that it refers to a counterfactual. The report's meaning is that these jobs were not actually created, but that this was the fault of the peso crisis, not of NAFTA. As we have already pointed out, this conclusion rests on the indefensible assumption that NAFTA and the peso crisis were unrelated. In fact, apart from this, Gould's findings should not be cited at all, since this result was not statistically significant even at the 10% confidence level (Gould 1996). In sum, even USTR's (1997) specific claim based on Gould's analysis is not a claim that any US job creation actually occurred in the US during 1994-96, except perhaps temporarily during 1994.

USTR (1997) also cites the finding by DRI (1997) that NAFTA, separate from the peso crisis, boosted US net exports with Mexico either by about 3% per year (based on aggregate data), or by about 12% per year (based on sectoral data). It translates this into a positive impact on US output and then suggests that the net employment impact must also have been positive. Like Gould's conclusion, this finding is based on the idea that NAFTA was independent of the peso crisis, an idea we challenge earlier in this paper.

Finally, one other caveat must be mentioned with respect to the effect of exports on jobs. There is ample reason to believe that US multinationals engage in transfer pricing, at least in the maquiladora sector, as a way of reducing the profits they report in Mexico. There are evidently two motivations for firms to do this. First, Mexican law mandates that each firm share 10% of its profits each year with its workers. While this law is much honoured in the breach, firms are more able to evade it if they show few or no profits.

Second, until US tariffs on imports from Mexico are completely eliminated, the tariff is levied on value added in Mexico over and above the US components contained in the imports. In practice, recently about three-fifths of the value of imports from "production-sharing" (typically maquiladora) plants in Mexico has been subject to tariff (ITC 1997:3-32). If firms report value added in Mexico as a small percentage above the cost of Mexican wages, this reduces the tariff bite, and means that the amount of profit reported is very small.

For both reasons, firms are therefore likely either to overstate the value of components exported from the US to their plants in Mexico, or to understate the value of finished goods imported back into the US. In either case, the US trade balance with Mexico will be reported at an inaccurately positive level. In late 1994, the Mexican government announced that, henceforth, arm's-length pricing would be required of firms (that is, transfer pricing would not be permitted) (Siegle 1994). However, the peso crisis followed shortly after, and we have not found evidence of whether enforcement of this decree has occurred.

Of course, we are interested here in the *change* in the trade balance. However, with an expanding volume of trade, any systematic measurement error will be amplified so that the change in the trade balance will be mismeasured in a positive direction. Hence, to the extent transfer pricing occurs in an attempt to reduce profits shown in Mexico, the trade data likely overstate the US trade balance with Mexico and hence overstate NAFTA's positive impact on US employment (or understate its negative impact).

In sum, in the case of US exports to Mexico, the export-jobs multiplier appears significantly to overstate the positive employment impact of NAFTA.

How do changes in US imports affect employment?

Assessing the employment impact of imports is even more controversial. Some authors, particularly those critical of NAFTA, have used the export-jobs multiplier to apply to changes in imports, or changes (positive or negative) in net exports. Use of the multiplier in this way has been criticized extensively by USTR (1997), Hinojosa et al. (1996) and Weintraub (1997), among others. While their criticisms are largely technically correct, we believe the size of the error they imply is small, and that the larger errors offset one another to a significant extent, at least in the case of trade between the US and Mexico.

The main reason is that, as reported in the ITC (1997) sectoral analyses, much of the trade between the US and Mexico is generated by "production-sharing" operations involving assembly plants which have relocated from the US to Mexico, and in such cases the employment impact is relatively easy to assess. In addition, they neglect one source of error which would cause the multiplier to understate the employment impact.

One problem raised with applying the multiplier to imports to obtain the employment effect is that in some cases increased US imports from Mexico represent a switch from importing from a different (often low-wage) country, rather than a switch from US production. If increased imports from Mexico do not represent an increase in total US imports, but are offset by reduced imports from another country, there should be no employment impact in the US. There is ample evidence that this is a significant factor in some sectors. In the apparel sector, growth in imports from Mexico during 1994-96 was accompanied by a decline in imports from Asian suppliers.

While Mexico's apparel exports to the US increased by 91% from $2.4 billion in 1993 to $4.7 billion in 1996, Hong Kong's apparel exports to the US declined by 1%, South Korea's declined by 39%, and Taiwan's by 11%. Apparel imports from China rose by only 2% over the same period (ITC 1997:6-24). To the degree that increased US imports are goods diverted from other countries, no US employment impact would be expected. None of the studies available assessed the extent to which this is true in practice in the aggregate.

It would be a mistake, however, to conclude that US imports of apparel were entirely diverted from other countries. In fact there was also a large shift of apparel production from the US to Mexico, like the movement by Guess cited above. As described in the statistical summary of the apparel sector earlier in the paper, ITC (1997) makes clear that substantial movement of garment production from the US to Mexico has occurred. This is confirmed by the certification of 11,532 apparel workers by mid-1997 under the NAFTA-TAA program as impacted specifically due to relocation of production to Mexico (DOL 1997). Additional apparel workers were certified due to the impact of imports from Mexico.

Second, it has been argued (USTR 1997: 24-25) that to the extent imports are cheaper than the same domestic goods, they save money for domestic purchasers (whether consumer or producers) who then spend that money on other goods or on expanding production. These are the gains from trade. While this point is true, its impact is offset, or possibly more than offset, by the fact that, when US imports come from lower-wage countries, if their lower wage cost is reflected in a lower import price, then a given dollar value of imported goods represents a larger employment impact than the same dollar value of US exports[3].

While neglect of gains from trade may cause a small overstatement of the employment impact of imports, neglect of the greater employment impact per dollar of imports with low-wage countries will likely be a much larger error in the other direction.

There is an additional reason why applying the export-jobs multiplier to US imports from Mexico can be expected to understate the negative employment impact. The export-jobs multiplier is an average, taken over a range of different export sector jobs with a range of wage levels. However, according to standard trade theory, imports to the US from a lower-wage country should be more labour- intensive than US exports. The jobs displaced in the US (the high wage country) are therefore likely to be lower-wage than the average job in the US export sector. For example, the single largest category of US workers certified under NAFTA-TAA was apparel workers. Hence in this respect as well, the export-jobs multiplier applied to imports from Mexico will understate US job displacement.

Several other arguments which are raised in USTR (1997), ITC (1997) and Hinojosa et al. (1996) against use of the export-jobs multiplier are more or less technically correct, but their impact is likely to be small. For example, USTR (1997:24) observes that trade, including imports, creates indirect jobs in transportation, communication, finance, insurance and other sectors. It is true that indirect employment linked to imports, such as transportation jobs, is not typically counted in these studies. But there is no reason to think the net effect of this factor is large.

If we are thinking of imports caused by relocation of production abroad, indirect jobs such as transportation jobs will be destroyed in one location and created in another, or some existing jobs may continue to exist. However, if the cost of such indirect services were substantial, they would add to the retail cost of imported goods in the US, and the increased imports would not occur at all because the imports would not be significantly cheaper than domestic goods. While technically correct, then, to our knowledge this effect has not been shown by any study to be substantial, and is not likely to be so.

USTR (1997) has also argued that importing from Mexico, for example, is advantageous to the US because it is better than importing from, say, Asia. The reason is that imports from Mexico have higher US domestic content, on average, than imports from Asia.

There are two problems with this argument. First, it is a mistake to compare *all* US imports from Asia with *all* US imports from Mexico. Instead, the comparison should be confined to those firms that actually do relocate production, or are likely to relocate production—the import propensity of marginal firms, not of average firms or of a nation as a whole. Those firms are disproportionately US-based multinationals, and it is likely that the US domestic content in *their* US imports—from Asia as well as from Mexico—is higher than the average of all US imports from these countries.

Second, even if there is some net US employment gain in importing from Mexico rather than from Asia, this is not necessarily the relevant comparison; there is still a net employment *loss* in importing from Mexico rather than producing the same goods in the US ITC (1997) reports that for a number of sectors a central explanation for changes in trade is the relocation of production to Mexico in order to take advantage of lower Mexican wages and establish or expand production-sharing arrangements.

USTR (1997:25) argues, too, that the export-jobs multiplier, applied to imports, overstates the negative impact of these imports because it assumes that indirect jobs (of input suppliers) are eliminated along with direct jobs. That is, it assumes, for instance, that textile jobs are eliminated along with jobs in the apparel factories to which the textile producers sell inputs. This is technically correct. However, this factor must be weighed against the undercounting noted above for imports from lower-wage countries.

An additional issue is raised by Hinojosa et al. (1996) as well as ITC (1997): if the US produces no close substitute for imported goods, or if the US is unable to meet its domestic demand for a good (such as oil), then these imports do not displace US domestic output and employment. In principle, this point is valid. But a very small proportion of US imports from Mexico fall into these categories, and only a tiny proportion of the increase in US imports from Mexico during 1994-96 fit this description; it is limited to a few agricultural products like coffee and avocados, as well as petroleum.

The vast majority of US imports from Mexico are manufactured goods which either are currently produced in the US, or were produced there until recently: TVs, computers, vehicles, clothing and leather goods, furniture, and so on. Thus, while technically true, this point has little relevance, at least with respect to Mexico.

SUMMARY: HOW TRADE AFFECTS EMPLOYMENT

Let us summarize our analysis of the employment impact of a change in exports, and then of a change in imports. The net employment creation of an increase in exports is overstated in two significant ways: (1) counting as exports some goods (like some electronic components) which were actually trans-shipped rather than produced in the US, and (2) counting exports which result from relocation and are therefore offset by a reduction in domestic demand and so have no net US employment impact.

The USTR category "jobs supported by exports" sidesteps the issue, but no study has calculated net job creation accounting for these factors, because the data needed are not available. Thus the export-jobs multiplier, if incorrectly interpreted as employment gain due to exports, overstates the positive employment impact of increased exports.

To summarize the employment impact of imports, application of the export-jobs multiplier to imports understates employment impact in a major way and overstates it in a major way. The understatement comes from the fact that lower wages abroad imply larger US job losses per dollar of imports. The fact that imports are displacing employment which is apparently lower-wage than the average wage on which the export-jobs multiplier is based contributes to even greater understatement. The overstatement of negative US employment impact flows from the inclusion of increased US imports from Mexico which represent relocation of production but reduced US imports from some third country. Finally, several other minor factors discussed above do imply some small additional overstatement of the negative US employment impact of increased US imports.

Since applying the export-jobs multiplier to exports probably seriously overstates job gains, and applying it to imports probably somewhat overstates job losses, applying the multiplier to the change in net exports (as EPI(1997) has done) probably yields a fairly good ball-park figure for the net employment impact. In a rapidly growing economy such as the US economy during 1994-96, however, much of this impact is felt as a slower rate of employment or wage growth than is normal during such a boom, rather than as actual *net* US job loss in most sectors. The sectoral analyses in ITC (1997) confirm that in most sectors this is the case. However, a few sectors, notably apparel, have been somewhat hard hit.

In the next section we evaluate an alternative method of estimating employment impact, which was used by Hinojosa et al. (1996).

The Armington method of estimating employment impact

Hinojosa et al. (1996) use a different method to calculate the job impact of imports[4]. That method is to use available information on the degree to which purchasers typically switch from imported to domestic goods in response to an increase in the price of imports, or switch from domestic to imported goods in response to a decline in the price of imports.

This information is summarized in "Armington elasticities", which in this case were estimated from data on all US trade, not on trade specifically with Mexico or Canada. Hinojosa et al. (1996) applied these numbers to US. manufacturing trade with Mexico and Canada to estimate how changes in US imports from these countries during 1994-96 must have affected US domestic production in these sectors.

Finally, the study applied the export-jobs multiplier to each sectoral change in domestic output to estimate how US employment was affected. Its conclusion was that NAFTA had a very small net positive impact, with exports creating 98,000 jobs and imports eliminating 91,000, for a net gain of 7,000 jobs over the period 1990-1996. About 4,000 jobs were found to have been created on net from 1990 through 1993, and about 3,000 more from 1994 through 1996.

While this procedure makes sense to some degree, in some respects it can be expected to understate the impact of an increase in US imports from Mexico and Canada. It assumes that the only impact of increased imports within a sector (say clothing) is a reduction in US production within that sector (that is, of clothing); it does not consider the possibility that US consumers who begin buying clothing, for instance from Mexico, may be switching from spending that money on something other than US clothing.

In this respect, the impact of increased imports is to some extent understated. (However, the authors note that several aspects of their procedure would result in overstating the impact of an increase in US imports from NAFTA countries. It is difficult to judge whether the net effect is overstatement or understatement.)

Moreover, the Armington elasticities assume that the mechanism which caused the quantity of US imports to increase was a decline in the price of those imports[5]. However, US imports from Mexico sometimes have risen even though no price change has occurred; this is possible because much trade is intra-firm. For example, in 1993, before the peso crisis, US automakers were exporting from Mexico between 47% (Ford) and 63% (GM) of their Mexican output (*EFI* 2/27-3/05/95, Suppl.). After the peso crisis, these automakers in Mexico began exporting a much higher proportion of their output, because the huge jump in Mexican interest rates caused sales of autos in Mexico to plummet; it is not clear that changes in vehicle prices occurred, or were in any way a cause of increased auto imports into the US from Mexico.

For years, auto prices have increased about 2-4% per year; only for 1998 models was it expected that price increases would be more moderate—mostly due to competition from Japanese auto prices because of depreciation of the yen (Reitman and Simison 1997). It appears that firms producing vehicles much more cheaply in Mexico, but continuing to produce the same vehicles in the US, would have no incentive to reduce prices, because a price reduction would make their US-made vehicles unprofitable. In this case, it would be inappropriate to apply the Armington elasticities. Instead, it seems reasonable to suppose that in 1995 automakers reduced the rate of growth of US domestic production, more or less one for one, to make room for the increase in imports from Mexican plants.

Thus, in this case the Armington elasticities would likely understate the true impact on US employment of the increase in auto imports from Mexico. As it happens, during 1995 auto production was expanding in the US, so that, in spite of increased auto imports from Mexico, no net negative impact on US auto employment occurred.

In general, the Armington method seems less suited to estimation of employment effects of relocated production than to estimation of employment effects from trade alone. ITC (1997) notes for many sectors that production-sharing and hence intra-firm trade accounts for much of sectoral trade. When the decision to import instead of to produce domestically is made within a firm, the decision will not necessarily follow the same pattern as when trade is among firms, and there is no reason in theory

NAFTA's Impact on US Labour Markets 153

why Armington elasticities should provide a good predictor of impact on domestic output. At the very least, it is to be hoped that the Hinojosa et al. final report, when issued, should provide a substantial discussion of this issue.

In sum, the advantage of the Armington method is that it takes some account of the fact that an increase in imports cannot be expected to have a 100% offsetting effect on domestic output in the same sector. However, it is not clear that application of the method in Hinojosa et al. (1996) is adequate to produce sensible estimates of net employment impact.

We now turn to a discussion of gross employment impact.

GROSS JOB DISPLACEMENT AND THE NAFTA-TAA EVIDENCE

The NAFTA Trade Adjustment Assistance program (NAFTA-TAA) provides benefits to workers whose jobs in goods production are certified by the US Department of Labour to have been adversely impacted by imports from Mexico or Canada, or else by relocation of production to either country. Such workers also may apply for the general TAA program which was already in existence before NAFTA and which offers a similar array of benefits; in practice many have applied for both.

During 1994-96, 182,000 workers (or their unions or employers) applied for NAFTA-TAA, and all but 13,000 of these cases were decided by the end of 1996, resulting in certification of 100,000 workers. By July 1997, this number had grown to 134,492 workers (DOL 1997). Data on NAFTA-TAA certifications by two-digit SIC sector are provided in Table 5, and by state in Table 6.

ITC (1997) points out that the number of workers certified under NAFTA-TAA should not be taken as a count of all affected workers. Many workers may have not applied due to lack of information, or applied only for general TAA due to differences in the training requirements or other features (ITC 1997:3-8). Some workers, particularly transportation and warehouse workers—even if they can prove they were impacted by NAFTA trade or plant relocation—have been denied certification because NAFTA-TAA is restricted to workers who produce tangible goods.

In addition, workers who belong to unions appear to have been more likely to submit applications, evidently due to better access to information and better support. Of all workers who applied for NAFTA-TAA, 36% had their applications submitted by labour unions, far higher than the 18.4% of manufacturing workers in the US who are represented by unions (CLC 1997:61).

This suggests that workers who did not belong to unions were considerably less likely to file applications for NAFTA-TAA, even if their jobs were truly impacted. Hence, if workers impacted by trade with Mexico or Canada, or US investment in these countries, are representative of all US manufacturing workers, then we may estimate the true number of workers displaced at about twice the number certified.

On the other hand, employers of higher-wage unionized workers are more likely to shift production to Mexico, and such firms are likely to be more affected by cheaper imports, implying that the true number of workers displaced is less than twice the number certified—perhaps in the neighbourhood of 180,000 or so during 1994-96, and perhaps 230,000 or so by August 1997.

This number, however, would include not just workers impacted by NAFTA, but workers impacted by trade with NAFTA countries or US investment in those countries, whatever the cause. Even if NAFTA had never been approved, the long-term trend toward shifting production from the US to Mexico would surely have continued, as more firms learned how to do business in Mexico; thus some of the jobs lost can be attributed to this long-term trend rather than to NAFTA.

Likewise, the Mexican economic reforms gave further impetus to this long-run trend. Several studies, including Hinojosa et al. (1996) and DRI (1997), suggest that NAFTA's tariff liberalization had remarkably little impact, and that most effects seen in 1994 were due to longer-term trends. The peso crisis is agreed to have had a much greater impact on US jobs. Thus, for example, the perhaps 180,000 workers hypothesized above to have been impacted from all these causes during 1994-96 might hypothetically include perhaps 90,000 who lost jobs due to NAFTA (including its effects through the peso crisis); perhaps 45,000 who lost jobs due to the non-NAFTA aspects of the peso crisis; and perhaps another 45,000 who lost jobs due to other causes such as the long-term trends.

However, we are not now able to determine the true number of displaced workers who fall into each of these categories. In sum, due to the various offsetting factors recounted here, the likely number of workers actually displaced by NAFTA (the gross negative employment impact) is probably not far different from the number certified for NAFTA-TAA.

ASSESSING EMPLOYMENT EFFECTS: AN OVERVIEW

Let us now try to make sense out of the wildly different numbers presented in different studies assessing NAFTA's employment impact on the US. We will see that, because they refer to different categories or scenarios, they are not quite as far apart as they seem.

USTR (1997) makes three main claims. First, it claims that during 1993-96 the increase in US exports to Mexico and Canada has "supported" an increased 311,000 US jobs, 189,000 supported by increased exports to Canada, and 122,000 supported by increased exports to Mexico. As explained in an earlier section, USTR does not say how many of these are newly created jobs rather than existing jobs whose output is now exported as input to relocated plants in Mexico or Canada.

In a large number of sectors, ITC (1997) emphasizes that changes in trade have been mainly driven by an increase in co-production arrangements between the US and Mexico or the US and Canada, in the case of Mexico mainly to take advantage of low wages. And in some sectors (such as apparel) the ITC specifically attributes the decline in US employment to the shift of production to Mexico. Thus, only a fraction of the jobs newly "supported by exports" are newly created jobs.

Moreover, we cannot assume these result from NAFTA's effects; some are due to such causes as the business cycle upswing in Canada. In addition, the exports on which USTR's estimates were based apparently included rather large US grain exports to Mexico, which would have very little direct job impact because the grain sector is among the most capital-intensive in the US economy.

Hinojosa et al. (1996) estimate the impact of increased US exports to Canada and Mexico post-NAFTA as generating only 31,158 jobs, about one-tenth the USTR estimate. Some of the sources of the large difference in Hinojosa's and USTR's estimates include the fact that Hinojosa et al. restrict their analysis to manufacturing trade, and the fact that they calculate only direct job effects, not indirect effects. Given the size of the discrepancy, however, it seems likely that there is some additional explanation for the difference in estimates.

While it would be appropriate to go on to estimate the impact of the much larger increase in imports from Mexico and Canada, USTR (1997) does not do so, citing the lack of adequate general methods to estimate the employment impact of imports. USTR does, however, make other claims about overall employment effects. One is that the number of US workers displaced because of trade with Canada and Mexico (but not necessarily as a result of NAFTA per se) during 1994-96 must lie between 100,000 (the number of workers certified for NAFTA during those three years) and 32,000 (the estimated number of workers who, once certified, actually applied for NAFTA-TAA benefits during those three years). The other workers certified may have applied for general TAA benefits, or possibly taken new employment and applied for neither type of benefit.

A frequent reason for displaced workers to apply for general TAA benefits is the tight time restriction written into the NAFTA-TAA program. The NAFTA-TAA program (but not the general TAA program) requires that, once certified, a worker must enroll in a training program within six weeks of certification, or within 16 weeks of being laid off. If there is no appropriate training program that begins during the requisite time frame, the worker has little alternative but to apply for general TAA benefits. Thus the number 32,000 provides little information about how many were affected by NAFTA.

As is argued above, it is also unjustified to assume that the number certified represents the true number of workers impacted by trade and relocation of production within North America; I have argued that the true number should be close to twice the certified number. However, the number impacted specifically by NAFTA itself is only a fraction of this total.

USTR (1997) makes a third claim, about a hypothetical (or counterfactual) situation. It cites the DRI (1997) result that, *if the peso crisis had not occurred*[6], NAFTA would have resulted in net creation of 90,000 to 160,000 US jobs. Unfortunately, however, the peso crisis *did* occur, in a particularly catastrophic form, and I have argued that the political and economic pressures generated by the NAFTA debate bear an important share of the blame. Thus I reject USTR's (and DRI's) claim.

Even those who accept it, however, cannot interpret it as the net employment effect that actually occurred during 1994-96 from trade with Mexico and Canada, and even they must concede that a significant number of US jobs were displaced by the worsening of the US trade balance with NAFTA partners during that period.

At the opposite pole, EPI (1997) estimated the employment impact of the worsening US trade balance with Mexico and Canada at 420,208 jobs (including both jobs which were actually eliminated and jobs that failed to be created), of which 169,498 arose from the worsening of the US-Canada trade balance and 250,710 from the worsening of the US-Mexico trade balance. The study arrived at this conclusion by applying the Department of Commerce export-jobs multiplier to the change in the trade balance.

Since this estimate of overall 1994-96 negative employment impact is the only one among the studies reviewed which both included jobs which failed to be created, and also included impact due to all causes of changes in trade during 1994-96, it is quite naturally larger than other numbers cited here. This number may be somewhat high, since it ignores the fact that some of the increased imports were a diversion of US imports from Asian countries. In addition, of course, it is to be expected that the number will be adjusted downward as the peso appreciates and the US trade deficit with Mexico shrinks. Indeed, one such adjustment was made by EPI in late 1997.

Since the EPI analysis is based on changes in US *net* exports, implicitly it accounts both for job creation and job destruction, arriving at a net change in employment. The NAFTA-TAA data suggest, as I have argued, that at least 180,000 or so jobs have been eliminated due to all causes related to trade and investment among NAFTA countries, and probably half of these are directly attributable to NAFTA.

We could then combine USTR's number of 311,000 jobs newly supported by exports to NAFTA countries with ITC's sectoral analyses indicating that a sizeable fraction of these exports probably come from existing suppliers whose customers moved offshore, and therefore imply no job creation in the US. Perhaps 50,000 to 100,000 jobs were actually created by new exports, then—again, some but not all of them due to NAFTA, since exports were on an upward trend long before NAFTA.

Suppose further that we make the extremely rough estimate that something like 200,000 additional jobs failed to be created due to trade and investment among NAFTA countries (EPI's 420,000, less 180,000 jobs estimated actually to have been eliminated, less an arbitrary 40,000 to account for diversion of imports from other countries). Of those hypothetical 200,000 jobs which failed to be created, again not all would be due to NAFTA, but perhaps half might be.

This hypothetical calculation would lead to a net negative employment impact due to NAFTA of about 190,000 (90,000 actual jobs eliminated due to NAFTA and 100,000 which failed to be created for that reason), and a gross employment impact of 90,000. (The estimate of jobs created, based on USTR (1997), would have been implicitly offset by jobs destroyed by imports, since the 420,000 EPI figure is based on net exports and so has already offset imports against exports.)

While these numbers are highly hypothetical, they seem to be reasonable educated guesses based on the considerations outlined above. They are the basis for our conclusion that the impact of NAFTA on US employment has almost certainly been negative.

NAFTA AND WAGES

The total annual income loss to US workers displaced by NAFTA due to the period during which they are unemployed (net of replacement income from unemployment benefits or TAA) was during 1994-96 probably in the range of one to two billion dollars, at most. In contrast, if there turns out to be any measurable negative effect of NAFTA on US wages, even a one-time \$.01 per hour loss in the US average wage would mean an income loss to labour of over \$2 billion. (And a disproportionate amount of this loss would be borne by the same dislocated workers, as they take jobs on average at lower wages than they previously earned.) The dollar impact on labour of measurably slower growth in real US wages, or an actual decline in the real wage, is potentially a larger effect than displaced workers' lost income while unemployed.

Has NAFTA affected US wage growth, relative to the level which would have occurred in the absence of NAFTA? It is not easy to tell, and none of the studies reviewed here reach a definitive conclusion on this point.

NAFTA occurred against the backdrop of a long-term stagnation in real hourly compensation (wages plus benefits) in the US. For more than two decades, US labour has been unable to secure in the form of compensation a constant share of productivity increases. For example, from 1979 to 1994, productivity in non-farm business sector increased at an average annual rate of 1.0%, while real hourly compensation in the sector increased at an average of only 0.5% yearly. And production and non-supervisory workers, who account for more than 80% of wage and salary employment, have fared much worse.

Moreover, the situation worsened in recent years: from 1989 to 1994, the rate of growth of productivity continued to be 1.0%, while the rate of growth of real hourly compensation was just 0.3% (Mishel, Bernstein & Schmitt 1997:134-6).

In the US manufacturing sector, from 1987 through 1996 productivity grew at an average annual rate of growth of 2.4%, while real hourly compensation fell, so that workers actually received a less than zero share of productivity increases. Moreover, in 1995 the lag of real hourly compensation growth in manufacturing behind productivity growth was 3.1 percentage points (with 3.2% productivity growth and 0.1% growth in hourly compensation), larger than in any year since 1987.

In 1996 the lag was exactly the same, at 3.1 percentage points, with 3.3% productivity growth in manufacturing and 0.2% growth in hourly compensation (BLS 1997). This historical trend, which shows no sign of major reversal, understandably makes US labour skeptical of arguments for free trade which rest on economists' confidence that the benefits of productivity growth will sooner or later be shared with labour.

Some pre-NAFTA studies suggested that NAFTA would shift the composition of employment toward a mix that on average was higher-skilled and higher-wage than before NAFTA. Has such a shift occurred? It is difficult to give a definitive answer. On the one hand, data on NAFTA-TAA certifications suggest that lower-wage jobs have been dispropor-tionately displaced; at least, the sector with the largest number of NAFTA-TAA certifications is the apparel sector, whose average wage (ITC 1997) in 1996 was just $7.89 per hour.

In principle, elimination of lower-wage manufacturing employment could increase the *average* wage in manufacturing, just by changing the mix of jobs, but without raising any individual worker's wage or creating any new higher-wage employment. Indeed, the apparel sector analysis in ITC (1997) explains that this type of effect occurred during 1994-1996 within the apparel sector itself: many lower-wage jobs went to Mexico, while the higher-skill, higher-wage jobs, such as in cutting, remained in the US, raising the average apparel wage as 130,000 production jobs were eliminated.

USTR (1997) asserts that the average wage in the US export sector is 13-16% higher than the average wage in the US. This fact is juxtaposed with USTR's assertion that 311,000 more jobs were "supported by ex-ports" in 1996 than in 1993, and seems intended to imply that the average wage ought to rise. However, even if the skill mix in *manufacturing* shifted toward a higher average skill level (even perhaps with creation of little net new high-skill employment, and shrinkage in total manufacturing employment), we would have to ask what happened to the displaced work-ers.

Did those unable to find jobs in manufacturing crowd into lower-wage, perhaps service sector employment, and on average suffer wage cuts? If so, this would be consistent with previous findings on the experi-ence of displaced workers. And if so, any increase in the average manu-facturing wage due to disproportionate elimination of low-wage manu-facturing jobs would be accompanied by higher weighting of the non-manufacturing average wage in computing the overall average wage; thus the overall average wage would likely fall.

None of the studies reviewed here found that NAFTA had a significant positive or negative effect on US labour compensation as a whole, in most cases because they did not carry out any substantial study to assess that effect. ITC (1997) did find that, of the industries identified through econometric analysis to have been affected by NAFTA, industries with earnings reductions outnumbered those in which there were earnings increases. However, it drew no conclusion about overall impact.

ITC (1997) also assessed NAFTA's effects on average wages in some specific sectors, and found these wage effects to be negligible except in the apparel sector. There, the rise in the average wage in apparel was attributed to the elimination of low-wage jobs and the resulting change in composition of employment, as explained above.

Estimates of NAFTA's productivity effects are no more conclusive. While ITC (1997) cited substantial changes in productivity in various sectors, it did not attribute them to NAFTA, consistently describing NAFTA's influence as negligible.

One channel through which NAFTA might well affect workers is that employers' threats to close plants and relocate them abroad might have a chilling effect on worker organizing and the level of unionization, and thereby on the average wage level. A study by Bronfenbrenner (1996) found that NAFTA has created a climate in which employers have threatened or carried out plant closings in order to avoid unionization. Since the average wage premium for unionized workers relative to comparable non-union workers has been estimated at about 20% in recent years (Mishel et al. 1997:200), discouraging unionization can be expected to have a negative impact on real wages. None of the studies reviewed here estimated this impact. The Bronfenbrenner study is described at length in the following section on labour rights.

NAFTA AND LABOUR RIGHTS

A study of the effects of plant closing or threat of plant closing on the right of workers to organize in the US, conducted by Bronfenbrenner

(1996), sheds light on ways in which NAFTA might have indirectly driven down US wages, or slowed their growth. The study was commissioned by the North American Commission for Labour Cooperation, established by the labour side agreement to NAFTA, and was conducted in the summer of 1996.

Bronfenbrenner studied more than 500 union organizing campaigns and more than 100 negotiations for a first contract. She found that a majority of employers threatened to close all or part of the plant during the organizing drive, either in captive audience meetings, or in letters to employees, or in conversations between supervisors and one or more employees. The threats were often crude, and included posting maps of North America with an arrow from the current plant site pointing to Mexico, and attaching shipping labels to equipment in the plant with addresses in Mexico. Among those campaigns in which threats were made, in 10% of the cases the threat was specifically to move to Mexico, while in other cases the threats were more vague, but sometimes made reference to NAFTA.

Bronfenbrenner found that plant closing threats were effective, on average: where such threats occurred during an organizing drive, union wins were 33%, while where no such threats occurred, the union win rate was 47%. Moreover, in 15% of the plants where the union won the election, the employer did shut down all or part of the plant within two years of the election, in most cases before a first contract was reached.

The 15% shutdown rate within two years of a union winning an election was three times the rate found by researchers during the late 1980s, before NAFTA. The report concluded that NAFTA had created a climate which had emboldened employers to threaten more aggressively to close plants, or else actually to close plants, in order to avoid unionization.

Conclusion

Standard cost-benefit analysis calls for evaluating any policy change by determining whether the winners gain more than the losers lose, and therefore could in principle compensate them. It is then hypothetically possible, with redistribution, for the policy change to make no one worse off, and some better off. On this basis, it is not clear that NAFTA has qualified. There have clearly been winners and losers: firms that have shifted production to Mexico to take advantage of lower wages have been winners; dislocated workers and the communities in which they live have been losers. But the gains may not have exceeded the losses: the ITC (1997) was unable to detect a net gain in US GDP due to NAFTA.

Other studies have claimed that NAFTA, apart from the peso devaluation, did bring about a small boost in US GDP, but if NAFTA was in any significant way a cause of the peso crisis—as we argue it was—this finding would be reversed. In the long run, of course, abstracting from short-run macroeconomic fluctuations, gains from trade must be realized.

Standard trade models predict that labour, particularly unskilled labour, in the US is likely to suffer a net loss in real income, and this would be counteracted only by sufficiently strong scale economies. Evidence of such substantial scale economies has been challenged, at least for Mexico, as pointed out above. While no significant statistical evidence of real wage losses in the US has emerged, neither is there evidence of real wage gains. And there are a couple of reasons to suspect that a negative wage impact has occurred in the US, even though it might be small.

One reason is the detailed sectoral analyses in ITC (1997), which describe widespread shifts of production to Mexico, particularly to the maquiladora sector, to take advantage of lower wages and duty reductions. Another is the conclusion reached by Bronfenbrenner's (1996) study, that NAFTA has encouraged US employers to brandish plant relocation, and to use plant relocation, as a means of discouraging union organizing.

Moreover, the losers have not been fully compensated for their losses. A survey of studies of the cost of protectionism concludes that the cost of protecting a single job is often over $100,000 (Coughlin, Chrystal and Wood 1995). This amount may be thought of as the size of the gain to the winners after trade liberalization, which in principle is the maximum amount available to offer compensation to the losers. If trade adjustment assistance were available in even half this amount per displaced worker, quite probably labour would have far fewer complaints about NAFTA.

It was initially argued that NAFTA would attract inward foreign investment from outside North America, and this has happened to some degree. Ironically, however, this shows the effectiveness not of free trade but of protectionism. What it says is that protectionism works to some extent in attracting foreign investment if the protected market is large and attractive enough, and includes a low-wage location for production to serve that market. But it is questionable to what extent labour can achieve any gains from this arrangement, or even avoid net losses. What we know so far about the experience of US labour under NAFTA provides little encouragement on this score.

ENDNOTES

1   This trend is often referred to as an increase in the wage premium for a college education, but in view of the stagnation in average real wages and the decline in the real wage for low-skilled workers, it seems more apt to describe the phenomenon as an increase in the penalty for the lack of a college education.

2   Such studies predicted employment impact, assuming a constant real wage; other studies or scenarios predicted real wage impact, assuming constant employment.

3   For this to occur it only requires that the import price recorded in the trade data be lower than would be recorded as an export price if the same good were domestically produced; transfer pricing might bring this about, whether or not the lower wage cost of the imported good was reflected in a lower retail price to US customers.

4   This was a preliminary report by the North American Integration and Development Centre in Los Angeles, a rough draft for which the final report had not yet been issued at the time of this writing. The numbers should therefore be viewed as very tentative only, and indicative of the range of results to be anticipated from the method used.

5   In fact, there appear to be technical problems in the application of the method: even though price change is hypothetically the mechanism which causes substitution away from domestic goods to comparable imported goods, at one stage in the procedure it is assumed that prices are unchanged over the time period in question. It appears to this author that the method ought first to be validated by application either to an artificially constructed (hence known) set of data, or to historical known data, to determine whether the method arrives at the correct result.

6   This is meant in the statistical sense that, in an econometric regression, absent the effect of the decline in the value of the peso, there would have been net creation of 90,000 to 160,000 jobs.

BIBLIOGRAPHY

Agosin, Manuel and Ricardo Ffrench-Davis. 1995. Trade Liberalization and Growth: Recent Experiences in Latin America. *Journal of Interamerican Studies and World Affairs* 37(3): 9-58 (Fall).

[BLS] Bureau of Labor Statistics. 1997. http://stats.bls.gov:80/datahome.htm. PRS 30006092, PRS 30006152.

Banco de México. 1996. *The Mexican Economy 1996*. Mexico, D.F.

Blecker, Robert A. ca. 1997. NAFTA and the Peso Collapse: Not Just a Coincidence. Economic Policy Institute Briefing Paper.

Bourgignon, Francois and Christian Morrisson. 1989. *External Trade and Income Distribution*. Paris: OECD.

Bronfenbrenner, Kate. 1996. *The Effects of Plant Closing or Threat of Plant Closing on the Right of Workers to Organize*. Report to the Labor Secretariat of the North American Commission for Labor Cooperation. New York State School of Industrial and Labor Relations, Cornell University. September 30.

[CLC] Commission for Labor Cooperation, North American Agreement on Labor Cooperation. 1997. *North American Labor Markets: A Comparative Profile*. Bernan Press and the CLC.

Coughlin, Cletus C., K. Alec Chrystal, and Geoffrey E. Wood. 1995. Protectionist Trade Policies: A Survey of Theory, Evidence, and Rationale. Ch. 20, pp. 323-338 in Jeffry A. Frieden and David A Lake, *International Political Economy*, 3rd edition, New York, St. Martin's Press.

[DOL] U.S. Department of Labor. NAFTA-TAA Office. 1997. [NAFTA]-TAA Certified Plants, by Two-Digit SIC Code, data printout.

[DRI] DRI/McGraw-Hill, International Group. 1997. "The Impact of NAFTA on Mexican Trade: An Empirical Study." April, photocopy.

Danby, Colin. 1997. *Mexican Financial Liberalization 1989-1993*. Ph.D. Dissertation, University of Massachusetts, Amherst.

[*EFI*] *El Financiero International* (English). 1995. February 27-March 5, Supplement.

[EPI et al.] Economic Policy Institute, Institute for Policy Studies, International Labor Rights Fund, Public Citizen's Global Trade Watch, Sierra Club, U.S. Business and Industrial Council Educational Foundation. 1997. *The Failed Experiment: NAFTA at Three Years*. June 26. Photocopy, Washington, DC: Economic Policy Institute.

[ERP] *Economic Report of the President 1997* [http://www.gpo.ucop.edu/info/erp.html].

Freeman, Richard B. 1995. Are Your Wages Set in Beijing? *Journal of Economic Perspectives* 9(3): 15-32 (Summer).

Gould, David M. 1996. Distinguishing NAFTA from the Peso Crisis. *The Southwest Economy* (September/October).

Hinojosa Ojeda, Raúl, Curt Dowds, Robert McCleery, Sherman Robinson, David Runsten, Craig Wolff and Goetz Wolff. 1996. *North American Integration Three Years After NAFTA: A Framework for Tracking, Modeling and Internet Accessing the National and Regional Labor Market Impacts.* University of California at Los Angeles, School of Public Policy and Social Research, North American Integration and Development Center.

[INEGI] Instituto Nacional de Estadística, Geografía e Informática. 1997. *Industria Maquiladora de Exportación.* Series *Estadísticas Económicas,* Feb.

[ITC] U.S. International Trade Commission. 1997. *The Impact of the North American Free Trade Agreement on the U.S. Economy and Industries: A Three-Year Review.* Investigation No. 332-381. Publication 3045. June.

[ITC] U.S. International Trade Commission. 1991. *The Likely Impact on the United States of a Free Trade Agreeement with Mexico.* USITC Publication 2353. February. Washington, DC: United States International Trade Commission.

Kouparitsas, Michael. 1996. A Dynamic Macroeconomic Analysis of NAFTA. *Economic Perspectives* 21(1):14-36, Federal Reserve Bank of Chicago (January/February).

Mishel, Lawrence, Jared Bernstein and John Schmitt. 1997. *The State of Working America 1996-97.* Washington, DC: Economic Policy Institute.

Reitman, Valerie and Robert L. Simison. 1997. Ford to Announce Flat Prices for 1998 Models Prices. *Wall Street Journal* August 1, 1997.

Richardson, J. David. 1995. Income Inequality and Trade: How to Think, What to Conclude. *Journal of Economic Perspectives* 9(3): 33-55 (Summer).

Scheeres, Julia. 1997. Guess Decides to Move to Mexico. *El Financiero International* 6(32): 13 (January 27-February 2).

Scott, Robert E. 1997. North American Trade After NAFTA: Rising Deficits, Disappearing Jobs. Economic Policy Institute Briefing Paper. Washington, DC: Economic Policy Institute.
Siegle, Candace. 1994. Tax attack. *World Trade* 7(8): 104-5.

Torres, Craig and Thomas T. Vogel, Jr.. June 14, 1994. Some Mutual Funds Wield Growing Clout in Developing Nations. *Wall Street Journal.*

[USTR] U.S. Trade Representative. July 1997. *Study on the Operation and Effects of the North American Free Trade Agreement.*

Tybout, James R. and Daniel M. Westbrook. 1995. Trade Liberalization and the Dimensions of Efficiency Change in Mexican Manufacturing Industries. *Journal of International Economics* 39(1-2):53-78 (August).

Weintraub, Sidney. 1997. *NAFTA at Three: A Progress Report*. Washington, DC: Center for Strategic and International Studies.

Wood, Adrian. 1995. How Trade Hurt Unskilled Workers. *Journal of Economic Perspectives* 9(3):57-80.

APPENDIX

TABLE 1

TOTAL U.S. TRADE WITH NAFTA COUNTRIES, 1993-1996

Total trade flows	1993	1994	1995	1996	1993-96	1993-96
			Value (million current dollars)			
U.S. imports from:						
Mexico	38,668	48,605	61,721	74,179	35,511	91.8%
Canada	110,482	128,753	144,882	156,299	45,817	41.5%
U.S. exports to:						
Mexico	40,265	49,136	44,881	54,686	14,420	35.8%
Canada	91,866	103,643	113,261	119,123	27,257	29.7%
U.S. trade balance with:						
Mexico	1,597	531	(16,840)	(19,493)	(21,090)	
Canada	(18,616)	(25,110)	(31,621)	(37,176)	(18,560)	

Source: ITC (1997), page xx.

TABLE 2

NAFTA VEHICLE AND VEHICLE PARTS TRADE, 1993-1996

MOTOR VEHICLE AND VEHICLE PARTS SECTOR TRADE		1993	1994	1995	1996	Absolute change, 93-96	% change, 93-96
			Value (million current dollars)				
US imports from:	Mexico	8,293	11,047	14,767	18,821	10,538	127.1%
	Canada	34,782	39,534	41,836	43,399	8,617	24.8%
US exports to:	Mexico	5,289	6,200	5,119	6,014	725	13.7%
	Canada	23,084	27,505	28,669	29,837	6,753	29.3%
US trade balance with:	Mexico	(3,004)	(4,847)	(9,648)	(12,807)	(9,803)	
	Canada	(11,698)	(12,029)	(13,167)	(13,562)	(1,864)	

MOTOR VEHICLE SECTOR TRADE		1993	1994	1995	1996	Absolute change, 93-96	% change, 93-96
			Value (million current dollars)				
US imports from:	Mexico	4,626	5,937	8,386	###	7,088	###
	Canada	###	###	###	###	6,936	25.8%
US exports to:	Mexico	513	1,083	372	1,168	655	###
	Canada	###	###	###	###	1,092	9.8%

AUTO PARTS SECTOR TRADE		1993	1994	1995	1996	Absolute change, 93-96	% change, 93-96
			Value (million current dollars)				
US imports from:	Mexico	3,667	5,110	6,381	7,107	3,450	94.3%
	Canada	7,864	8,442	8,337	9,545	1,681	21.4%
US exports to:	Mexico	4,776	5,117	4,747	4,846	70	1.5%
	Canada	###	###	###	###	5,661	47.4%

Source: ITC (1997), pages 6-52 and 6-60. Includes Standard Industrial Classification (SIC) Industry Nos. 3711, Motor Vehicles and Motor Vehicle Equipment; 3716, Motor Homes; 3691, Storage Batteries; 3694, Electrical Starting and Ignition Equipment for Internal Combustion Engines; 3714, Motor Vehicle Parts and Accessories; 3715, Truck Trailers; and 3792, Travel Trailers and Campers.

TABLE 3

NAFTA APPAREL TRADE, 1993-96

Apparel sector trade	1993	1994	1995	1996	Absolute change, 1993-96	Percentage change, 1993-96
		Value (million current dollars)				
U.S. imports from:						
Mexico	2,449	2,877	3,673	4,670	2,221	90.7%
Canada	616	788	987	1,186	571	92.7%
U.S. exports to:						
Mexico	1,139	1,411	1,567	1,975	836	73.4%
Canada	606	672	768	785	179	29.5%
U.S. trade balance with:						
Mexico	(1,310)	(1,466)	(2,106)	(2,695)	(1,385)	
Canada	(10)	(116)	(219)	(401)	(391)	

Source: ITC (1997), page 6-30. Standard Industrial Classification (SIC) 23, which in-cludes apparel and other textile products produced by cutting and sewing, as well as some nonapparel textile products like home furnishings (curtains, sheets, towels, etc.) - but not apparel products made in knitting mills, which fall under SIC 22, textile mill products.

TABLE 4

NAFTA ELECTRONIC COMPONENTS AND PRODUCTS TRADE, 1993-1996

ELECTRONIC COMPONENTS & PRODUCTS		1993	1994	1995	1996	Absolute change, 93-96	% change, 93-96
			Value (million current dollars)				
US imports from:	Mexico	5,453	7,956	10,082	12,360	6,907	126.7%
	Canada	5,456	6,692	8,419	8,931	3,476	63.7%
US exports to:	Mexico	4,992	6,549	7,002	8,905	3,913	78.4%
	Canada	7,533	8,777	10,559	11,446	3,917	51.9%
US trade balance with:	Mexico	(461)	(1,407)	(3,080)	(3,455)	(2,994)	
	Canada	2,077	2,085	2,140	2,515	438	

RADIO AND TV EQUIPMENT		1993	1994	1995	1996	Absolute change, 93-96	% change, 93-96
			Value (million current dollars)				
US imports from:	Mexico	2,405	3,851	5,087	6,048	3,643	151.5%
	Canada	295	484	639	784	489	234.1%
US exports to:	Mexico	1,803	1,798	1,696	2,042	539	33.6%
	Canada	1,116	1,363	1,565	1,601	489	43.8%

COMPUTERS		1993	1994	1995	1996	Absolute change, 93-96	% change, 93-96
			Value (million current dollars)				
US imports from:	Mexico	854	1,388	1,804	2,916	2,062	243.8%
	Canada	2,169	3,026	3,950	3,328	1,160	53.5%
US exports to:	Mexico	1,082	1,314	1,112	1,784	702	64.9%
	Canada	3,057	3,642	4,256	4,475	1,419	46.4%

TABLE 4 (CONT'D)

NAFTA ELECTRONIC COMPONENTS AND PRODUCTS TRADE, 1993-1996

COMMUNICATIONS EQUIPMENT						Absolute change,	% change,
		1993	1994	1995	1996	93-96	93-96
			Value (million current dollars)				
US imports from:	Mexico	317	444	551	713	396	124.9%
	Canada	948	1,091	1,324	1,846	897	94.6%
US exports to:	Mexico	466	564	420	598	132	28.3%
	Canada	854	882	1,054	1,357	503	58.9%

ELECTRONIC COMPONENTS SECTOR TRADE						Absolute change,	% change,
		1993	1994	1995	1996	93-96	93-96
			Value (million current dollars)				
US imports from:	Mexico	1,877	2,273	2,640	2,683	806	42.9%
	Canada	2,044	2,091	2,496	2,973	930	45.5%
US exports to:	Mexico	1,941	2,873	3,774	4,481	2,540	130.9%
	Canada	2,506	2,890	3,684	4,013	1,506	60.1%

SOURCE: ITC (1997). This category is an aggregation of four less aggregated categories in the ITC report, and includes Standard Industrial Classification (SIC) Nos. 3571, Electronic Computers; 3575, Computer Terminals; 3577, Computer Peripheral Equipment, Not Elsewhere Classified; 3651, Household Audio and Video Equipment; 3663, Radio and Television Broadcasting and Communications Equipment; 3671, Electron Tubes; 3661, Telephone and Telegraph Apparatus; 3669, Communications Equipment, Not Elsewhere Classified; 3672, Printed Circuit Boards; 3674, Semiconductors and Related Devices; 3675, Electronic Capacitors; 3676, Electronic Resistors; 3678, Electronic Connectors; and 3679, Electronic Components, Not Elsewhere Classified.

TABLE 5

NAFTA-TAA CERTIFICATIONS,
BY TWO-DIGIT SIC CATEGORY

SIC 2-digit category		Number of workers certified for NAFTA-TAA
1	Crops	2,212
2	Meat products	105
10	Metal mining	1,208
13	Oil and gas extraction	1,054
15	General contractors & operative builders	19
17	Special trade contractors	50
20	Food and kindred products	2,649
22	Textile mill products	4,779
23	Apparel and other textile products	29,247
24	Lumber and wood products	5,547
25	Furniture and fixtures	2,820
26	Paper and allied products	4,734
27	Printing and publishing	1,432
28	Chemicals and allied products	2,111
29	Petroleum and coal products	21
30	Rubber and miscellaneous plastics products	3,690
31	Leather and leather products	5,873
32	Stone, clay and glass products	4,076
33	Primary metal industries	4,457
34	Fabricated metal products	6,650
35	Industrial machinery and equipment	6,010
36	Electronic and other electrical equipment	22,176
37	Transportation equipment	10,182
38	Instruments and related products	5,058
39	Miscellaneous manufacturing industries	2,968
49	Electric, gas and sanitary services	4,062
50	Wholesale trade - durable goods	173
51	Wholesale trade - nondurable goods	557
73	Business services	572
76	Miscellaneous repair services	56
87	Engineering and management services	4
Total workers certified for NAFTA-TAA		134,552

Source: Department of Labor, NAFTA Trade Adjustment Assistance.

TABLE 6

NAFTA-TAA CERTIFIED WORKERS, BY STATE
AS OF MID-JULY 1997

State	Workers	State	Workers
North Carolina	####	West Virginia	1,288
Texas	####	Kansas	1,184
Pennsylvania	####	Kentucky	1,016
New York	####	Alaska	780
California	7,476	Louisiana	778
Georgia	6,186	Arizona	684
Indiana	5,811	Connecticut	631
Tennessee	5,640	Montana	613
Arkansas	5,397	Maine	432
New Jersey	4,471	Wyoming	392
Ohio	4,413	Vermont	361
Wisconsin	4,405	Minnesota	336
Michigan	3,783	North Dakota	300
Washington	3,445	Utah	292
Missouri	3,329	New Mexico	242
Illinois	2,902	Oklahoma	230
Florida	2,804	Nebraska	220
Iowa	2,785	New Hampshire	139
Oregon	2,550	Maryland	86
South Carolina	2,305	Idaho	83
Virginia	2,166	Nevada	76
Colorado	1,990	South Dakota	65
Alabama	1,383		
Massachusetts	1,315	TOTAL	#####

Source: Department of Labor, NAFTA Trade Adjustment Assistance Office.
Note: Certifications are for Jan. 1, 1994 to July 18, 1997.

TABLE 7

NAFTA-TAA CERTIFICATIONS, BY REASON AND YEAR

	Number of workers certified for NAFTA-TAA, Jan.-July 1994-July 1997	Number certified			
		1994	1995	1996	1997
C1: Mexico production shift	####	9,008	####	####	###
C2: Canada production shift	####	2,471	4,150	2,789	1,369
C3: Mexico import by business	####	3,296	2,073	5,146	958
C4: Canada import by business	8,102	1,495	3,919	1,389	1,299
C5: import, country unspecified	####	1,029	5,700	8,805	4,466
C6: Mexico import by customers	####	431	3,714	4,287	2,502
C7: Mexico import by customers	6,452	2,773	2,713	874	92
C8: Import by customers, unspecified	1,787	636	620	281	250
C9: Other	3,592	0	0	0	3,592
Total	####	21,139	####	####	###

Source: Department of Labor, NAFTA Trade Adjustment Assistance Program.

Note: data are for January 1, 1994 through July 18, 1997, and 1997 figure is through this date.

Mexican Labour Markets Under NAFTA

By Maria Teresa Gutiérrez Haces

" ...we want a world with a place for everyone. "[1]

INTRODUCTION

In order to objectively analyze the impact of NAFTA on the structure of employment and wages in Mexico, one must start by looking at the main economic indicators over a longer period than the negotiation and implementation of NAFTA (1991 to 1997). For the purpose of our analysis it is relevant to go back to 1985 when the process of trade liberalization began in Mexico.

Any analysis that seeks to examine the evolution of employment and wages must take into account not only the effects of trade and investment liberalization, but also those of structural adjustment programs of which they are a part. Structural adjustment programs in Mexico have involved the following elements: privatization of state-owned enterprises; a change in the method of regulating economic activity; the promotion of a trade strategy based on non-petroleum exports; control of inflation; wage restrictions; and an effort to maintain stability in the balance of payments. All these measures have directly affected wages and employment.

During the process of trade liberalization, a large number of companies have tried to reorganize their productive structures, retrain their employees, and reorient their marketing strategies. This process of "business adaptation" has meant in many cases a reduction in the number of jobs, changes in duration and rhythm of the work-day, and company downsizing and closure. These aspects will be analyzed later in this paper.

During the negotiation stage of NAFTA, official statements focused on the promise of a few key benefits that supposedly would result from the treaty. The way in which these were presented to civil society was crucial, as it would have been very difficult to negotiate NAFTA had there not been a minimum consensus in Mexico.

Among the expected benefits were the following: an increase in the competitiveness of the national economy; growth in employment; and a significant increase in wage levels. The first of these was aimed at the national and transnational business sector, and the last two were meant to ease the fears of a large number of Mexicans who had suffered from a worsening of employment and wage levels in the 1980s.

In this paper we will demonstrate how the NAFTA promises have not been fulfilled, especially those related to sustainable economic development. We will firstly analyze briefly the recent macroeconomic performance of the Mexican economy. Secondly, we will review labour market trends in the era of economic liberalization and NAFTA and finally, we will present the main conclusions from the analysis.[2]

MACROECONOMIC PERFORMANCE

Gross Domestic Product

Mexico's GDP grew at an average annual rate of 1.7% from 1986 to 1994, lower than the rate of population growth, implying a decline in living standards. The only year in this period with a negative growth rate was 1986 when GDP growth was -3.8%. Subsequently, GDP growth accelerated, peaking at 5.1% in 1990.

During the Salinas administration (1988-94), GDP growth took on a classic "bell shape" (Salas y Rendón, 1996:81). Economic growth, the main priority of the Salinas government, did not develop a sustainable trend (Tables 1 and 2). Furthermore, the crisis of December 1994 caused a dramatic drop in GDP, reaching the level of -6.2% in 1995. (OECD, 1997, p. 175.) More recently, GDP growth became positive again, with a rate of 4.6% estimated for 1996, and is projected to increase 3.7% and 5.5.% in 1997 and 1998 respectively. (Dehesa y Camarena, 1997:89.)[3]

TABLE 1

EVOLUTION OF MEXICO'S GDP BY BROAD DEVELOPMENT PHASES

Phase	Period	Average Annual GDP Growth Rate %
Take off	1940-1954	5.8
Growth with stability	1955-1972	6.7
Growth with broken stability	1973-1981	7.0
Crisis and adjustment	1982-1987	3.5
1995 Crisis	1995	-6.2

Source: adapted from Samaniego, 1997:68

TABLE 2

EVOLUTION OF SELECTED ECONOMIC INDICATORS
(PERCENTAGE OF GROWTH IN RELATION TO THE PREVIOUS YEAR)

Year	1989	1990	1991	1992	1993	1994	1995
GDP	4.2%	5.1%	4.2%	3.6%	2.0%	4.4%	-6.2%
Employment	3.6%	1.9%	5.5%	5.4%	4.5%	1.4%	-1.0%
Productivity	1.4%	2.2%	1.4%	-0.2%	-1.7%	1.2%	6.2%
Unemployment/EAP	29.5%	29.5%	30.9%	32.9%	34.7%	35.3%	-
% Wages/GDP	25.5%	28.1%	28.9%	21.8%	15.7%	10.1%	-

Source: OECD. 1997:175

With respect to GDP per capita, we have already noted that the rate of population growth exceeded that of GDP. Assigning GDP per capita for 1980 an index of 100, it had dropped to 85 by 1988. During the Salinas administration, the GDP per capita index rose slightly to 89 in 1994 (Hiernaux, 1996:20.)[4]   Thus, market liberalization did not improve the situation of Mexican families. GDP per capita was more than 10% below the average level reached in the 1978-82 oil boom period, the final stage under the import-substitution model.

This assertion is further strengthened if we recall that between 1950 and 1970 the average annual growth rate in GDP was 6.6% and a population growth rate of 3.2%. Between 1978 and 1982, the Mexican economy grew at rates exceeding 8%. This economic peak has no precedent in any previous period, nor has it been surpassed in the trade liberalization period. (Samaniego, 1997:55.)

In the first three years of NAFTA (1994-96), GDP per capita dropped 3.2%. GDP per capita at the end of 1996 was 7.8% lower than in 1981, the last year of real growth before the first crisis.

GDP per capita fell 10.0% during the administration of Miguel de la Madrid (1982-88), while growing 11.2% during the administration of Salinas de Gortari (1988-94) (RMALC, 1997). Far from demonstrating the success of the neoliberal economic model, within months of Salinas's departure came the financial crisis and the collapse of GDP per capita by 6.9% in 1995, the second largest decline in the economy this century, surpassed only in 1932. (RMALC, 1997:20, citing INEGI data.)

Despite the changes made to the Mexican economy during 1988-94, there were few changes in the sectoral composition of the economy. In the *primary sector* (agriculture, forestry and fishing) there was a steady decline in its contribution to GDP, from 6.3% in 1988 to 5.8% in 1995 (Tables 3 and 4). This drop was possibly due to the steady decline in importance in the rural economy. From 1988 to 1995, the average rate of growth of this sector was 1.2%, among the lowest after mining and construction.

The manufacturing sector's share has been stable, at almost one-quarter of GDP—24.3% in 1988 and 24.4% in 1995. The December 1994 crisis does not seem to have affected the size of the manufacturing sector in relation to GDP. However, in 1990, 1991 and 1992 there was an upturn

TABLE 3

MEXICO'S GROSS DOMESTIC PRODUCT: SECTORAL COMPOSITION (PERCENT)

By Category	1988	1989	1990	1991	1992	1993	1994	1995P
Agriculture, forestry and fisheries	6.32	6.07	6.10	5.99	5.72	5.79	5.55	5.81
Industry	24.27	24.72	25.11	24.90	25.08	24.67	24.76	24.39
Mining	1.45	1.39	1.37	1.33	1.30	1.29	1.27	1.31
Manufacturing	17.12	17.73	18.02	17.88	17.97	17.51	17.45	17.75
Construction	4.15	4.05	4.21	4.24	4.36	4.41	4.58	3.74
Electricity, Gas and Water	1.55	1.55	1.51	1.46	1.45	1.46	1.46	1.59
Services	61.35	61.17	60.75	61.06	61.15	61.50	61.64	61.76
Internal Trade, Restaurants, and Hotels	19.44	19.51	19.73	20.08	20.40	20.03	20.49	18.74
Transportation, Storage, Communications	8.40	8.45	8.32	8.25	8.39	8.56	8.91	9.06
Finance, Insurance, Real Estate	14.09	13.99	13.91	13.97	14.10	14.58	14.73	15.63
Personal, Community and Social Services	21.74	21.50	21.11	21.16	20.73	21.01	20.37	21.09
Banking	-2.31	-2.28	-2.32	-2.40	-2.47	-2.68	-2.85	-2.77
Subtotal of gross value added	91.95	91.95	91.95	91.95	91.95	91.95	91.95	91.96
Net tax on goods and services	8.05	8.05	8.05	8.05	8.05	8.05	8.05	8.04
Total GDP	100.00	100.00	100.00	100.00	100.00	100.00	100.00	100.00
By Sector								
Public sector	20.44	19.75	19.15	17.32	14.92	14.92	14.68	na
Private sector	79.56	80.25	80.85	82.68	85.08	85.08	85.32	na

Source: Statistical annex to Dr. Zedillo's 2nd Presidential Report, 1996.

TABLE 4

GROWTH OF MEXICO'S GROSS DOMESTIC PRODUCT BY SECTOR (PERCENT CHANGE)

	1989	1990	1991	1992	1993	1994	1995p	1988-1995p
By Category								
Agriculture, forestry and fisheries	-0.03	5.63	2.32	-0.97	3.08	0.18	-1.81	1.17
Industry	6.14	6.71	3.36	4.37	0.29	4.81	-7.58	2.48
Mining	-0.29	3.39	1.04	1.26	1.84	2.54	-3.45	0.88
Manufacturing	7.89	6.77	3.43	4.16	-0.67	4.07	-4.57	2.93
Construction	1.75	9.19	4.88	6.68	3.02	8.43	-23.30	0.91
Electricity, Gas and Water	4.47	2.59	0.39	3.07	2.56	4.77	2.11	2.84
Services	3.88	4.35	4.77	3.76	2.53	4.65	-5.99	2.50
Internal Trade, Restaurants, and Hotels	4.62	6.21	6.08	5.30	0.09	6.78	-14.14	1.88
Transportation, Storage, Communications	4.80	3.46	3.43	5.29	4.03	8.71	-4.54	3.53
Finance, Insurance, Real Estate	3.50	4.45	4.70	4.58	5.45	5.42	-0.39	3.94
Personal, Community and Social Services	3.06	3.15	4.48	1.51	3.32	1.26	-2.88	1.96
Banking	2.96	6.72	8.12	6.50	10.82	11.06	-8.96	5.11
Subtotal of gross value added to basic prices	4.20	5.07	4.22	3.63	1.95	4.42	-6.16	2.41
Net tax on goods and services	4.20	5.07	4.22	3.63	1.95	4.42	-6.20	2.40
Total	4.20	5.07	4.22	3.63	1.95	4.42	-6.17	2.41
By Sector								
Public sector	0.66	1.90	-5.73	-10.75	1.93	2.75		
Private sector	5.11	5.85	6.58	6.64	1.95	4.71		

Source: Statistical annex to Dr. Zedillo's 2nd Presidential Report, 1996.

TABLE 5

EMPLOYMENT IN MANUFACTURING (1)
(INDIVIDUALS)

	1986	1987 (2)	1988	1989	1990	1991	1992	1993 (3)	1994	1995	1996
YEARLY AVERAGE	946,330	948,079	945,622	967,673	969,038	952,850	916,709	1,440,217	1,394,321	1,271,067	1,312,835

1/ Up to 1992, information reflects data from the Monthly Industrial Survey which is an assessment of approximately 3218 manufacturing plants, which account for 72% of the total manufacturing production value reported in the Economic Census of 1989. Starting in 1993, information reflects data from the Monthly Industrial Survey assessing approximately 7000 manufacturing plants, which account for 80% of the total manufacturing production value reported in the Economic Census of 1994. For the last 4 years, information corresponds to the new series of 205 types of activities.
2/ For 1987, amounts to the end of June were revised and up-dated by INEGI.
3/ Starting in 1993, amounts are preliminary and were revised and up-dated by INEGI.

Source: National Institute of Statistics, Geography and Information (INEGI)

EMPLOYMENT IN THE MAQUILADORA SECTOR (1)

	1986	1987	1988	1989	1990	1991	1992	1993	1994 (2)	1995	1996
YEARLY AVERAGE	249,833	305,253	369,489	418,533	447,606	457,352	505,698	542,074	583,044	643,502	754,858

1/ Information corresponds to the total number of plants in operation of the "maquiladora" industry.
2/ Revised and up-dated amounts by INEGI.

Source: National Institute of Statistics, Geography and Information (INEGI)

Table 6
Growth of Manufacturing of the Maquiladora Sector
for Specific States, 1975-88 (Selected Years)
(Percent)

	1975		1980		1985		1988	
	Manufact. % of GDP	Maquiladora % of manuf.	Manufact. % of GDP	Maquiladora % of manuf.	Manufact. % of GDP	Maquiladora % of manuf.	Manufact. % of GDP	Maquiladora % of manuf.
Baja California	18.10	21.36	17.89	17.89	17.15	31.44	19.20	57.60
Sonora	11.82	15.69	12.06	17.75	13.37	15.62	16.89	22.82
Chihuahua	14.15	24.12	15.07	34.11	18.29	49.14	22.02	69.26
Coahuila	24.71	2.13	26.93	1.72	29.07	2.82	34.96	4.76
Nuevo León	37.59	na	35.54	na	37.14	na	42.93	na
Tamaulipas	13.74	13.38	14.09	17.36	13.55	33.58	16.91	56.05
Sub-total border states	22.53	7.19	22.87	8.13	24.15	12.70	28.61	20.23
Federal District	26.62	0.00	26.97	0.00	27.53	0.00	29.56	0.09
México	39.53	0.00	38.06	0.00	40.20	0.00	43.63	0.00
Jalisco	23.67	0.00	23.36	0.00	26.81	0.00	28.29	2.23
other states	16.79	0.60	16.18	0.98	15.88	1.38	19.81	1.36
Country total	23.34	1.56	23.03	1.80	23.36	2.94	27.00	4.99

Source: Author's calculations, based on Salinas de Gortari's Sixth Presidential Report, 1994.

in manufacturing growth. In the first years of the Salinas administration these were very high, 6.1% in 1989 and 6.7% in 1990. This was due to an upturn in manufacturing and construction in 1989-90. However, during 1990 and 1991 growth started to weaken, falling to almost zero during 1993.

The crisis of 1994 was particularly hard on the manufacturing sector. Manufacturing GDP declined by -7.6%, more than the overall decline of GDP overall (-6.2%). Maquiladora sector employment has grown rapidly, rising from 369,489 in 1988 to 754,858 in 1996, and jumped to an estimated 890,412 in the first half of 1997 (Zedillo, Informe, 1997). Between 1994 and 1996, maquila manufacturing GDP jumped by a record 12.2%, and the job growth by an even greater 13.8%.

The dynamism of manufacturing GDP is due to the dynamism of the maquiladoras, leading many observers to refer to the process of "maquilization" of Mexican manufacturing. The participation rate of the maquila sector in manufacturing GDP went from 1.6% in 1975 to 5% in 1988, and has continued to grow—15.2% in 1995 and 20.2% in 1996 (calculated from Zedillo, 1997).

Despite the increasing weight of the maquiladora sector in the manufacturing, there are important qualifications. The accumulated total maquiladora exports for the years 1994-1996 was $94.2 billion. Total exports from oil and its derivatives (through the state-owned oil company, PEMEX) was only $27.6 billion during this period. However, the trade balance (exports minus imports) was markedly different. The maquiladora trade surplus was $17.1 billion for the years 1994-1996, while oil and derivatives posted a $23.2 billion surplus during this period.

Thus, despite the high level of maquiladoras exports, the net benefit to the Mexican economy in terms of foreign exchange is lower than that of the traditional oil exports.

Services GDP increased at an average annual rate of 2.5% between 1988 and 1995. However, this average obscures some internal disparities. The most buoyant were financial services with an average growth of 13.9% per year during this period, banking with 5.1%, and transportation, communications and storage with 3.5%. These figures reflect the unprecedented expansion of the financial and banking sectors.

At the same time, the expansion of the transportation sector is related to the growth in the external sector and movement of goods within the country and abroad. This has been noticeable in ports, airports, and customs offices. Moreover, it has been necessary to expand the highway system and modernize ports and airports. This has been accompanied by significant privatization of communications and transportation infrastructure.

For example, sea freight grew by 7.4% per year from 1988 to 1995. The number of airline passengers increased by 54.6% in the same period. Freight by road increased by 22.7% annually (data taken from various tables in the Zedillo, Informe, 1996). The share of services in total GDP has, like manufacturing, been relatively stable. (Table 4)

Finally, one of the major changes in composition of GDP has been the decline in the public sector, from 20.4% in 1988 to 14.7% in 1995, reflecting the privatization of the Mexican economy.

The growth of GDP has not been stable in recent years. There was a sharp decline even before the crisis of 1994, which considerably aggravated the situation. Moreover, this growth has been concentrated in the external sector, to the detriment of the domestic market.

During the NAFTA era (1994-97), the largest annual growth has been in communications and transportation (12.4%), due in part to domestic and foreign private investment in telecommunications. The next largest are electricity (11.8%), manufacturing, especially the export component (9.8%), and mining (including oil) (8.1%).

Distribution of the GDP by sectors has been stable during the period, but there have been differences within sectors. Notably, the growth of the financial and banking sub-sectors (6.6%) has been driven by foreign portfolio investment and liberalization. By contrast, sectors linked to the internal market decreased or showed little dynamism. Construction dropped by 7.6%. Despite international tourism, the internal trade category (restaurants and hotels) fell by 6.1%. The agricultural sector grew only 3.1%. The case of the manufacturing sector is noteworthy: two branches alone—*machinery and equipment, and food processing*—make up 52.1% of manufacturing production (RMALC 1997:20).

Foreign Investment

Here we will analyze the main aspects of foreign investment: its origin, sectoral and regional composition and its presence in the Mexican financial system and stock market.

Growth in foreign investment has been seen as one of the most important benefits arising from NAFTA and the liberalization of trade and investment. Foreign investment has in fact grown significantly in the last few years. The increase in the volume of foreign investment that began in 1990 led to an increase in the trade deficit. The deficit grew from $882 million in 1990 to $18,464 million in 1994. (Zedillo, Informe, 1997.)

The Salinas government's foreign investment strategy involved changing legislation to allow investment in government bonds and in the Mexican stock market (Bolsa de Valores). With the implementation of NAFTA, the Mexican financial system underwent fundamental change, namely the influx of foreign portfolio investment into the stock market. As of August 1997, there were 127 foreign financial institutions, of which 24% were US, 12% Japanese, 7% German, 7% French, 6% UK, 6% Canadian, 5% Swiss, 3% Korean, 3% Dutch, 3% Cayman Islands, 2% Israeli, and 2% Italian.

According to figures from the Association of International Financial Intermediaries (AIFI) in a study by G. Howard, foreign financial institutions accounted for more than 15% of the equity base, more than 35% of total bank deposits, and 30% of company credit. Also, foreign investment accounted for more than 9% of total credit instruments, including money markets, government instruments, capital markets, exchange markets, etc. Most foreign bank finance went into commerce, hotels, and restaurants, construction and manufacturing.

Foreign control of Mexican banks increased: Banco Santander controlled 70% of Banco Mexicano; Banco Bilbao Vizcaya 65% of Mercantil-Probursa; Bank of Montreal 16% of Bancomer; Shanghai Bank 20% of Banco Serfin; BCH de Espana y de Portugal 16% of Bital; Bank of Nova Scotia controlled Inverlat. Nevertheless, three Mexican Banks, Banamex, Bancomer and Serfin, still account for 50% of all financial activity.

The strategy followed by foreign financial groups is linked to the same transnational interests that influenced the NAFTA negotiations. Their Mexican affiliates are focusing their operations on corporate finance, and for the most part their Mexican presence is a form of "insurance against nationalizations, economic crises, and devaluations." Their direct control of the national market is minuscule: for example, JP Morgan 0.3%, Bank of America 0.1%, Chase Manhattan 0.1%, Bank of Tokyo and Desdner Bank .04%

The financial liberalization also brought an influx of foreign investment banks in the stock market—beginning with Barings in November 1994 and most recently Deutche Morgan Grenfell (January 1998)—serving institutional investors in industrialized countries. The increased inflow of foreign investment was not only due to NAFTA-driven financial liberalization, but also due to high interest rates and protection against devaluation.

Financial deregulation helped to bring $31.6 billion during 1994-96, of which 65% was reported to the Registro Nacional de Inversion Extranjera (NIE), 8.9% was fixed assets imports by the maquiladora, 19% was reinvested earnings, and 8.9% was intra-company transfers.

In 1993 only 31% of foreign investment was direct compared to the years before 1989 when 86% was direct. More recently, the FDI share has increased again—78% in 1994, 95% in 1995, 67% in 1996, and 62% in 1997 (preliminary, Zedillo, Informe, 1997)—due to the drop in stock market and other portfolio investment.[5]

An important component of foreign investment flowing into Mexico went to the stock market and not directly to productive sectors. In 1991, for example, almost two-thirds of foreign investment went to the stock market. This proportion was reduced in 1994 and 1995, but was growing again in 1996, and especially in 1997. In 1996, stock market investment accounted for 33.5% of total foreign investment (Zedillo, 1997,:119).

Preliminary 1997 figures (INEGI and Informe Annual, 1997) indicate that foreign investment in the stock market has been around $2.3 billion. By contrast, FDI in the maquiladoras was only $948 million in 1996 and $604 million in 1997 (preliminary).

TABLE 7

SHARE OF FOREIGN DIRECT INVESTMENT IN TOTAL FOREIGN INVESTMENT
($ MILLIONS AND PER CENT)

Year	Direct Investment $ Mill	Total $ Mill	%
1989	2499.7	2913.7	85.8%
1990	3722.4	4978.4	74.8%
1991	3565.0	9897.0	36.0%
1992	3599.6	8382.7	42.9%
1993	4900.7	15617.0	31.4%
1994	14692.8	18776.7	78.3%
1995	9270.6	9790.0	94.7%
1996	8051.4	12101.2	66.5%
1997p	3762.5	6090.2	61.8%

Source: author's calculation based on Anexo Económico del 3o Informe del Presidente Zedillo.
p: preliminary figures

TABLE 8

FOREIGN INVESTMENT IN MEXICAN STOCK MARKET AS A SHARE OF TOTAL
FOREIGN INVESTMENT ($ MILLIONS AND PERCENT)

Year	Total $ Mill	Stock Market $ Mill	%
1989	2913.7	414.0	14.2%
1990	4978.4	1256.0	25.2%
1991	9897.0	6332.0	64.0%
1992	8382.7	4783.1	57.1%
1993	15617.0	10716.3	68.6%
1994	18776.7	4083.9	21.7%
1995	9790.0	519.4	5.3%
1996	812101.2	4049.9	33.5%
1997	6090.2	2327.7	38.2%

Source: Author's calculation based on Anexo Económico del 3o Informe del Presidente Zedillo,
1997.

As of July 1997, foreign investment in the stock market was valued at $53.3 billion, an increase of 15.6% over the previous month and 55.3% compared to December 1996 (El Financiero, 12 August 1997). Foreign investment in Mexican financial instruments in the first half of 1997 increased 55.3% to $53.4 billion.

Foreign investment is concentrated in seven sectors: automotive, telecommunications, construction, services, electronics, gas, petrochemicals and finance. These sectors are expected to account for 60% of total foreign investment in the next few years. The Mexican Council of Investment stated that the 100 leading transnationals in these sectors increased their 1997 investment by 13.6% over 1996. These companies are part of the 500 companies that together account for 70% of Mexico's trade, with an estimated value of more than $65 billion. (Cappi Mario, El Financero, July 1997.)

Manufacturing accounted for 50.6% of the total FDI stock in February 1995 (OECD, 1996: 130), compared with 77.4% in 1982. The drop was the result of the rapid growth in foreign direct investment in services (38.5% compared to 11.8% in 1982). In the *internal trade* sector, there was a small increase in proportion of FDI, 9.4% compared 8.6% in 1982. In mining, the respective figures were 1.1% and 2.2%.

The National Commission of Foreign investment, in its statistical bulletin on direct investment in Mexico (January-April 1997), reported $310 billion registered with the Registro Nacional de Inversion Extranjera (RNIE), a 22% increase over the same period in 1996. There was a $407 million inflow of foreign investment into the maquiladora during January-April 1997, a 42% increase over 1996. According to Banco de Mexico estimates, the reinvested earnings of foreign-owned companies in the first quarter of 1997 grew 21.3%, and inter-company transfers were $245 million, a 57.4% decline from the previous year. These are the four components that the commission takes into account in calculating foreign investment.

Of the $717 million inflow of FDI during January-April 1997, $310 million was registered with the RNIE and $407 million was imports of fixed assets by maquiladoras. The manufacturing sector received $541 million, of which $407 million was fixed asset imports by maquila com-

TABLE 9

SECTORAL DISTRIBUTION OF FOREIGN DIRECT INVESTMENT FLOWS*
($ MILLIONS)

SECTOR	1996 $ Mill	1997 $ Mill
TOTAL	541.1	716.7
Agriculture	0.0	0.3
Extractive	1.4	1.6
Manufacturing	415.9	541.4
Elect. & Water	0.0	0.9
Construction	0.0	10.2
Commerce	46.0	23.0
Transp/Com.	0.0	52.9
Financial	25.8	73.5
Serv. (other)	52.0	2.9

Source: Informe Estadístico sobre el Comportamiento de la Inversión Extranjera Directa en México. Comisión Nacional de Inversiones Extranjeras.

*January to April

panies—$279 from the US, $98 million from Korea, $22 million from Japan, and $9 million from other countries. (CNIE, 1997:11)

The bulk of imports of fixed assets by the maquiladora during 1994-97 was *metal products and machinery and equipment,* $2.7 billion or 84% of total manufacturing direct investment in the maquiladoras. (Table 10)

The country origin of foreign direct investment has also become more diversified. The United States' share of foreign direct investment dropped from 66.3% of the total in 1983 to 59.1% at the beginning of 1995. Canadian direct investment rose from 1.4% in 1983 and 7.2% in 1994, dropping sharply to 2.1% in 1995, then rising to 8.7% in 1996 and 5.5% in 1997. Thus, Canada's share of FDI flows during 1994-97 averaged 5.9%, while the US share of FDI flows was 62.1%.

TABLE 10

MAQUILADORA: FIXED ASSETS IMPORTS BY MANUFACTURING SECTOR
($MILL AND PER CENT)

Sector	1994		1995		1996		1997	
	$ Mill	%	$ Mill	%	$ Mill	%	$ Mill	%
Manufact.	777.0	100	1,098.6	100	947.6	100	406.8	100
Food/bev,	1.9	0.2	4.2	0.4	2.9	0.3	0.5	0.1
Metal/Mach,.	640.4	82.4	953.8	86.8	775.6	81.8	347.8	85.5
Petrol/Plásticos.	45.8	5.9	39.0	3.5	58.7	6.2	19.4	4.8
Non Metallic min.	3.5	0.5	3.7	0.3	3.7	0.4	1.7	0.4
Basic metals	6.1	0.8	3.9	0.4	5.3	0.6	1.9	0.5
Other	79.3	10.2	94.0	8.6	101.4	10.7	35.5	8.7

Source: Comisión Nacional de Inversión Extranjera. Informe Estadístico, Jan-April 1997.

In conclusion, the surplus in the capital account contributed to the financing of a growing disequilibrium on the current account, with portfolio investment playing a major role. One of the most serious problems with portfolio investment is its volatility. The majority of investment in the Mexican stock market does not stay longer than 72 hours in spite of the fact that at the end of 1997 it had the second highest profitability in the world, exceeded only by Switzerland.

This kind of investment favours an international élite of speculators but does not generate sustained growth, employment and wage increases. Mexico has converted itself into a country that is very attractive to international investors, but not for millions of Mexicans who daily face conditions of extreme poverty. For them the collapse of equity markets in Asia or even in Mexico has little significance. Even though private consumption has recovered its 1994 level (after having fallen 9.5% during the crisis) and growth has resumed, Mexico's economic project continues to be exclusionary for most.

Trade

Starting in 1983, the Mexican government began to reduce tariffs and other trade barriers. This liberalization took place unilaterally, expos-

Table 11

Stock of Foreign Direct Investment by Sector

	Total	Manufact-uring	Services	Commerce	Mining	Agri culture
(US$ millions)						
1982	10,786	8,347	1,272	926	237	5
1983	11,470	8,944	1,285	984	252	5
1984	12,900	10,213	1,407	1,016	258	6
1985	14,629	11,379	1,842	1,125	276	6
1986	17,053	13,298	2,165	1,277	307	6
1987	20,930	15,699	3,599	1,255	356	22
1988	24,087	16,719	5,477	1,502	381	10
1989	26,587	17,701	6,579	1,889	390	29
1990	30,310	18,894	8,782	2,060	484	90
1991	33,875	19,857	10,920	2,447	515	135
1992	37,473	20,958	15,620	3,198	524	174
1993	42,374	23,279	14,351	3,958	579	209
1994	50,401	26,483	18,517	4,594	591	217
1995 *	54,123	27,382	20,853	5,066	603	218

* Figures for January and February.

Source: Secretariat of Trade and Industrial Promotion

Table 12

Foreign Direct Investment Stock by Country of Origin

	TOTAL	USA	Canada	U.K.	Germany	Switz.	Japan	France	Others
(US $ millions)									
1983	11,470	7,601	162	351	973	588	780	229	786
1984	12,900	8,513	195	396	1,125	648	816	237	970
1985	14,629	9,840	230	452	1,181	789	895	248	994
1986	17,053	11,047	270	556	1,399	823	1,038	565	1,355
1987	20,930	13,716	290	987	1,446	918	1,170	596	1,807
1988	24,087	14,958	324	1,754	1,583	1,005	1,319	749	2,395
1989	26,587	16,772	361	1,799	1,668	1,199	1,335	765	2,688
1990	30,310	19,080	417	1,914	1,956	1,347	1,456	946	3,194
1991	33,875	21,466	791	1,988	2,041	1,415	1,529	1,447	3,198
1992	37,473	23,118	580	2,414	2,126	1,730	1,616	1,516	4,373
1993	42,375	26,622	654	2,603	2,237	1,832	1,690	1,593	5,143
1994	50,401	30,626	817	3,703	2,612	1,885	2,390	1,656	6,713
1995 *	54,123	31,971	1,338	3,723	2,690	1,811	2,403	1,681	8,435

* Figures for January and February

Source: Secretariat of Trade and Industrial Promotion

TABLE 13
FOREIGN INVESTMENT [1]
(MILLIONS OF DOLLARS)

Item	1988	1989	1990	1991	1992	1993	1994	1995	1996 p
TYPE OF INVESTMENT									
Foreign(annual flow)	3,157.1	2,913.7	4,978.4	9,097.0	8,382.7	15,617.3	12,110.1	7,257.8	4,897.9
Registered FDI [2]	3,157.1	2,499.7	3,722.4	3,588.0	3,000.0	4,000.7	8,028.2	6,738.4	1,946.2
Stock market [3]		414.0	1,258.0	6,332.0	4,783.1	10,716.6	4,083.9	519.4	2,952.7
REGISTERED FDI (ANNUAL FLOW) [2]									
By economic purpose									
Assembly plants	1,020.0	982.4	1,192.9	963.6	1,100.8	2,320.5	3,204.0	3,821.7	1,225.6
Services	1,877.4	1,102.2	2,203.1	2,138.0	1,700.0	1,730.7	4,166.5	2,160.3	613.1
Trade	246.8	386.3	171.4	387.5	750.9	759.9	635.7	702.3	104.6
Natural resource extraction	24.9	9.5	93.9	31.0	8.6	55.1	12.0	48.5	1.9
Agriculture	-12.0	19.3	61.1	44.9	39.3	34.5	8.0	5.6	0.0
By country of origin									
USA	1,241.6	1,813.8	2,308.0	2,386.5	1,651.7	3,503.6	4,004.5	4,337.6	977.2
Holland	218.2	47.8	126.1	119.5	83.1	88.3	385.7	615.4	5.8
Canada	33.9	37.5	56.0	74.2	88.5	74.2	163.5	153.8	407.7
Germany	136.7	84.7	288.2	84.7	84.9	111.4	374.9	535.9	14.9
Japan	148.8	15.7	120.8	73.5	86.9	73.6	699.7	145.9	63.9
U.K.	767.6	44.7	114.4	74.2	426.8	189.2	1099.5	143.8	50.5
Switzerland	86.3	194.4	148.0	67.5	315.3	101.7	52.9	158.1	13.4
France	152.4	16.5	181.0	500.5	69.0	76.9	63.2	77.9	28.9
PERCENTAGES									
Annual flow of total foreign investment/GDP [4]	1.7	1.3	1.9	3.1	2.3	3.9	2.8	2.6	na
Annual flow of registered FDI/GDP [4]	1.7	1.1	1.4	1.1	1.0	1.2	1.9	2.4	na
Annual flow of registered FDI/ gross creation of fixed assets [4]	9.4	6.6	8.0	6.1	5.0	6.6	9.6	15.1	na
Annual flow of registered FDI/ gross creation of imported fixed assets [4]	47.9	32.5	34.8	26.4	19.8	28.6	38.2	49.2	na
Annual flow of registered FDI/ gross creation of private fixed assets [4]	12.3	8.7	10.5	7.8	6.3	8.3	11.9	19.1	na

FOOTNOTES

1/ Revised and up-dated information by the organization.
2/ From 1986 to 1994, it includes amounts registered under the Foreign Investments National Registry (RNIE), and those authorized by the Foreign Investments National Commission (CNIE). Starting in 1995, information is not comparable with that of previous years since actual foreign investment registered under RNIE is added to the value of temporary imports of fixed assets by the "maquiladora" industry.
3/ 1992 and 1993 amounts were revised and up-dated by SECOFI.
4/ For this comparison, FDI was converted from US dollars into national currency based on the exchange rate used for the conversion of foreign currency flow.
p/ preliminary figures to the month of June

Source: Secretariat of Trade and Industrial Promotion (SECOFI)

ing Mexican business to international competition with little time to adjust (OECD, 1996).

Mexican exports until 1987 were dominated by crude oil and its derivatives. Petroleum accounted for 31.3% of total exports. By the end of 1994, petroleum exports made up only 11.2%. Non-petroleum exports grew at an annual rate of 16%, from 68.7% in 1987 to 87.9% in 1994. This growth corresponds to a strong expansion of maquila exports—26.4% per year during 1987-1996. (Zedillo, 1997.) However, non-maquila manufacturing exports also grew by an annual 9.5% during the same period.

A key element of the changing structure of exports was the *transportation equipment* category, which grew from 13.8% of non-maquila exports in 1981 to 38.5% in 1993. This was due to the expansion of the Mexican auto industry as part of the continent-wide integration of this industry. Auto sector integration, the most advanced of all manufacturing sectors, has had important consequences in the redistribution of employment in the three countries. It should be noted that, despite the December 1994 crisis, transportation equipment exports did not decline, indicating their dependence more on the continental economy rather than on the ups and downs of the domestic Mexican economy.

Moreover, exports of machinery and equipment increased from 14.1% in 1981 to 24.0% ot total exports in 1993. (Maquiladora exports have been almost exclusively machinery and equipment, i.e., transportation and electronic equipment). Thus, a key role assigned to the Mexican economy in the continental division of labour was the production of industrial goods in a few traditional sectors.

Imports of consumer goods went from 4.1% of total imports in 1987 to 12.0% in 1994. Intermediate goods are still the largest component of Mexican imports, but they fell from 81.9% of total imports to 71.3% during this period. Finally, capital goods accounted for 14.0 % of imports in 1987 increasing to 16.8 % in 1994. As can be seen, the opening of the economy has a direct impact on final consumption. More alluent Mexicans were looking for new products, unavailable on the national market or of better prices and/or quality. The result was a decrease in domestic industrial production of consumption goods and a negative impact in employment.

In 1994, two-thirds of imports were intermediate inputs for the manufacturing sector (Table 14). One-half of these went to the *machinery and equipment* sector. The structure of manufacturing imports for the maquiladoras resembles the structure of exports, which is understandable given the nature of the maquila sector. In 1994, one-quarter of all imports to Mexico were by the maquiladoras.

TABLE 14

MERCHANDISE IMPORTS (US $ MILLIONS)

	1987	1990	1991	1992	1993	1994	1995 (Jan-June)	Growth rates 1987-94
Total imports	18,812.4	41,593.4	49,878.3	62,129.4	65,366.5	79,374.0	35,223.0	22,8%
Consumer goods	767.6	5,098.6	5,639.5	44.1	7,842.4	9,511.0	2,666.0	43.3%
Intermed. goods	15,414.2	29,705.2	35,768.2	42,829.6	46,468.3	56,542.0	28,123.0	20.4%
Maquiladora	5,507.0	10,321.4	11,694.3	13,936.7	16,443.0	20,494.0	12,315.0	20.7%
Other	9907.2	19,383.8	24,073.9	28,892.8	30,025.3	36,049.0	15,804.0	20.3%
Capital Goods	2,630.6	6,789.6	8,470.6	11,555.7	11,055.9	13,322.0	4,435.0	26.0%

Source: Banco de Mexico

In 1989, the non-maquila sector began to experience deficits, which rose to more than $20 billion in 1992. The maquila sector, as expected, showed a surplus of more than $5 billion in 1992. Thus, liberalization caused a large deficit in Mexico's merchandise trade balance. The success of the maquila sector has not been able to offset the deficit, given that its activities are based on imports for re-export. The low value-added, high-import content of maquila production means that the level of exports do not greatly exceed the level of imports.

One of the most notable effects of the crisis of 1994 was the reduction of the manufacturing deficit. This was due to the reduced import capacity of Mexican firms because of the peso depreciation and the collapse of domestic demand due to job loss. The peso depreciation acted as a new tariff limiting the growth of Mexican imports. The contraction in Mexican purchasing power created a mini-crisis for US retailers along the Mexico-US border, temporarily affecting US exports to Mexico and ending the rosy expectations of the great "market of Mexican consumers."

TABLE 15
MERCHANDISE TRADE BALANCE [1] ($ MILL)

	1986	1987	1988	1989	1990	1991	1992	1993	1994	1995	1996 p
TOTAL EXPORTS [2]	21,804	27,800	30,882	38,171	40,711	42,892	46,196	51,886	60,882	78,642	48,408
"Maquiladoras"	5,646	7,105	10,146	12,329	13,873	15,833	18,680	21,853	26,269	31,103	16,917
Non-"maquiladoras"	16,158	20,495	20,546	22,842	26,838	26,855	27,516	30,033	34,613	48,438	28,551
Petroleum Industry	6,307	8,630	6,711	7,876	10,104	8,166	8,306	7,418	7,445	8,423	5,362
Crude oil [3]	5,580	7,877	5,883	7,292	8,921	7,265	7,419	6,485	6,624	7,420	4,914
Other	727	753	828	584	1,183	902	887	933	821	1,003	447
Non-petroleum related	15,496	18,970	23,980	27,295	30,607	34,521	37,889	44,468	53,437	71,119	40,107
Agricultural	2,098	1,543	1,670	1,754	2,162	2,373	2,112	2,504	2,678	4,016	2,293
Natural Resource Extraction	510	576	660	605	617	547	356	278	357	545	225
Manufacturing	12,888	16,851	21,650	24,936	27,828	31,602	35,420	41,685	50,402	66,558	37,589
- "Maquiladora"	5,646	7,105	10,146	12,329	13,873	15,833	18,680	21,853	26,269	31,103	16,917
- Non-"maquiladora"	7,242	9,746	11,504	12,607	13,955	15,769	16,740	19,832	24,133	35,455	20,672
TOTAL IMPORTS (FOB)	16,784	18,812	28,082	34,766	41,593	49,966	62,129	65,367	79,346	72,453	41,341
"Maquiladoras"	4,351	5,507	7,808	9,328	10,321	11,782	13,937	16,443	20,466	26,179	14,013
Non-"maquiladoras"	12,433	13,305	20,274	25,438	31,272	38,184	48,192	48,924	58,880	46,274	27,329
Consumption goods	846	768	1,922	3,498	5,098	5,834	7,744	7,842	9,510	5,335	2,911
Intermediate goods	12,983	15,414	22,133	26,499	29,705	35,545	42,830	46,468	56,514	58,421	33,488
"Maquiladoras"	4,351	5,507	7,808	9,328	10,321	11,782	13,937	16,443	20,466	26,179	14,013
Non-"maquiladoras"	8,632	9,907	14,325	17,171	19,384	23,763	28,893	30,025	36,048	32,242	19,475
Capital goods	2,954	2,631	4,027	4,769	6,790	8,588	11,556	11,056	13,322	8,897	4,942
TOTAL TRADE BALANCE	5,020	8,788	2,610	405	-882	-7,278	-15,933	-13,481	-18,464	7,069	4,127
"Maquiladoras"	1,295	1,598	2,338	3,001	3,552	4,051	4,743	5,410	5,803	4,925	2,904
Non-"maquiladoras"	3,725	7,190	272	-2,596	-4,434	-11,329	-20,676	-18,891	-24,267	2,164	1,223

1/ The sum of partial figures may not coincide with the total as a result of rounding-up of the former. From 1991 onwards, the flow of exports and imports includes the gross value of trade operations in the "maquiladora" industry. This criteria was applied to the whole table in order to make amounts comparable. 2/ Include currency re-valuation. 3/ Include natural gas, oil products and petrochemicals. 4/ Unadjusted dollars. December-December. n.d.: Not available. p/ preliminary figures to the month of June. Source: Bank of Mexico

Mexico's trade surplus at the end of 1997 fell to $400 million, an 80% drop over 1996. Due in part to 9.2% appreciation of the peso, this also reflects a sluggish export capacity and continuing strong demand for imports. There are two problems here. One is the floating peso which affects exports and imports, and the high import content of domestic production which affects the price of consumer products. The second is controlling wages as a means of inflation control, which in turn affects demand and thus import capacity.

The exchange rate impact on employment was downplayed in the NAFTA debate. It is wrong to think that the relocation of firms is the sole cause of unemployment; worse is continuing the IMF policies of inflation control. Family consumption has been eroded in the last 10 years, making it extremely difficult to purchase imports from the US or Canada.

As we have seen, the productive base in Mexico is very hetrogeneous since the large exporting firms with external finance are more dynamic, while the smaller companies dependent on the domestic market have more difficulty surviving due to the shock of economic opening and NAFTA, but also because official government policy supports the former and is detrimental to the latter.

The peso devaluation and economic compression during 1995-96 were the only means for correcting the trade disequilibria. Under NAFTA, the following consequences for trade are evident:

1. Imports grow rapidly and government regulates this disequilibria through exchange rate devaluation at the expense of the productive base.

2. The Mexican dependency on the US seems irreversible (as is the case with Canada) and neither NAFTA nor agreements with the EU or APEC will alter this situation. The US is the preferred market and neither Mexicans nor Canadians are disposed to change their trade and investment strategies. According to SECOFI, Mexico is now the largest foreign supplier of 684 product lines to the US and the second largest supplier of another 1,200. Between 1993 and 1996, Mexico replaced Asia as the largest supplier of textiles and clothing, supplanted

Germany as the third largest supplier of autos, and has become the fourth largest supplier of steel.

3. The denationalization of banking, railways, telephones, etc.
4. The conversion of the country from a semi-industrialized economy to an "emerging market," thanks to international speculation.
5. The growth of Mexican exports has been, according to many, illusionary. In 1983, each dollar of exports (including the maquila) contained 88 cents of domestic inputs. By 1994, the domestic component of exports had fallen to 42 cents for every dollar of exports. The total net growth of exports (i.e., minus imported inputs) during this period was 1% annually, less if dollar inflation was included. (Vazquez Tercero, 1995.)

TABLE 16

DEGREE OF NATIONAL INTEGRATION OF MEXICAN EXPORTS

($ MILLIONS AND PER CENT)

Year	Exports Gross	Exports Net	National Integration %
1983	25,953	22,736	87.6%
1985	26,757	22,168	82.9%
1987	27,600	19,800	71.7%
1990	40,711	25,006	61.4%
1991	42,668	23,936	56.1%
1992	46,196	22,756	49.3%
1993	51,886	23,968	46.2%
1994	60,882	25,695	42.2%

Source: Vazquez Tercero.Comercio Exterior 1995.

Earlier we showed how Mexico prepared for economic opening and NAFTA through legal changes such as the Decree on the Maquiladora Export Industry and the Automotive Decree. The first widened the scope of the maquiladora, ending the monopoly of the northern border region, but it also broadening the participation of foreign investment and deregulated the requirements for domestic inputs.

The Automotive Decree ended the requirement for high national value added. This change reduced the use of domestic inputs, negatively affecting the domestic work force and productive base. Both the transnationals and the maquiladora began to use inputs from their own affiliates. After this, the negotiation of a national content provision in NAFTA was not difficult because the real changes had already been made.

When the national content rule of origin became "regional," the responsibility of the government to "watch over employment' of Mexicans disappeared and was replaced by a 62.5% North American content rule. The fact that the maquila has less than 2% Mexican value added or that export manufacturing has low value added is of little concern since what is now important is "North American" content. Mexican exports don't, obviously, contain 100% domestic value-added; so if they want to export to the US or Canada they must incorporate a share of the value added of one of these countries, which implies that NAFTA is not an economic fortress but a captive market (Gutiérrez Haces, 1993, 1997).

LABOUR MARKET

The labour force in Mexico has grown rapidly in the last few decades. From 1950 to 1990 it tripled, going from 8.3 million in 1950 to 24.6 million in 1990. The National Employment Survey of 1995 reported the labour force at 35.6 million.

The female labour force has grown much more rapidly than the male component. In 1995, women made up 32.2% of the total labour force. From 1991 to 1995 alone, the female labour force grew by an annual rate of 4.5% compared to male growth of only 2.8%.

The participation of women in the labour market in 1996 and 1997 jumped to 35% of the labour force as a direct consequence of the fall in family income. In 1980 one in five women were in the labour market, Today the ratio is one in three. However, this increased participation is not necessarily reflected in the family economy because these women receive on average 30% less than men for the same work.

The increase in female labour is also explained by other factors. First, there has been an increase in education and training levels of women.

Second, there has been less social pressure on women to stay at home and raise the children. Third, the emerging labour market has required a new labour force capable of adapting to new forms of work organization, notably in the maquiladoras where female labour predominates.

The Secretaria del Trabajo y Prevision (STPS) has publicly acknowledged that women experience more violations in their conditions of work. The new federal regulations of health, safety and workplace environment claim to remedy this situation but are in fact ineffectual in light of the corruption between labour officials more interested in personal gains from companies than really watching for workplace violations.

TABLE 17

INDICATORS OF UNEMPLOYMENT AND UNDEREMPLOYMENT [1]
ECONOMICALLY ACTIVE POPULATION (PER CENT)

Item	1989	1990	1991	1992 [2]	1993 [3]	1994 [4]	1995 p	1996 [5]
OPEN UNEMPLOYMENT RATE (TDA) [6]								
Annual average	3.0	2.8	2.6	2.8	3.4	3.7	6.3	5.9
GENERAL PRESSURE RATE (TPRG) [7]								
Annual average	5.8	5.1	4.8	5.5	6.6	6.4	9.8	9.3
OPEN UNEMPLOYMENT RATE IN ADDITION TO THOSE EMPLOYED WHO WORK LESS THAN 15 HOURS PER WEEK (TOPD1) [8]								
Annual average	6.8	6.1	6.1	6.5	7.7	7.8	10.8	10.5
UNEMPLOYMENT RATE IN ADDITION TO THOSE EMPLOYED WHO WORKED LESS THAN 35 HOURS PER WEEK (TOPD2) [9]								
Annual average	21.0	20.5	20.8	21.6	23.0	22.1	25.9	26.2
RATE OF CRITICAL EMPLOYMENT CONDITIONS (TCCO) [10]								
Annual average	20.1	16.8	14.3	14.1	14.2	13.7	15.7	16.9

FOOTNOTES

1/ Indicators in this table come from the National Survey on Urban Employment.

2/ Starting in January, amounts correspond to 32 urban areas. Starting in July, they correspond to the aggregate of 34 urban areas.

3/ Starting in April, amounts correspond to the aggregate of 35 urban areas and starting in October they refer to 37 urban areas.

4/ Starting in October 1994 amounts correspond to the aggregate of 38 urban areas and starting in December they refer to 39 urban areas.
p Preliminary figures.

5/ Starting in January 1996 amounts correspond to the aggregate of 41 urban areas. Amounts for the third quarter correspond to July.

6/ Individuals aged 12 and over who, during the week of the survey, did not work, were available or work or were seeking to incorporate themselves into an economic activity during the two months prior to the week of the survey and did not succeed.

7/ Reflects the percentage of unemployed and employed population looking for work with the intention to change employment or to secure additional employment, in relation to the economically active population.

8/ Proportion of the economically active population who are unemployed or employed but working less than 15 hours during the survey week.

9/ Proportion of unemployed and employed individuals who worked less than 35 hours per week in relation to the economically active population.

10/ Proportion of employed population that is working less than 35 hours per week due to market conditions, who work over 35 hours per week for monthly salaries below the minimum wage, or who work more than 48 hours per week earning less than two minimum wages.
p/ Preliminary figures

Source: INEGI.

TABLE 18

ESTIMATES OF SIZE OF THE INFORMAL SECTOR
(PER CENT OF TOTAL EMPLOYMENT)

A) Non-remunerated owners, self-employed individuals, and workers

1979	Total	17.0
1983	Total	20.3
1988	Total	24.3

B) Workers in enterprises not registered with the Office of National Revenue

1987	Urban	26.4
1993	Urban	20.3

C) Workers without social insurance

1980	Total	44.6
1991	Total	44.5
1993	Total	47.5

D) Self-employed individuals and workers of small enterprises [1]
(less than 5 workers)

1987	Urban	38.6
1993	Urban	42.3
1995	Urban	44.4

1 Non agricultural activities

*Sources: a) Rendon y Salas (1991), b) Hernandez (1996), c) and d) Secretariat of OECD based on
IMSS, INEGI, ECSO 1979, ENE 1988, 1991, 1993, and ENEU.*

From 1990 to 1996, the employed labour force increased from 30.5 million people to 35.2 million. But the level of waged labour was practically stable—from 12 million in 1991 to 11.9 million in 1996. Thus, the labour force increase was entirely unwaged or self-employed workers. Waged labour participation in the total labour force fell from a 39.4% to 33.7% during this period.

There has been a notable growth of waged labourers in the agricultural labour force (4% annually from 1991 to 1995), whereas self-employed agricultural labour declined by 3.6%. This is indicative of the increasing difficulty of subsistence farming and the need to resort to waged labour and piece-work to survive, as an alternative to urban migration or crossing the northern border.

In the non-agricultural sector, although there was growth in the proportion of waged labourers and piece-workers (3.5%), there was an even higher growth of self-employed workers (4.0%) during 1991-95 (Samaniego, 1996: 71.)

There was a decline of employment in the agricultural sector from 1991 to 1995. This trend is a long-term one, and relates to the structural transformation of the Mexican economy from one with a strong agricultural base to one with an increasingly industrial and urban composition. In the last few years, manufacturing employment levels have been stable, at about 15% of the total in 1991 and again in 1995. (Sanmaniego, 1996: 72.)

However, what is most important is the structural transformation of employment within this sector. While in 1986 employment in the maquila sector made up 26.4% of the labour force in manufacturing, in 1994 it made up 41.8%, and it passed the 50% mark in 1995. Non-maquila employment in manufacturing grew from a total of 696,497 in 1986 to 811,277 in 1994, an eight-year growth of only 114,780 jobs, a mere 14,347 per year. Worse still, in 1995 non-maquila employment in manufacturing dropped to 627,585: in other words, to less than in 1986. This reflects the fragility of the non-maquila economy, which has not been able to adapt to the new conditions of liberalization and NAFTA.

Thus, the least "transnationalized" sector of Mexican manufacturing is the one that has been most negatively affected by liberalization and the crisis. It has been overwhelmed by the maquila sector and some of the transnationalized maquila-type sectors, such as the automobile industry. The promise that NAFTA and trade liberalization would modernize and rejuvenate domestic Mexican manufacturing has not materialized.

According to INEGI's Encuestra Industrial Mensual, overall employment in manufacturing grew 5.5% from May 1996 to May 1997, while employment in the maquiladora sector grew 20.8%. Total maquila employment as of October 1997 was 963,199.

One sector that benefited from liberalization was *internal trade* and *restaurants and hotels*. Increasing travel to Mexico in the context of liberalization and currency depreciation stimulated significant growth in hotels and restaurants. The increase came mostly from business travellers, but also in tourism from the United States, Canada and Latin America. Internal trade has been stimulated by the entry into Mexico of chains such as Wal Mart and other retailers.

This TNC-driven restructuring of the retail and tourism sectors helps to explain the annual employment growth of 6.1% from 1991 to 1995, surpassed only by the transportation and communications sector. However, the 1994-95 crisis has substantially dampened growth and employment in the internal trade sector. Tourism, on the other hand, benefited from devaluation and thus employment in hotels and restaurants continues to increase. The transportation sector benefited greatly from the increase in exchanges of goods and people. This is reflected in the rate of growth in employment of this branch of 6.4% between 1991 and 1995.

Finally, the neoliberal policy of putting the public sector "on a diet" has had a considerable impact on the reduction of employment. Employment in this sector fell from over 1.5 million in 1986 to 900,000 in 1995. This was due mainly to the reduction in employment within the central government, rather than the parastatal firms in which employment overall has remained stable despite job reductions at PEMEX and CFE. Employment has also increased at the Social Security Institute (IMSS).

In 1995, according to the criteria used by INEGI, 95.3% of the labour force was employed, down from 97.8% in 1991. Women made up 32% of the employed labour force in 1995, up from 30.4% in 1991. The rate of growth in unemployment among women has been slower than among men in recent years. Female unemployment grew 15.7% from 1991 to 1995, compared to 31.1% for men. The unemployment rate for men was 4.6% in 1995 compared with 5.0% for women (Samaniego, 1996: 70; RMALC, 1997: 52).

The open unemployment rate declined steadily from 1986 to 1991, to a low of 2.6%. Unemployment climbed to 6.3% in 1995, 5.5% in 1996, falling to 4.1% in 1997 (Informe Presidencial, 1997: 51). Supplementary indicators more accurately reflect the reality of unemployment in Mexico. The rate of seasonal unemployment separates the seasonally unemployed from those employed but not actually working. Mexican surveys consider those who did not work the previous week for economic or seasonal reasons as nevertheless employed (Salas y Rendón, 1996: 89). Seasonal unemployment is approximately equal to, or slightly above, the official unemployment rate, which doubled the unemployment to 12% or higher in 1996.

In addition, the Mexican government has an employment indicator for those in critical conditions of employment. This includes employees who work less than 35 hours per week for market reasons, those who work more than 35 hours per week but earn less than the minimum monthly wage, and those who work more than 48 hours per week earning less than double the minimum wage. The working population experiencing critical conditions of employment reached 17.7% of the total in the third quarter of 1996. Adding these raises unemployment to 24.5% of the economically active population.

Looking at the sectoral distribution, service sector unemployment grew substantially from 1991 to 1993. The peso crisis of 1994 caused unemployment to grow substantially in 1995 in services, construction, and manufacturing.

Unemployment in construction resulted in part from the suspension of public and private projects due to lack of funds, but also to high interest rates and the substantial increase in bank liabilities that caused a large rise in business and personal bankruptcies, a situation which has led to the formation of an activist organization of debtors called El Barzón. The high unemployment rate in the construction industry is worrisome, given the traditional role of this sector in absorbing unskilled workers with few resources. Also, the increase in unemployment in urban areas has led to worsening violence and general insecurity.

Because of the lack of public programs to support the unemployed, the loss of employment does not necessarily mean a period without work, but often the transfer to another job (or jobs) with lower pay and shorter hours, or to self-employment. This leads to an increase in the informality of employment, with a lack of formal contracts and labour protection, and the worsening of wages and benefits.

The informal economy is growing to unprecedented levels. In Mexico City this is reflected in the increasing numbers of street vendors and the inability of the authorities to control the use of public roadways. The phenomenon of street vendors, formerly restricted to the central areas with a high volume of pedestrian traffic, has spread to other parts of the city, including the suburbs.

TABLE 19

SALARY DIFFERENTIALS BETWEEN WORKER GROUPS (IN PERCENTAGES)

	1984	1989	1992
Non-tradable/tradable [1]	85.8	97.3	107.7
Manufacturing for internal/external markets [2]	69.1	83.3	82.7
Non-unionized/unionized.	75.1	86.1	96.8
Non-border states/border states.	93.8	79.1	95.2
Rural/urban.	55.6	45.6	55.1
Women/men.	76.7	71.6	74.7
Poorest states/other states [3]	91.8	82.2	86.5

FOOTNOTES
1/ Tradable: mining, manufacturing; non-tradable: public services, trade, transportation, communications, construction.
2/ Those exporting a % of their total production above the average: chemicals, basic metals, metallic products, machinery and equipment.
3 /Oaxaca, Guerrero, Chiapas and Hidalgo.

Source: Alarcon and McKinley (1995)

The OECD provides an estimate of the informal sector in Mexico (OECD, 1997: 83; see also Table 18). Of the four definitions used for the informal sector, the one that gives the highest rates is that based on the number of self-employed workers in establishments with fewer than five workers. According to this definition, the informal sector made up 38.6% of employment in 1987, growing to 42.3% in 1993 and to 44.4% in 1995.[6]

A high percentage of the employed population works only a few hours per week. According to Salas and Rendón (1996: 101), 5.7% of the employed population worked less than 15 hours per week. For male workers it was 3.8%, for female workers 9.9%. These percentages increased considerably before the crisis; for men the rate rose to 4.9% in 1993, while for women it went up to 12%, making an average rate of 7.1% for both sexes. This occurred during the growth cycle, not in the wake of the crisis. Thus the evolution of the economy has tended to make employment more precarious.

Wages and Productivity

The minimum wage, which is set by social agreements between the state, business and unions, has been decreasing in real terms. In the last ten years, from 1987 to 1997, its level dropped 50%. But the minimum wage is no longer an accurate reference point. For example, the average wage paid has been twice the minimum wage during this period. For manufacturing, the average wage paid was 3.4 times the minimum wage in 1987, rising to 7.6 times in 1994 and 7.2 times in 1997 (Calculations from Zedillo,1997: 56).

One might expect that wages in maquiladoras would be higher than in the rest of the manufacturing sector. However, in 1987 the average wage in the maquiladora was only 67.6% of the wage non-maquila sector. By 1994 this relation has dropped to 57.7%, though after the crisis it climbed again to 63.3%.

Average wages are not determined by the relation between non-maquiladora and maquiladora sector, but by other factors. Wages in the maquiladoras seem to respond to international competitiveness considerations, while non- maquiladora activities are responding to domestic labour market pressure, wage regulations and local demand.

Differences in wages between micro and small enterprises on one hand, and medium and large enterprises on the other, are quite significant. The average wage in the second group (medium-large) was 1.44 times higher than in the first one in 1987. For 1994, this relation increased to 1.52 times, and for 1997 it climbed to 1.69 times. In other words, the gap in wages between the medium-large group of enterprises and the micro-small is increasing steadily. This can be explained by the better performance of medium and large enterprises, which were better equipped to confront the opening of the economy and the new competition.

TABLE 20

AVERAGE ANNUAL LABOUR PRODUCTIVITY (PERCENTAGE GROWTH)

Sectors	1970-1980 (%)	1981-1986 (%)	1987-1991 (%)
Mining	-0.65	-0.11	1.26
Manufacturing industry	2.60	0.26	3.35
Food, beverages and tobacco	2.69	-0.65	2.40
Textiles, clothing, leather	1.13	-0.76	3.44
Wood and wood products	1.77	3.14	0.24
Printing	2.66	0.88	2.75
Chemical, petroleum deriv., plastics	5.45	2.77	-0.22
Non-metalic minerals, except oil products	3.21	-0.45	3.21
Basic metalic industries	2.13	3.05	3.85
Machinery and equipment	3.13	-1.85	9.07
Others	-4.03	-4.06	-2.07
Construction	-0.44	-2.82	-3.99
Electricity, water, gas	5.14	1.79	-6.35
Retailing, restaurants, hotels	3.75	-2.75	1.63
Transportation, communications	2.29	-2.40	1.31
Financial services	0.13	0.44	1.52
Government services	0.32	1.57	1.37
Total	1.85	0.02	0.90

Sources: INEGI, Banco de México, Diseño de Estrategias.

TABLE 21

AVERAGE ANNUAL CAPITAL PRODUCTIVITY (PERCENTAGE GROWTH)

Sectors	1970-1980 (%)	1981-1986 (%)	1987-1991 (%)
Mining	-4.02	-0.05	-2.25
Manufacturing industry	1.35	0.36	8.24
Food, beverages and tobacco	4.69	4.20	3.08
Textiles, clothing, leather	4.30	2.61	9.24
Wood and wood products	-2.88	8.63	9.74
Printing	2.65	2.76	7.60
Chemical, petroleum deriv., plastics	4.18	4.06	4.11
Non-metalic minerals, except oil products	-0.26	0.82	7.09
Basic metalic industries	-2.42	2.22	8.05
Machinery and equipment	3.56	-7.43	16.73
Others	-5.41	-2.78	11.11
Construction	1.37	7.43	13.36
Electricity, water, gas	-0.98	1.99	-6.01
Retailing, restaurants, hotels	2.97	-3.01	3.12
Transportation, communications	-1.91	-2.71	-3.05
Financial services	0.51	3.48	-3.68
Government services	-3.73	1.52	1.96
Total	0.78	1.56	2.16

Sources: INEGI, Banco de México, Diseño de Estrategias.

In manufacturing, the gap between wages paid in medium-large enterprises versus micro-small was practically the same as the gap for the overall economy. In 1987 it was 1.48 times, increasing to 1.59 in 1994 and 1.78 in 1997. Some sectors, such as transportation and communications, or production and personal services, have a much higher average wage and a larger wage difference according to size of enterprise (see Zedillo, 1997: 58).

Regarding productivity, Albero-Semerena (1997) presents figures which allow us to make some interesting comparisons between economic development models in Mexico. The 1970-80 period was the last phase of import substitution period, as well as the oil boom period (1978 to 1981). During this period labour productivity was increasing at an average of 1.9% annually. Only *mining, other manufactures and construction* showed negative growth. Oil and petrochemical industries, as well as electricity, water and gas, all had large increases in labor productivity.

The second period, 1981 to 1986, was a time of recession, a transition from protected economy to an open one. Therefore, labor productivity was decreasing at 0.02% per year as an average for the economy as a whole. Except for *wood industries, basic metal industries, government services*, all sectors showed poor productivity performance,

Finally, the last period, 1987-1991, was the opening of the economy and the first stage of Salinas presidency. During this period, GDP grew steadily, as did labour productivity. But the rate of growth of labour productivity overall during this period was lower than GDP growth, and quite irregular between sectors. For example, the state-controlled sectors which were not, or only partially, privatized—chemical, petroleum derivatives and plastics—had negative labour productivity growth, as did electricity, water and gas. On the other hand, machinery and equipment showed an increase in labour productivity of 9.1% per year, the highest of the manufacturing sector. But the most impressive result is that manufacturing labour productivity grew 3.4% annually during 1987-1991.

Capital productivity overall increased 2.2% per year between 1987 and 1991, much greater than the labour productivity increase in this period of 1.0 % per year. In manufacturing, capital productivity grew 8.2 % per year during 1987-1991. In construction, a boom sector during the

Salinas era, capital productivity increased at an annual rate of 13.3%.

Alberro observes a major difference in productivity performance between tradeable good sectors (high) and non-tradeable (low or negative): "...the gap between productivity and real average earnings has also followed the same pattern: growing faster in the tradeable goods sector and slower in the non-tradeable goods sector" (Alberro, 1997: 10).

Alicia Puyana suggests that the increase in productivity during 1990-1993 was due to a "...process of inter-sectoral rationalization, implying the exit of unproductive and lower size units with an increase in the production concentration in the biggest and most modern enterprises..." (Puyana, 1995: 61-62).

This suggests a correlation between productivity performance and tradeable sectors, where foreign direct investment is greater and the size of production units is larger. But these sectors have also had negative impacts on employment and plant closures because of intense competition between enterprises. Changes in labour and production factor substitution have been central for the productivity increase during this opening period.

Puyana states: "The commercial reforms have induced a very rapid obsolescence of capital and the appreciation of peso vis. the dollar, increases the cost of labour relative to capital. This accelerates the rate of capital investment with more modern technologies. The signing of NAFTA can facilitate the access to new technologies and force the enterprises to compete with lower price margins, increasing this way the obsolescence of capital. Then the productivity of capital is increased relative to labour...this phenomenon appeared in Mexico even before NAFTA..." (Puyana, 1995: 64.)

The concentration of production, exports and profits is occurring in a small group of highly competitive enterprises. The annual report on Mexico's 500 largest enterprises (published by Expansión) reflects this situation. In the top group are: the three big auto producers, the Mexican telephone company, and others with a secure position in the new order. On the other hand, a growing number of companies are increasingly vulnerable to collapse when a crisis occurs, as in 1994, with strong negative impacts on employment and living standards.

Distribution of Income and Earnings

The distribution of income in Mexico has been regressive in recent years, with an unprecedented growth in the income of the top one-tenth of the population. This has been recognized by the OECD, which states: "During most of the 1980s, high and unpredictable inflation and the free trade economy have combined to produce an increase in the inequality of income, such that real per capita income fell by 15% between 1981 and 1988." (OECD, 1997: 100.)

Between 1980 and 1990, there was a steady reduction in the portion of GDP going to labour, from 36% in 1980 to 25.9% in 1988, and then to 24.7% in 1990 (OECD, 1992: 277). Although the figures are slightly different in the Presidential Reports, the trend is the same. The remuneration of workers has been a decreasing component of GDP throughout the period of economic liberalization. This means that labour income (due to the freezing of salaries and benefits) has become a less important factor of production. This improves productivity, but at the same time worsens living conditions for workers.

Productivity grew steadily from a base of 100 in 1993 to 125 in 1996 (Zedillo, Informe, 1996: 55). Thus, the crisis may have negatively affected GDP and employment, but has improved labour productivity. The remaining workers clearly have not received remuneration proportional to their increase in productivity.

There has been a major decline in the average real wage per worker, starting in 1981. There was a slight improvement in 1989, at the beginning of the Salinas administration. However, in 1993, wages were still much lower than in 1981. The real minimum wage has declined steadily, due to the policy of freezing wages to support gains in productivity. (OECD, 1997: 100.) Wages in the maquila sector have improved only modestly from 1985 to the present. Meanwhile, wages have worsened in the traditional non-maquila manufacturing industry.

Finally, there has been a growing gap between the real wages of white-collar and blue-collar workers—in other words, between skilled and unskilled labourers (OECD, 1997: 102). This reflects the unequal education levels among workers, and also helps to explain the increasing income inequality in Mexico. (Table 23, OECD, 1997: 100.)

There has been an increase in the wage gap between those working in tradeable vs. non-tradeable goods sectors, between export-oriented vs. domestic manufacturing, between border vs. non-border states, and between women and men. Salary differences by geographic region and by gender have persisted and even increased. The same is true for different activities, such as industry and maquiladoras. According to the 1997 OECD Report, this is due to differences in labour productivity.

There have always been wage differences related to certain factors such as sex, skill level, professional and general work experience, and geographic region. However, trade liberalization and NAFTA have accentuated these differences. This is apparent if one takes into consideration whether a firm is export-oriented or not, if one looks at the level of transnationalization of the firm and the appreciation or devaluation of the peso. For example, between 1989 and 1993, businesses probably reduced their wage costs in pesos due to appreciation of the peso. On the other hand, the devaluation of the peso in 1994-95 did not result in salary improvements for Mexican workers.

The depreciation of the peso has resulted in a 15% increase in productivity and a 23% decline in real wages since 1994, according to data from INEGI and the Banco de Mexico. According to Zuniga (La Jornada, September 1997), the increase in production volumes and the drop in real wages have made Mexican exports more competitive; it is the Mexican workers, with their work and diminished purchasing power, who are sustaining the apertura policies of the government.

The enhanced competitiveness of Mexican exports is due to three factors: 1) real wages have fallen 18% from the beginning of 1994 to the beginning of 1997; 2) taking into account inflation, the peso is still 12% below where it was before the 1994 devaluation; and 3) increases in labour productivity have not resulted in higher wages.

The process of wage renegotiation had become very tense at the end of 1997 because labour, especially the Congresso del Trabajo and the independent unions, were unwilling to accept the minimal increases proposed by the Labour Secretary in spite of the growth and productivity gains. The vice-president of the Congreso del Trabajo, Elizondo Kauffman, reflected the mood of discontent in response to the 14% increase in the minimum wage put forward by the Labour Secretary: "I would ask the Secretary to explain to a worker why he has to travel six hours a day by minibus, work eight hours per day and earn only 27 pesos per day (about $US3.00)...Why do micro and macro gains not permit them to give their families a life of dignity in accordance with clause 123 of the Constitution? (La Jornada, September 1997.)

Social Security

Social security coverage is an important aspect of the conditions of the labour market. In 1991, of 30,534,000 in the work force, only 8,779,000 were permanently insured under the Mexican Social Security Institute (IMSS) and 2,018,000 under the Social Security Institute for State Workers (ISSTE); including public universities, a combined coverage of 35.4%. By 1995, those insured under IMSS numbered 8,501,000, with 2,180,000 under ISSTE, out of a total of 33,881,000 employed workers—a drop in coverage to 31.5%.

This situation is troublesome, given that the social security benefit allows a worker to get medical attention, to receive retirement pay and other social benefits. This backward step in access to benefits is even more dramatic today, not only because of reductions in the amount and access to benefits, but also because the process of partial privatization of certain services and the creation of a new pension system (AFORES) is gradually altering the social security regime for waged workers.

According to INEGI and the statistical annexes of the Presidential Reports, the current levels of social insurance coverage (1996) by sectors of the economy are as follows: agriculture, 4.8%; manufacturing, 56.7%; construction, 13.0%; trade, 26.8%; and transportation and communications, 36.2%. There has been a decline in social security coverage in all the sectors, with the exception of manufacturing. In 1991, coverage was as follows: agriculture, 5.9%; manufacturing, 64.8%; construction, 12.9%; trade, 33.7%, and transportation and communication, 47.3%.

Thus, there has been a substantial worsening of working conditions in recent years. Moreover, the quality of benefits provided is also diminishing despite an increase in employment in the institutions affiliated with IMSS and ISSTE. (An increase in the social security bureaucracy, though not an increase in the number of doctors and nurses.)

Gender

Although the participation of women in the labour force has increased—a positive development in the sense that it means greater participation of women in Mexican society—it also raises several problems which are exacerbated in an open neoliberal economy. First, the entry of women into the labour market starts from the basis of unequal conditions for women in that same market; female jobs are generally more poorly paid.

At the same time, the arrival of a new female labour force, to the extent that it replaces the male labour force, represents a loss in the level of union awareness and militancy in defending labour rights. This implies that the new labour force is more vulnerable to exploitation by unscrupulous employers.

Furthermore, the integration of women into the labour market does not mean a change in gender roles at home. Thus, even more than before, women are performing a double role: both earning income and managing the household. They perform nearly all the unpaid and unrecognized labour that is done in the domestic sphere. Finally, the position of women in the labour market is more tenuous than that of men, to the extent that their unemployment levels are higher than those of men.

The greater participation of women in the labour force has not meant a significant improvement in their living conditions, but often a worsening of conditions. At the same time, the speed of structural adjustment, in the context of liberalization and NAFTA, has prevented an effective adjustment of gender relations to this new reality. It has also meant that women have not had time to define their new position in responding to the demand for work in the labour market. Mexican feminist movements are in the process of developing and communicating to women workers alternative strategies on these issues, but they have been slow in coming.

Even the international institutions are beginning to admit publicly that the policies of structural adjustment have had human costs which are highly explosive. The impact of structural adjustment policies on women are not always visible in the statistics, since the increase in their work load is hard to measure. No estimates are available for the number of families in which the crisis has left fathers unemployed who then abandon their families. Thus, the number of women who have had to assume sole-provider responsibility for the family has increased with unemployment.

The number of social service organizations has diminished, which means that low-income women have less access to child care, maternity support, etc. This problem has become accentuated because there are fewer within the family who can care for the children, pick them up from school, line up for medical care, buy subsidized milk, etc. A woman with a double work day begins to work at 4:30 a.m. Finally, the economic crisis has returned older women, the traditional support of working mothers, to the formal and informal labour markets.

Regional

Up to now, we have been analyzing the impact of NAFTA on the economy and labour at the national level and by sectoral divisions. However, as many writers have observed (Benko and Lipietz), there are "regions that win and regions that lose" in the process of restructuring of national economies in the context of global change. In this paper we shall make reference only to a few key variables, based on Hiernaux (1996).

Mexico City has been harshly affected by the restructuring of the economy since 1982. The loss of industrial jobs has been acute, especially in the highly protected traditional areas that have not been able to survive foreign competition. More recently, there has been a recovery, reflected in a significant increase in the participation of the Federal District (DF) in GDP. Thus, while the national GDP grew 3.0% annually from 1988 to 1993, the DF experienced an annual growth rate of 5.6% during this period.

Since population growth levelled off in the DF during the 1980s, with an annual rate close to zero, there was a significant increase in GDP per capita. Recalling that national GDP per capita in 1980 had an index of 100, falling to 89 in 1993, GDP per capita in DF went from 160 in 1980 to 250 in 1993. In other words, GDP per capita for the DF widened from 60% above the national level in 1980 to 250% above in 1993.

Mexico City has acquired a central role in continental relations, with an increase in the number of foreign firms locating their Mexican head offices in the DF, even when most of their investments are in other areas of the country. Moreover, the most important Mexican-owned firms have increasingly located in Mexico City, at the expense of medium-sized cities or the other large cities, such as Monterrey and Guadalajara.

Paradoxically, however, the labour market of the large metropolitan areas is also the one which shows the highest levels of unemployment, along with more severely affected areas such as the oil towns that have not recovered from the restructuring in their industry.

An important conclusion of this study is that the economic opening and growth evident in some sectors of the economy due to NAFTA do not resolve the employment problems of the large cities. Rather, it worsens these problems and also brings negative social consequences and political instability. Moreover, economic liberalization has reinforced regional inequalities. While these inequalities were traditional in Mexico, they were diminishing slowly under the import-substitution model.

Consider, for example, the case of Chiapas. In 1980 the GDP per capita in this state was 75% of the national average and 50% of the DF. By 1993, GDP per capita had fallen to 46%, to less than half the national average, and less than 20% of the GDP per capita in the DF. These figures give some indication of the cause of the Chiapas uprising that started on the day of NAFTA's implementation.

Although there are no regional employment figures, INEGI does organize information by large cities. Open unemployment rates are provided for the principal Mexican cities (Cited Hiernaux, 1996: 18). The cities in the poorest states are not necessarily those with the highest unemployment, given that restructuring has been most extensive in the industrial cities. Such is the case of Monclova, a steel-manufacturing town in the northern state of Coahuila, with the highest urban unemployment rate in the country in 1995 (8.4%).

Looking at the relationship between ethnicity, employment, and the liberalization of trade, there have been no studies analyzing in detail the effect of continental integration on indigenous people. However, the regions which are most negatively affected by NAFTA are those with a high presence of indigenous communities. The decline in basic social conditions has become so critical in those areas that the Mexican government decided to launch a number of economic and social development initiatives in through the National Solidarity Program (PRONASOL). However, the short duration of this program, along with numerous problems with its implementation, suggests that it has not been sufficient to remedy the appallingly poor living conditions of the indigenous regions.

Moreover, one finds the highest incidence of labour rights abuse in the indigenous areas, including child labour, payment below the minimum wage, and lack of social benefits of any kind, not to mention the violence and mistreatment which have been repeatedly denounced by human rights organizations. Expectations that NAFTA might bring new work opportunities have only been partially realized by a few activities linked to tourism or the sale of handicrafts. The latter have found new outlets in certain art markets at the international level. However, these activities are minor and incapable of improving the income of communities in an integral way.

Concluding Observations

A first point to consider is that before economic opening, the Mexican government strategy had a single logic which applied to the internal market as well as the macro economy. For decades the economic project supported import-substitution linked to the internal market, and the key word during these years was *produce*.

From the moment the direction of economic policy changed, there appeared two contradictory logics. One focused on the internal market, but was not based on protectionism and import-substituting industrialization, and the other focused on macro-economic objectives conditioned by the needs of globalization. Policies benefited those sectors linked to the world and particularly the North American economy.

While the first logic supported a production project linked to national productive sectors and the domestic market, the second logic focused on production for export and left the internal market to drown in imported products.

The productive base in Mexico has always been unequal and hetrogeneous. Economic opening and NAFTA caused a deepening of these characteristics. Clearly, not all enterprises can convert into exporters. On the other hand, while many Mexican companies embraced the challenge of becoming exporters, many small and medium-sized foreign companies and some transnationals began to fill the vacuum in domestic production left by Mexican enterprises.

The logic of opening was justified by the rapid growth of the maquiladoras and of non-petroleum exports without considering the sectors that remained excluded. For example, the strategy of export diversification had consequences in employment and petroleum activity. For decades petroleum was almost the only export. One has to ask: did non-traditional export volumes really increase, or are we talking simply of a fall in international prices? New investment went solely to the most competitive sectors, usually transnationalized and, disturbingly, to speculative investment activity.

Economic opening accentuated the two sectors of the economy and civil society tended to fracture in accordance with its link to one of the two sectors. In the open sector are exporting firms, maquilas, automotive, and those traditional sector companies that were able to restructure themselves toward exports—beer, glass, cement, steel, part of textiles—among others. Paradoxically, these companies which survive by exporting, but within NAFTA, benefited from a projectionist negotiation which extended the period of tariff removal and protected them from foreign competition thanks to regional content provisions. This is especially the case with automotive and textiles.

The dualization of the Mexican economy does not necessarily mean more labour and higher wages in the export sector. One of the major problems of this dualization is that the open sector, due to the demands of competitiveness, needs to expand its activity into the traditional sector, which in turn means future rounds of restructuring and employment losses.

The import-substitution industrialization model sustained itself for 40 years because it depended on a broad social consensus. To the extent that it stopped being redistributive it lost credibility. One of the great paradoxes of the current era is that the model of economic openness was imposed through a structural adjustment strategy that did not have consensus among the great majority of Mexicans, but had a consensus within the corporate community and transnational finance. Moreover, this model did not distribute income positively.

In the long term, a reintegration of the productive structures that were ruptured by the NAFTA national treatment clauses is unlikely, but rather a greater transnational penetration in the highest profitability areas.

The liberalization of markets, and particularly NAFTA, have altered many aspects of Mexican economy, society, and politics. Among these is the profound restructuring of the production system—the disintegration of traditional areas of the economy and the rise of new ones. Traditional sectors that were protected by the previous economic model were hit hard by liberalization, resulting in a major loss of employment in all the traditional sectors.

In contrast, employment in the maquila sector has expanded rapidly. This form of work organization flowing from economic relations between Mexico and (principally) the United States has become the new industrial paradigm of the country. We have shown that this has had a major impact on the balance of trade, on the nature of investment, and above all on employment.

Numerous studies concur that the maquiladoras are regressive in terms of working conditions for Mexicans. Therefore, its expansion, replacing traditional industrial production, has meant an enormous step backwards for Mexican workers.

The cycle of GDP growth which started with liberalization and continental integration has been extraordinarily short, meaning there are no durable effects. The negative consequences of the 1994-95 crisis are still evident, even though GDP has shown some recovery and open unemployment levels have fallen somewhat.

Some economic sectors appear to have benefited from the crisis, among them tourism, the maquilas, banking and financial services. Even though these sectors generate employment, they do not have the capacity to absorb either those who have become unemployed due to restructuring or those who are entering the labour market.

The entry into force of NAFTA has not resolved past problems of employment, the integration of women, regional or ethnic inequalities. On the contrary, it has aggravated these problems by offering global rather than local solutions which are difficult to put into practice in the short-run.

There is not much chance that Mexican society will be able to maintain control over its economy, and particularly over the creation of urgently needed jobs, when entire segments of the national economy are falling apart, replaced by activities supported in the name of globalization.

The government is counting on the fact that the economic opening and NAFTA will provoke a modernization effect coming from the North. The reality is very clear: the modernization has touched and transformed few economic and social sectors in Mexico. While the Mexican government preaches the virtues of modernization, the majority of Mexican businessmen, a large number of unionists and the government itself think that competitiveness has been achieved through the super-exploitation of labour and miserable wages.

In political terms, it is the governability of the Mexican economy that is at stake. There is a reduction in the areas where public policy can intervene and shape economic activity, particularly in light of the opposition victory in the July 6, 1997 elections. Currently, the margin of manoeuvrability in creating employment and improving working conditions is very narrow.

The NAFTA side agreements on labour and the environment have been a dead letter, both because of the disinterest shown by the governments in dealing with such problems, and because of their fear that growth may be constrained if businesses are more closely regulated in matters of labour and the environment.

NAFTA has some positive elements. Some social and economic sectors have become more dynamic, more competitive, and more quality conscious. This is not sufficient, however, to sustain a model for the country that is acceptable for all. The creation of jobs in Mexico should continue to be the highest priority, ahead of the country's integration into the world market.

Endnotes

[1]   From words of welcome to the Encuentro Intercontinental por la Humanidad y contra el Neoliberalismo" Chiapas, 1996.

[2]   This analysis was done originally with statistical information available in Mexico as of August 1997. In December 1997 several adjustments were made to the content of the final report based on the Informe Presidencial and its economic annexes released annually on September 1 and on annual economic evaluations released in December.

[3]   Information published recently in *El Financero* (29.12.97) citing data from INEGI (Instituto Nacional de Estadistica Geografia e Informatica) indicated growth of 7.2% in 1997 and inflation of 16.3%

[4]   GDP per capita in 1992 was $21,418 in Canada, $21,449 in the United States, but only $2,930 in Mexico, according to the OECD, The disparity between Mexico and its partners is striking.

[5]   Total foreign investment is calculated starting from FDI (maquilas, reinvestment of earnings, and intra-company transfers) to which is added stock market investment. This methodology is also used by the National Commission of Foreign Investment and is consistent with INEGI. On the other hand, institutions outside Mexico use different criteria which creates confusion. Moreover, statistical information on foreign investment in the stock market has only been available since 1989, and in the maquiladoras since 1994. According to official Mexican figures (Tables 13 and 14), the stock of foreign direct investment in 1982 was US$10,786 million. By 1995 it had reached US$54,123 million.

It should be noted that there is a difference between the OECD and Government of Mexico figures. The latter reports an inflow of $18,777 million for 1994, whereas the OECD reports $8,026 million. This is because the OECD bases its calculations on information coming from only five sectors: industry, services, commerce, mining and agriculture, without taking into account foreign investment in the stock market. Nor is it clear what its concept of industry includes, since in the Mexican statistics the term applies to processing, services, extractive and agriculture.

6   All the definitions, except the one based on the registry of firms with the tax office, show an increase in the size of the informal sector. The decreasing indicator is a reaction to increasing pressure to register firms by the Ministry of the Treasury and Public Credit.

BIBLIOGRAPHY

Alberro Semerena, José Luis. "Productivity and Economic Performance of the Mexican Economy. 1970-1996", Commission for Labor Cooperation, Dallas, Texas, Preliminary Version, 1997.

Banco de Comercio Exterior. "Veiticinco Años de Analisis de la Revista Comercio Exterior" (CD-ROM).

Campbell. Bruce, "NAFTA and the Canadian Labour Market" Revista Momento Económico #92, Instituto de Investigaciones Economicas, UNAM, México, 1997.

Comision Nacional de Inversiones Extranjeras. "Informe Estadístico sobre el Comportamiento de la Inversión Extranjera Directa en México", enero-abril 1997.

Commission for Labor Agreement. "North American Labor Markets. A Comparative Profile", NAALC, Dallas,E.U. 1997.

De la Garza Toledo, Enrique "Labor and Free Trade Agreement:México Three Years Later", Documento Inédito, UNAM, México, 1996.

Dehesa, Mario y Camarena Zavala, Rafael. "Tendencias Recientes del Empleo en México", Revista El Economista Mexicano, Colegio Nacional de Economistas, México, vol.1, #2,1997.

El Financiero, periódico, Información 1997, (CD-ROM)

Expansión Revista, "Frontera Norte La Tierra Prometida" Informe Especial: TLC y Maquiladoras, vol. XXIX, #726, México 1997.

Gónzalez, Maria Luisa. "Estadísticas sobre el Mercado de Trabajo Femenino",Instituto de Investigaciones Económicas,UNAM, México,1997.

Gutiérrez-Haces Teresa, "La Negociación del TLCAN a partir del Borrados de Dallas", Revista Problemas del Desarrollo Latinoamericano#90, Instituto de Investigaciones Económicas, UNAM, México, 1992.

Gutiérrez-Haces. T, "L'Accord de Libre Echange Nord-Americain: Les Contraintes de la Transition et de la Réforme d'Etat au Mexique", capítulo del libro "Integration Economique Integration Sociale? Presses de de l'Université de Québec, Canada, 1994.

Gutiérrez-Haces. Teresa, "Reexaminando el TLCAN desde la Perspectiva de la Crisis Mexicana", en el libro "Mexico and the Americas, ANUIES, México, 1996.

Gutiérrez-Haces.T, "Balance de la Apertura Económica y el TLCAN en el Sexenio de Salinas de Gortari" capítulo del libro "Le Sexennat de Carlos Salinas de Gortari", edit. L´Harmattan, Paris, 1997.

Gutiérrez-Haces.T, "Experiencias y Coincidencias de una Vecindad Bajo el Libre Comercio", capítulo del libro "La Integración Comercial de México a Estados Unidos y Canadá", editorial siglo XXI, México, 1993.

Gutiérrez-Haces.Teresa, "Historical Background of the Continental Integration: Towards New Challenges for México", Documento, CERLAC- York University, 1991.

Guzmán, Alenka "Productividad y Especialización Manufacturera en México, Canadá y Estados Unidos", Revista Comercio Exterior, vol. 47 # 3, México, marzo, 1997.

Hernández Laos. E, "La Productividad y el Desarrollo Industrial en México", Fondo de Cultura en México, 1985.

Hernández Laos.E, "México Competitividad Laboral y Tipo de Cambio", Revista Comercio Exterior, vol.46,#7, México, 1996.

Hernández Licona, Gonzalo. "Efectos de la Pobreza Familiar sobre la Tasa de Participación, Horas Trabajadas y el Desempleo en México", Revista El Economista Mexicano, Colegio Nacional de Economistas, vol.1,#2, México,1997.

Hiernaux Nicolas. D, "Desigualdades Sociales y Exclusión en la Reestructuración Económica y Territorial de México", Documento Universidad Autónoma Metropolitana Xochimilco, 1996.

Hiernaux Nicolas.D, "Reestructuración Económica y Cambios Territoriales en México Un Balance 1982-1995", Revists Estudios Territoriales # 43, Universidad de Andalucía, España. 1995.

Hinojosa, Dowds, Mc Cleery, Robinson, Runsten, Wolff, Wolff. "North American Integration Three Years After Nafta: A Framework for Tracking, Modeling and Internet Accessing the National and Regional Labor Market Impacts". North American Integration & Development Center, University of California, E.U.,1996.

INEGI, "Estadísticas de la Industria Maquiladora de Exportación", 1997, México.

INEGI, "Indicadores de Empleo y Desempleo", Mexico, 1996 y 1997.

INEGI. "Censos Económicos"(CD-ROM)

INEGI. "Cuentas Nacionales de México"(CD-ROM)

INEGI. "Empleo Urbano".(CD-ROM)

INEGI. "Estadísticas Históricas de México", Material Electrónico,CD- ROM
INEGI. "Ingreso-Gasto de los Hogares" vol. 1y 2.(CD-ROM)

INEGI. "Sistema de Cuentas Nacionales de México, Producto Interno Bruto por Entidad
    Federativa", 1993, México.

Jornada, periódico, Información 1997, (CD-ROM)

López Dóriga, Joaquín. "El Mercado Laboral en el Proceso de Ajuste: el caso de
    México",Revista El Economista Mexicano, Colegio Nacional de Economistas, vol.1,#
    2, México,1997.

Marquez Padilla, Carlos. "La Fijación de los Salarios y el Problema del Empleo en los
    Países de la OCDE. Una Refexión desde la Perspectiva de México", Revista El
    Economista Mexicano, Colegio Nacional de Economistas, vol.1, #2., México, [997.

OCDE. Estudios Económicos de la OCDE México, "Politicas y Mercados de Trabajo",
    Paris, 1997.

OCDE. Estudios Económicos de la OCDE: México, 1991/ 1992, Paris, 1992.

OCDE. "Investment Policies in Latin América and Multilateral Rules on Investment",
    Paris, 1997.

OCDE. "Reconciling Economy and Society Towards a Plural Economy", Paris, 1996.

OCDE. "Trade Liberalisation Policies in México", Paris, 1996.

OECDE. Economic Surveys: México, 1995.

Portos.I, Pacheco.E. Parker.S ,Girón.A, González Marin.M, Cooper.J, Rodríguez
    Chaurnet.D, Jusidman.C, Pérez Enríquez.I, et als, "La Condicion Laboral y Social
    de la Mujer en México y América Latina", Revista Problemas del Desarrollo
    Latinoamericano # 106. Instituto de Investigaciones Económicas, UNAM, 1996.

Puyana, Alicia. "Las Reformas Económicas en América Latina y sus Efectos sobre los
    Niveles de Pobreza", documento, El Colegio de México, México, 1995,

Rendón. T, 'Cambios Recientes en el Empleo en México". entrevista, Notas Censales,
    INEGI, #9, 1994, México.

Salas, Carlos y Rendón, Teresa, "Ajuste Estructural y Empleo: el caso de México", Revista
    Latinoamericana de Estudios del Trabajo, año 2, #2, México 1996.

Salinas de Gortari. Carlos, "Anexo Económico", Sexto Informe de Gobierno, Poder
    Ejecutivo Federal, México, 1994.

Samaniego Breach, Norma. "El Mercado de Trabajo en México", Revista El Economista
    Mexicano, Colegio Nacional de Economistas, México, vol. 1, #2,1997.

Sassen. Saskia, "La Movilidad del Trabajo y del Capital. Un Estudio sobre la Corriente Internacional de la Inversión y del Trabajo", Ministerio de Trabajo y Seguridad Social España, 1993.

Villarespe. Verónica, "Pobreza y gastos en politica social para México, Revista Momento Económico # 89, Instituto de Investigaciones Económicas, UNAM, México, 1997.

Zedillo, Ernesto, "Anexos Económicos" del 1o, 2o y 3o Informe de Gobierno, Poder Ejecutivo Federal, México, 1995,1996,1997.